THE EDUCATOR'S
GUIDE TO THE
CLARINET
Copyright Jan. 2002, Second Edition by
W. Thomas Ridenour
611 N. Royal Oak Dr.
Duncanville, Tx 75116
Phone: 1-888-AKUSTIK, FAX 1-972-572-8939
E mail: rclarinet@aol.com
Web site: www.ridenourclarinetproducts.com

Notice of Rights

No part of this publication may be reproduced, transmitted or shared in any form or by any means, electronic or mechanical, or stored by any information retrieval system, without prior written permission from the author. For information on getting permission for reprints and excerpts, or for purchase of additional copies, pleased write the author directly at 611 N. Royal Oak Dr., Duncanville, Tx. 75116, or by E-mail at Rclarinet@aol.com or through the Web site: www.ridenourclarinetproducts.com

Notice of Liability

The information in this book is distributed on an "As is" basis, with no warranty. While every precaution has been taken in the preparation of this book, neither the author nor Ridenour Clarinet Products shall have any liability to any person or entity with respect to any liability, loss, damage or injury caused or alleged to be caused directly or indirectly by the instructions contained in this book.

Procurement of Copies

Copies of The Educator's Guide to the Clarinet may be obtained directly from the author, by writing him at the above snail, E-mail or Web-site addresses, or from your local purveyor of printed material.

Cover design, graphics and text formatting:
Tom Ridenour
Editing and text proofing: Matthew Best, Emilia Ridenour, Teddy Ridenour

Proudly printed and bound in the
United States of America

ISBN 0-9717979-0-0

About the Author

Tom Ridenour is a native of Southeastern Kentucky where he attended Murray State University. At Murray he studied clarinet with David Gowans, John Sumrall and Donald Story, receiving a Bachelor's of Music in clarinet performance, graduating with honors.

After graduation, Tom then attended Yale University as a Charles Ditson Fellowship recipient, where he studied clarinet with Keith Wilson. At Yale Tom received a Master's degree in clarinet performance, again graduating with honors. Tom also did additional studies with Kalmen Opperman, David Weber, and Sigurd Bockman.

After graduation from Yale Tom lived in New England for over a decade and a half, teaching clarinet at Wesleyan University, Hartt College of Music and the University of Connecticut. In New England Tom performed extensively, being heard regularly on Connecticut Public Radio as a member of the group, Chamber Music Plus, toured as guest soloist with the New England String Quartet, performed frequently in New York City, and did numerous recording sessions at Radio City Music Hall and performed a solo recital on Boston Public Radio. Tom, with pianist Alan Lurie, also gave the North American premier of Robert Muczynski's Time Pieces for clarinet and piano. It was in those years that Tom also learned mouthpiece making from Ken Legace and Everit Matson, and began developing his own ideas concerning clarinet acoustics and design.

Over the years Tom has lectured at virtually every major music convention throughout the United States, and given master classes, lectures and performances at many of the major universities and educational institutions throughout the U.S. and Canada. He has written articles on virtually every aspect of the clarinet, and his numerous monographs have appeared in NACWPI and The Clarinet over the past two decades.

In addition to his work and contributions to the field of education, Tom worked for a time with one of the major musical manufacturers concentrating primarily on clarinet design during his tenure there. In 1997 Tom and his family moved to Dallas Texas where runs his own clarinet specialty business, Ridenour Clarinet Products, and serves as clarinet specialist for Brook Mays Music Company in Dallas, Texas. Tom continues to work with clarinetists of all skill levels, helping them with both equipment and acoustics. He is available for master classes, lecture demonstrations and workshops. Tom seeks to combine his skills as a performer, technician and teacher to present a complete approach to clarinetistry. He, his wife, Gay, and his five children presently reside in Duncanville, Texas.

Other books by Tom Ridenour

Tom has also written, Clarinet Fingerings: A Comprehensive Guide for the Performer and Educator. To date it has been through seven printings and is widely regarded as the standard work on the subject of alternate and third register fingerings. Copies of Clarinet Fingerings: A Comprehensive Guide for the Performer and Educator are available directly from the author, or from your local music and book dealers.

Dedication

Joseph Thomas and Shirley Ball Ridenour's marriage lasted only a few months short of sixty years. They had three children; myself, and twin girls who died shortly after birth. My father worked in the Kentucky coal mines for forty-seven years. My mother worked faithfully in the home for sixty. Their passings into the next world took place within forty days of each other.

They bought me my first clarinet when I was eleven, though I had washed out on the piano a few years earlier. The lessons they taught me by their examples take on increasing importance with the years; how to endure through difficulties, how to forgive, even when it is hard, the importance of never giving up and to cling to the hope of God's providential goodness in spite of all our personal weaknesses and failures; in the face of constant and often daunting difficulties despair was not a reality they would accept. Their final days on earth showed how love is tougher than all that life can throw at you, and ultimately triumphs over all else. To them and their memory, this book is respectfully and lovingly dedicated. Eternal thanks for the gift of life you gave me.

INTRODUCTION

Why This Book Was Written

Almost three decades of teaching and lecturing about the clarinet has left me with two very distinct impressions. The first is that large numbers of educators are somewhat perplexed about how best to go about teaching the clarinet. The second, is that many of these same educators are not exactly sure where to turn for help and advice. Certainly, there are lots of articles which have been written over the years, but few educators have the time to research all of the material, read it thoroughly and decide what may or may not be of practical use. The fact that some articles present information which seems to contradict the information found in others does not help matters. In fact, it may even leave the educator feeling more confused than ever. The whole process can be time consuming and frustrating, and I'm sure we all agree that music educators already have too little time and too many frustrations.

The text you now hold in your hands is my response to this situation. In it I have tried to provide all that is needed to effectively teach the clarinet. First, there are complete explanations of how the individual parts of the clarinet's various systems work, with an emphasis on understanding their interdependent nature and how the individual parts reinforce and buttress one another; success of the whole depends upon the perfection of the parts; perfection of the parts can only be rightly understood by seeing the whole. Next, the reader will find step-by-step teaching methods for each technique and lists of criteria which set valid and reasonable standards by which progress may be both directed and measured.

Finally, the individual parts of any system can derive their ultimate meaning only in the light of a Core Concept or Overarching, Primary Principle. For the clarinet this singular Principle is that of Efficiency. The Substance of this principle is the DNA which should be found in all the clarinet's systems, pedagogical, mechanical, acoustical and technical. Rigorous adherence to this Principle prevents the development of any one of the individual components of tone production from becoming merely arbitrary, and provides a safe-guard against any type of musical myopia to which the performer may be lured. Rather, such a core principle directs them in such a way that all the parts grow together into a consistent, harmonious Complementarity, becoming a truly unified, logical system, void of the slightest hint of internal contradiction or conflict. Understanding how this Principle is specifically expressed and practically and properly applied to the various concrete elements of playing technique and equipment is essential if the teacher is to grasp their true nature, meaning and relationship. This Unifying Principle provides the proverbial "flash of lightening at midnight" which instantaneously illuminates the entire landscape of clarinet playing, enabling the mind to survey each the parts without losing sight of the whole, as well as ensuring that the individual elements will be presented in a logical order, given a proper proportionality and assigned an objectively correct relationship in the hierarchy of techniques.

Who Might Benefit From this Book
Essentially, <u>The Educator's Guide to the Clarinet</u> is meant for anyone and everyone who is faced with the task of teaching and learning the clarinet, whether in the studio or the class room, whether in public schools or universities. It is especially hoped that it might be of use in college methods classes, where students are not only trying to learn clarinet fundamentals themselves, but also need to learn how to effectively teach them to beginners.

Presentation Order of the Material
The various pedagogical subjects presented in this book are discussed in the order of their importance to actual performance. For instance, the first thing one needs to know in order to begin a task is what it is that needs to be done; what the goal or point of the activity is. Therefore, we begin with a discussion on ways which teachers can present the concept of clarinet tone to the student and help the student get his or her own idea of what clarinet playing is about. Next, the clarinet is, in its essence, a wind instrument; nothing happens without the air. Therefore, the next chapter logically deals with teaching students to breathe and blow the clarinet correctly. Once this is done, the air needs to be channeled, shaped and directed properly. Therefore, because of its intimate relationship to and control of the air column, it stands to reason that the next chapter would be concerned with the use of the tongue, and so on.

Technical Development and Musical Style
Any method or approach to clarinet playing commonly raises a valid and important question in the mind of the thoughtful reader; one which should be satisfactorily answered. That question is: "Since styles and tastes are so diverse, how can anyone have the temerity to present a given method as the *only* way to approach the clarinet?" The simple answer to this question is, "Musically and aesthetically speaking, one can't. There are as many ways to use mechanics and techniques as there are players, and any attempt to dictate how they should be *musically* used

constitutes both a misunderstanding and an abuse of what such information is, and how it relates to the aesthetic, artistic and musical. In short, matters of musical taste must be left up to the individual."

Because of this, I have tried only to point out how the technical and mechanical aspects of clarinet playing work, shed light upon the interdependent nature of the system they form, and demonstrate their cause and effect relationship with the elements of music. In other words, I have tried only to give you the tools and show how they work. What sort of house should be built with them has been left up to you. Anything which seems to go beyond that in these pages should be taken with a substantially sized allotment of the proverbial grain of salt.

A Word to Advanced and Advancing Students

It is certainly possible for more mature students to familiarize themselves with this material with the intent of teaching themselves. However, *both* the use of this manual and private study with a fine teacher will create the optimum atmosphere for quick advancement. Whether you are working alone or with a teacher, you should also be aware that you must in some degree, always be your own teacher. This means that you need to learn to detach yourself from the act of clarinet playing to reflect upon and understand what you are doing and what effect is it having. Without this analytical, reflective effort on your part progress will not be what it should. To make the things you learn truly your own you must chew over and digest the material presented to you as a cow chews its cud. And remember, whenever you conceive of playing in one way but do another in reality, there has to be a problem with either your thinking, your acting or both. Never trust inconsistencies and always look for reasonable, yet simple (but not simplistic) solutions.

A Word to Teachers

Since this book hopes to satisfy a wide range of needs and uses, it is understandable that those who read it might react variously to its contents. Some of you may feel that your appetite has barely been whetted by what you find. In contrast, others may feel the way a little boy did about a book he was assigned for an oral book report. The book was entitled "All About Ants." His report was only one sentence. It read, "This book tells me more about ants than I care to know." If this is your case, I can only beg you to understand that anyone who attempts to write a book of this nature has two abiding fears: Obscurity of form and paucity of content. Therefore, in an attempt to eliminate at least one of these anxieties, I opted to offer what I felt the "average reader" would judge as too much information rather than too little: It is better to have an embarrassment of riches rather than a penurious insufficiency when it comes to information. Or as one public luminary whose name escapes me once observed, "I've been rich and I've been poor, and rich is better."

The primary goal of this book is to help you teach characteristic clarinet tone with confidence. The techniques and methods are all tried and true. But teaching clarinet tone requires more than the possession of correct techniques. It also requires that you as the teacher become highly sensitized to fine clarinet tone, especially in regard to tonal shape, so that you can very quickly detect when the students are failing to maintain the integrity of certain techniques. You might find it helpful to reflect on the words used in chapter I to describe characteristic clarinet shape, while listening closely to some of the recordings listed in the same chapter. Unless you are sensitized to what a truly focused tone is you will accept something less from your students.

The fact that exercises and musical examples have been held to a minimum was wholly a matter of practicality. There was simply no room for both thorough explanation of techniques and mechanics and extensive exercises for their development by the student. I hope that the two books of exercises which will follow the publication of this text will remedy the dearth of exercises in this present text and be useful for both teacher and student.

Although a great deal of time is spent in the text explaining how various mechanisms operate and interrelate, I recommend that such explanations not be presented to students, especially young ones. The student, with rare exceptions, is only slowed by having to reason and use the faculty of abstraction. You, as the teacher, are the only one who needs to know "how it works." The students only need to know "how it feels" to perform this or that function; how energies are exerted, not which muscles do the work. It is usually best to bypass the reasoning part of the intellect as much as possible, and appeal directly to the student's imagination by means of familiar "action images". One such example that comes immediately to mind is the action image of "blowing up a balloon so that it grows constantly larger at a steady rate". Such an act is easily seen in the mind's eye, and corresponds exactly to the kind of blowing needed to keep the tone "healthy."

The teacher is encouraged to be as creative as possible in devising action images for every technique and concept. Many teachers already do this intuitively. But making this method a conscious effort can be very effective, and may save you a thousand words of reasoned explanation in the classroom. "This is how it works," needs to be replaced with "It feels like..." "Think of it this way," needs to be replaced with "do it this way."

The more senses involved in the learning process the better. For example, having the student to play the mouthpiece into a tuner to learn correct voicing involves feeling the air, embouchure, right hand thumb, and tongue; hearing the sound, and seeing the amount of subtle pitch deviation they cause on the tuner. Thus three senses cross reference one another and are providing information to the student's intellect to help him or her learn to voice the sound correctly.

You may notice that no brand names are specifically mentioned in any of the equipment chapters. The reason for this is simple: brands come and go. This means mentioning them by name could quickly date the usefulness of the information provided here and even confuse the reader when he or she goes shopping for something no longer available. Therefore, a different tact was decided upon, that of discussing the qualities which need to be considered and looked for in each type of product and to formulate standards by which each brand may be judged; products come and go, but standards of quality and usefulness remain relatively stable.

Remarks on the publication of the Second Edition

I am gratified at the positive reception my little pedagogy has received from both educator and professional alike. Many have commented to me about how clear and easy the text is to read and that difficult and complex things were presented in ways which made them easily understandable. I, alas, cannot claim credit for such lucidity, but must restate my thanks to those who read the original text and offered the astute suggestions and insights which made it increasingly clear and easy to understand. With their assistance, some of the chapters were rewritten as many as twenty times. I also want to thank my friend Dr. Evelyn Pluhar for her careful reading of the Overview of The Clarinet added to this new edition. Her suggestions were very helpful. I have labored in this present edition to make further clarifications to those parts of the text which, upon reflection, seemed to me still obscure and in some cases, even confusing. In other instances, I expanded upon certain aspects of important subjects which seemed to me incomplete. I hope the reader agrees that what he beholds is, in point of fact, an improving rather than a worsening of the text. Other than clarificational changes and the overview offered after the acknowledgments, the text remains, in its fundamental contents, unchanged. It is my hope that the textural changes in the second edition will further clarify the contents for the reader, making each aspect of the pedagogy even more easily accessible to both clarinetist and non-clarinetist educator alike.

Tom Ridenour
Duncanville, TX
Jan. 2002

ACKNOWLEDGMENTS

I would like to take the opportunity to give specific thanks to a few of the many persons who have either directly or indirectly contributed to the writing of this book. First, there are my parents, who bought me my first clarinet (despite the fact that earlier I had washed out at the piano) and who generously supported me in countless ways all their lives. Their character and perseverance in the face of difficulty continue to be inspirational to me.

Next, I would like to thank my wife Gay, for her patient and understanding forbearance all the time it took me to get all this down on paper. Also, for all those who read the rough texts and offered countless invaluable suggestions a big hearty thanks. These include Pierce McMartin, Geoff Nudel, and Fred Lowrance. A special thanks to David Irwin, who faithfully and thoughtfully read over large amounts of the text and suggested numerous improvements. Thanks also to my good friend, fellow clarinetist and computer "geek," Ted Lane. Ted's knowledge consistently amazes me. His technical advise and formatting prowess was of tremendous help to a lesser "geek" such as I. Also, I would like to thank Prof. Richard Shanley of Baylor University for his helpful insights on articulation and breathing and his contributions to the discography. Matt Best and my daughter Emilia helped proof read the text and cleared up scores of obscurities, both flagrant and subtle. Thanks guys!

Thanks must also go to Debra Haburay and Amy Forbes of Forest Park Middle School in Lewisville, Texas. They were open enough to allow me to test out and apply many of the teaching ideas and concepts presented in this book in actual classroom situations. Their creative and imaginative suggestions and encouragement have been heartening. They also proved once again that you can teach an old dog new tricks...as long as they aren't too many of them.

I must also acknowledge my primary teachers, Keith Wilson and Kalman Opperman, who both contributed very different but equally essential things to my knowledge. Thanks must also go to my old friends and fellow clarinetophiles Ken Legace and Everit Matson. Both helped me learn how to make mouthpieces. Ken is especially significant in my own development in that he was the first person who made me suspect that thinking about the clarinet correctly could actually make a practical difference in how well I could learn to play it. In up to date parlance, you might say he showed me that it really was possible to work smarter, not harder. Thanks also to Dr. Lee

Gibson. Lee's dedication to pedagogy and his analytical, objective approach to clarinet equipment has been a true inspiration. For almost three decades he has generously and selflessly shared his knowledge of pedagogy and acoustics with the clarinet community. Lee's work demonstrated to me the value of thorough analysis and how it can improve and facilitate every aspect of clarinet performance and pedagogy.

I must not neglect to thank my students and the countless players who have availed themselves of my pedagogical, technical and acoustical skills over nearly two and a half decades. I owe them a great debt, for each, with hardly an exception, taught me something precious and valuable. I hope the following chapters might serve in their minds as compensation for all that I in ignorance failed to teach them.

Finally, sometimes those who affect us most are those who lived in another age. These are persons we can only know directly by their work. For me, one such person is the great philosopher and theologian, St. Thomas Aquinas. It was exposure to St. Thomas' thought which renovated my whole understanding of the nature of reality, and of created things, both in regard to their essences and their relationships. The fundamental laws and common sense principles which guided his thought turned out to be of the greatest practical use to me in the comparatively mundane and humble task of properly understanding and ordering what I have come to know about the clarinet. It would be hard for me to overstate the benefit and blessing his work has been to my own and to my life. Without his benign and beneficent influence, this book would have been very different, and perhaps would never have been written at all. I owe him an immense debt of gratitude, and to Fr. Jose A. Salazar M.S.A. as well, who introduced me to Thomistic thought in the winter and spring of 1981-82.

Finally, I would like to thank God Himself for the gift of life, the gift of music and the gift of love, by which we are inspired to share with others whatever good has been given to us. In that spirit, it is sincerely hoped that all those who consider this material find the information they need to help make the burden of their work lighter, their teaching more effective, and their students more successful.

It would give me the greatest pleasure to know that this little text might in some way ease the weight of someone else's burdens and illuminate what was previously obscure for yet another. The more clearly and correctly we think about the clarinet, the better we will all teach and play it. It is hoped that the information in this book will help many avoid the whole array of time consuming, frustrating mistakes, misconceptions and pitfalls that both I and others have encountered in our own teaching careers. Once mastered, the reader it encouraged to improve and expand upon all that is found in these pages. There is certainly ample room for both. What is presented here is by no means an end. It is offered here only as a beginning.

> Tom Ridenour
> Dallas, Texas
> January 20th,
> 2002 A.D.

The Necessity of Developing a Complete Overview of the Clarinet

Most of us have some passing familiarity with the ancient story of the blind men and the elephant. You may recall that being unable to see the elephant and having familiarity with only a part of the elephant's anatomy, each blind man mistook the part they knew for the whole. As a result, each ended up imagining the elephant to be a grotesque sort of creature, very, *very* different from what it truly is. The great 20th Century English apologist, Catholic theologian and publisher, Frank Sheed, used the somewhat more shocking image of "eyes on a plate" to make essentially much the same point. He wrote, "The human eye is very beautiful---in the human face. Put the same eye on a plate, and though in one sense it can be investigated more closely and thoroughly, it has lost its beauty and even its significance. A being who knew only eyes and not faces would not even know eyes. A being who knew masses of facts about each feature separately, but did not know how the features were arranged in a human face, could imagine only a nightmare and no face."

The fundamental point of both these examples is that knowledge, if it is to be complete, must have two dimensions or aspects. First, one must be familiar with the broad categories and principles within the subject itself; fundamental categories and principles that both unite and delineate the subject, categories and principles that follow from the very nature or essence of the subject itself and that encompass the whole of the matter, leaving nothing excluded. Secondly, one also needs the study of particular things, the encountering and correct application of which brings a greater enrichment, variety and depth to the subject. When one has attained such a complete understanding of a subject, one may admittedly not know every individual fact about it, but whenever a new thing is encountered, one knows readily where it belongs, how it relates to the whole, what it means and how to apply and develop it properly.

Of these two aspects or ways in which a subject may be known, knowledge of particulars always comes first. One might say that though particulars appear prior to fundamental principles in the learning process, the fundamental principles are primary in importance. For instance, students most often must spend a long time familiarizing themselves with particulars, all the while remaining unaware of the principles that, in reality, provide the conceptual foundation upon which all the particulars rest. But if knowledge is to ever mature into understanding, if mere cleverness is ever to turn to into wisdom, if material evidence and experience is to ever take on substantial, coherent meaning, there must come the time when one lifts one's eyes from the close scrutiny of individual things to see the whole to which they belong and which alone causes them to make sense in relationship to one another. In short, there comes a time when the student must see the proverbial forest hidden among the trees, with its vast and grand shapes, its sweeping contours and its sprawling landscapes. Only once this is seen, can one enter the forest without becoming lost or disoriented; only then can one engage in the process of the study and perfection of particular things without becoming myopic or creating something altogether disproportionate to the whole.

Since it is primary, at first blush it may seem odd to the reader that the conceptual foundation is apprehended and understood only secondarily. Yet it is not just the way of learning the clarinet but of all reality. The causes of the world we experience cannot, in point of fact, be apprehended directly, but are deduced only from their effects which we can perceive. And deduction requires reflection, and reflection requires mature, structured thought. To ignore or deny this fact, as many in our age have, is to ensure the ultimate purpose or reason for existence will and can never be understood. If one remains in such a frame of mind one remains, metaphorically speaking, just another lost soul wandering among myriads of trees. Perhaps such a one is very familiar with certain specifics in the forest. One may even be regarded in some quarters as an expert on this, that or the other. (As they say, in the land of the blind the one eyed man is king.) Yet, because such a one does not see the forest, one understands the true nature of the subject little better than each blind man understands the true nature of the elephant, his cleverness and natural gifts notwithstanding. This is tragic whenever it happens, and reflecting upon the consequences of such tragedy brings to light an important truism: one ultimately masters the forest or is mastered by it; swallowed up, in fact. Deficiency in such fundamental conceptual knowledge of the whole is, for the performer, even the so-called successful performer, a crippling one at best. And what is true for the performer is true a fortiori for the teacher! For the teacher, such a lack is altogether a disaster. This is because the teacher's whole work *should* be to lead students from familiarity with a subject's particulars to the appreciation of its deeper meaning and significance, and a fuller understanding of the principles that make up the underpinnings of its reality. And, obviously, one cannot give what one does not have. With this in mind, it should be easy to see that any pedagogue who fails to draw the reader's attention to the necessity of developing such awareness has, de facto, failed in both his primary and ultimate duty at the very outset! So goes the rationale for the following attempted, albeit brief, overview of the clarinet.

If what has been said up to now is true (and it is), if the possession of an overview of the clarinet is truly requisite in order to effectively teach it, the next logical question should be, "How does one best go about acquiring such an overview?"

First, it is helpful to understand that clarinet playing is the result of the coordination of three very different systems; the mechanical, acoustical and musical systems.
The mechanical system includes the subsystems of blowing, voicing and embouchure techniques.
The acoustical system includes the whole clarinet, from the tip of the reed and mouthpiece to the end of the bell.
The musical system includes the whole variety of pitches, colors, shapes and dynamics that the technical and expressive content of music itself places upon the clarinet and the clarinetist.

All the particulars one learns about clarinet pedagogy will fall under one of these broad categories. As one studies each particular aspect of playing or equipment one should be aware that a puzzle is being pieced together. Each piece helps answer fundamental questions such as, "How do the elements of the mechanical, acoustical and musical systems relate to one another? How are they connected? How do they work together? What are their inner relationships? How are they interdependent? Is there a common element that binds all the systems together? If so, what is it and how does it influence and affect each and how do each affect it?"

To better answer these and similar such questions it is further helpful to know the fundamental causes of clarinet tone. There are, with a bow to Aristotle, four causes; material, formal, efficient and final. For example, the material cause of a candle is wax, the formal cause is as a means of sustaining fire, the efficient cause is ye olde village candle maker, and the final cause is to give light so you can read the yellow pages and hopefully find a competent electrician! What a time for the electricity to go out!!! (Is there ever a good time?) Now to the clarinet:

1. The material cause of clarinet tone is primarily the air.
2. The formal cause of clarinet tone, is the intention to create musical sound with a reed instrument driven by the breath.
3. The efficient cause of clarinet tone is the performer.
4. The final cause, or ultimate purpose of clarinet tone, is the realization of the musical phrase.

What can delineating these causes ultimately tell us that will help us better understand the clarinet's systems and its pedagogy? First, it helps us see that clarinet tone is not an end in itself but a means. It's sole purpose is the production of elegant, sinuous and expressive musical phrases. Or as Vienese clarinetist Eric Simon once succinctly observed, "The function of tone is phrasing." This is very important to note because all too many clarinetists stop at only the formal cause in evaluating tone. Thus, whenever they play a new instrument they ask only, "How does it sound?" While this is important it is much more important to proceed to the ultimate and much more important and comprehensive question of, "How does it phrase?" Next, and just as importantly, laying out the causes helps one to more readily see the profound connection between the material and final causes of clarinet tone; the wind column and the musical phrase. These two phenomena are to one another as the soul is to the body, distinct but not separate. What happens to the one happens to the other. As the one changes the other changes in the same way and to precisely the same degree. Clarinet playing, in its most generic and essential understanding, is wind playing. To be sure it is and must become more than that, but it is and can never become less than that; the wind is inescapably present and primary at every point and in every aspect of the clarinetist's industries. One might say that the air column is the musical phrases' hidden, inaudible Foundation, its invisible Conductor.

Knowing the profound relationship of the air with the phrase is helpful in and of itself, but it also gives us a clue to help us begin understanding the relationship between and meaning of the mechanical and acoustical systems as well. The mechanical and acoustical systems are the intermediaries between the air and the phrase. In a technical sense, these two systems are all about the air. For example, any change or development in playing mechanics or acoustics which allows the air to operate more fluidly, securely, efficiently and sinuously to create beautiful, elegant and expressive phrases, is a positive change. Any change or development in mechanics and acoustics which requires increased amounts and degrees abrupt changes and modulations of the air (and embouchure) pressure to prevent tones from sticking out, or to make them speak, to secure predictable response, to create smooth intervallic connections or to mask harsh color or dullness, is a negative change. This plays out on a practical level by one asking one's self the following kinds of questions:

"Is this embouchure technique causing the reed to vibrate in a way that it uses the air best for resonance and yet requires only minimal modulation of it to achieve control and efficiency?"

"Does this clarinet have requisite balance in blowing resistance to facilitate beautiful, smooth intervallic connections without the necessity of inordinate and sudden modulations of the air speed, volume, shape or direction and concomitant changes in embouchure pressure?"

"Do I have to change my air volume, shape or speed for certain areas of this clarinet's range or at certain dynamic levels in order to mask bad color or secure predictable response?"

"Is this mouthpiece or mouthpiece/reed combination causing me to bite, lapse into other bad habits or change embouchure pressures to secure response, all of which prevent the air from flowing with unimpeded fluidity from register to register?"

Armed with an awareness and fundamental understanding of the clarinet's systems and subsystems and the causes of clarinet sound, one can begin to develop an effective pedagogy; a pedagogy based upon the true and objective nature of the clarinet's material and final causes; a pedagogy characterized by its completeness and proper proportionality; a pedagogy void of the slightest hint of internal contradiction or myopia. The more one reflects upon the particulars understood in the context of their proper categories the more one will see the immense organizational value and practicality of conceptual knowledge. Just to take one example, any given performance problem can be caused by a variety of things or combinations of things. The ability to see the particulars properly ordered in their categories can assist the teacher in quickly fabricating a laundry list of causes, systematically and accurately evaluating a student's problems in the light of these causes and finding the proper and effective solution. Experience will repeatedly show that far from being mere theoretical nonsense, useless esoterica or dreamy headed speculation, this conceptual knowledge based upon the objective nature of the elements of clarinet playing is of the greatest and most practical use, providing the teacher with a clarity and perspective that can be attained no other way. It is suggested that the reader will find it very helpful to habitually refer back to these broad categories as he or she considers the detailed discussions in the text. Each line has been written and each point has been made with the whole in mind, and each is better understood in that same spirit. Thinking of the clarinet in this way is, admittedly, not particularly easy, but it is not only practical and rewarding but necessary as well, for in the final analysis, it is the only thing that really works.

THE CHAPTERS AT A GLANCE

PART I: CLARINET PEDAGOGY

CHAPTER I: TEACHING THE CLARINET TONE CONCEPT

CHAPTER II: THE AIR: BREATHING AND BLOWING CORRECTLY

CHAPTER III: THE TONGUE: VOICING THE CLARINET TONE

CHAPTER IV: HOW TO TEACH CLARINET EMBOUCHURE

SUMMARY OUTLINE OF TONE PRODUCTION TECHNIQUES

CHAPTER V: HOW TO TEACH ARTICULATION

CHAPTER VI: TECHNIQUE: FINGER FUNDAMENTALS

PART II: CLARINET EQUIPMENT

CHAPTER VII: HOW TO TEST AND SELECT CLARINETS

CHAPTER VIII: ALL ABOUT CLARINET MOUTHPIECES

CHAPTER IX: FUNDAMENTALS OF REED BALANCING

CHAPTER X: CLARINET REPAIR AND MAINTENANCE

CHAPTER XI: ACCESSORIES FOR THE CLARINET

AFTERWORD

TABLE OF CONTENTS

DEDICATION iv
INTRODUCTION..v-ix
REMARKS ON THE SECOND EDITION...ix
ACKNOWLEDGEMENTS... x-xii
OVERVIEW OF THE CLARINET..xii-xvi
CHAPTERS AT A GLANCE xii
TABLE OF CONTENTS.. xiii-xxi

PART I:
CLARINET PEDAGOGY

CHAPTER I: TEACHING THE CLARINET TONE CONCEPT
The Two Essential Elements for Teaching Tone Concept 1-2
Developing the Auricular Concept 1-2
Developing an Intellectual Concept of Tone..1-2
Teaching the Characteristic Shape of the Clarinet Tone............................1-3
A Short List of Clarinet Recordings...1-4
The International Clarinet Association 1-6
In Conclusion 1-6

CHAPTER II: THE AIR: BREATHING AND BLOWING CORRECTLY
Part I: Basic Breathing and Blowing Techniques......................................2-2
The Natural Breath 2-2
The Full Breath 2-2
Using the Air: The Two Possible Methods of Expelling the Air 2-3
The Diaphragmatic Method of Blowing 2-4
The Results of the "Toothpaste Tube" Method 2-4
The Compression Method of Blowing 2-5
First Steps in Learning Compression Blowing..2-5
The Results of the Compression Method of Blowing 2-7
The Two Methods of Blowing and Other Instruments..............................2-8
What to Play 2-8
What to Notice 2-9
Habitually "Supporting" the Clarinet Tone 2-9
The Air and the Fingers 2-10
The Think/Play Exercise..2-11

PART II: Advanced Blowing Techniques: Playing Dynamics 2-13
What is Modulation of the Air? 2-13
Air Pressure, Air Volume and Playing Dynamics 2-13
The Tongue, the Soft Palate and Playing Dynamics 2-14
Putting it all Together 2-14
Review of the Relationship of Embouchure Pressure and Air Volume 2-16
Basic Exercise for Improving Modulation of the Air 2-17
Breath Attacks: Starting the Sound with the Breath 2-18
Methods of Beginning Tones with the Breath 2-18
The Decreasing Pressure Method 2-18
The Increasing Pressure Method 2-19
Conclusion 2-19

CHAPTER III: THE TONGUE: VOICING THE CLARINET TONE

Introduction 3-2
How the Tongue Affects the Air 3-2
Negative Effects of Poor Tongue Position on the Embouchure 3-3
Negative Effects of Poor Tongue Position on the Tone and Tuning 3-3
Beginning to Learn Correct Tongue Placement 3-4
Relating Aural Concept to Physical Technique 3-4
Using a Tuner 3-6
The High "C" Exercise 3-6
Results of the High "C" Exercise 3-6
Extending the High "C" Exercise 3-7
The Tongue and Playing Dynamics 3-8
Tongue Position and Properly Voicing the Registers 3-8
Tongue Position and Elimination of Undertones in the Upper Clarion 3-9
Learning How to Voice the Upper Clarion 3-10
The Tongue and the Third Register 3-10
Honks and Squeaks 3-10
Correct Voicing and Articulation 3-12
Clarinet Tone and the Oral Cavity 3-12
Conclusion 3-13

CHAPTER IV: HOW TO TEACH CLARINET EMBOUCHURE

Form and Function in Clarinet Embouchure 4-2
The Goal of Embouchure 4-2
The Paradox of Tone 4-2
The Relationship of Tone, Reed and Embouchure 4-3
Parts of the Embouchure and How They Work 4-4

Table of Contents

The Two Possible Methods of Controlling the Reed 4-4
The Jaw (and lower teeth) 4-4
Biting: What it is and its Effect on Tone 4-6
The Lips 4-6
The Lower Lip 4-7
The Upper Lip 4-7
The Chin Muscles 4-8
The Upper Teeth 4-8
The Right Hand Thumb 4-10
The Tongue 4-11
The Throat 4-11
How to Find the Best Angle for Playing the Clarinet 4-12
Friction-Style Embouchure, Clamp-Style Embouchure, Reed Vibration
and the Paradox of Musical Tone 4-12
How Much Mouthpiece Should be Snugged? 4-17
Trouble Shooting and Teaching Tips 4-18
Teaching Tips for Embouchure 4-18
Teaching Tips for Tongue 4-19
Teaching Tips for the Thumb 4-19
Teaching Tips for the Lips 4-19
How to Check for Biting 4-20
How to Teach a Beginner the Friction-Style Embouchure 4-21
Adding the Tongue Position 4-22
Use of the Tuner 4-22
Embouchure Development and Equipment 4-22
Part II: Playing French Embouchure 4-23
Fallacies and Factoids about Double-Lip Technique 4-23
Positive Benefits of Double-Lip Technique 4-24
Double-Lip as a Corrective for Poor Embouchure Habits 4-25
Learning Double-Lip 4-25
Double-lip and the Soft Palate 4-26
Initial Problems Learning Double-Lip and Their Solutions 4-26
Double-Lip and Finger Technique 4-27
Switching 4-28
Double-Lip and its Effect on Single-Lip 4-28
Double-Lip and Articulation 4-28
How Much Lip Should be Tucked 4-28
Some Pit Falls To Avoid 4-29
Double-Lip and Younger Players 4-29
Conclusion 4-30

SUMMARY OUTLINE OF TONE PRODUCTION TECHNIQUES

Putting it All Together SO-1
Teaching the Tone Concept SO-1
A Short Discussion on Tonal Shape SO-2
Concise Summary of the Elements SO-2
The Air Stream and Tongue SO-2
The Embouchure: Controlling the Reed SO-3
Effects of the Proper Coordination of Tongue, Air and Embouchure SO-4
Clarinet Tone Production at a Glance SO-5

CHAPTER V: HOW TO TEACH ARTICULATION

Introduction 5-2
Tongue Placement on the Reed 5-2
"Off-the-Reed-Tonguing" 5-3
Tongue Position in Tonguing 5-4
The Proper Tonguing Syllable for the Clarinet 5-4
Motion of the Tongue 5-5
The Embouchure in Tonguing 5-5
The Chin in Tonguing 5-5
The Air and Tonguing 5-5
Beginning Efforts at Tonguing 5-6
Some Things to Watch and Listen for 5-7
What to do Next? 5-7
Advanced Tonguing Techniques 5-8
Stop Tonguing 5-9
When to use Stop Tonguing 5-10
How to Play Tongued Attacks 5-11
Developing Speed 5-13
Tonguing on the Fingers 5-13
Conclusion 5-14

CHAPTER VI: TECHNIQUE: FINGER FUNDAMENTALS

Introduction 6-2
The Hands: General Comments 6-2
The Natural Handposition and Relaxation 6-2
How the Fingers Should Cover the Tone Holes 6-3
Finger Action and the Repair Condition of the Clarinet 6-3
The Left Hand 6-4

The Left Hand Index Finger 6-4
The Left Hand Thumb 6-6
The Left and Right Hand Middle Fingers 6-6
The Left Hand Ring Finger 6-7
The Left and Right Hand Pinkies 6-7
Developing Independence of the Pinkies 6-7
The Right Hand 6-9
The Right Hand Index Finger 6-9
The Right Hand Middle Finger 6-9
The Right Hand Ring Finger 6-9
The Right Hand Thumb 6-9
The Touchpoint System: The Cure for "Flyaway Fingers" 6-10
The Pinkies and the Touchpoint System 6-11
Complex Combinations 6-13
"Growing" a Traditional Technique 6-13
Published Material for Technical Development 6-13
Playing Over the Middle Break 6-14
Legato Finger Technique 6-15
Finger Technique and the Third Register 6-16
Conclusion 6-16

PART II:
THE CLARINET AND CLARINET EQUIPMENT

INTRODUCTION .... II-i
The Goal of Fine Equipment .... II-i
More About Acoustical and Mechanical Efficiency .... II-ii
Equipment and Artistic Preference .... II-ii
Reasonable and Unreasonable Expectations Concerning Equipment ...... II-iii
Your Attitude .... II-iii
Introducing the Clarinet: Basic Basics .... II-v
Parts of the Clarinet .... II-v
Pitch Range of the Clarinet .... II-v
The Throat Tones .... II-v
Tuning and the Throat Tones .... II-vi

The Throat Tones and Timbre .... II-vi
The Throat Bb .... II-vii
The Break Area .... II-vii
Pitch Tendencies of the Clarinet .... II-vii
The Bore of the Clarinet .... II-viii
The Clarinet's Bore Dimensions and What They Mean .... II-viii
The Tone Holes of the Clarinet and Undercutting .... II-ix
Tuning the Clarinet for Performance .... II-ix

CHAPTER VII: HOW TO TEST AND SELECT CLARINETS

Introduction 7-2
Playing Features to Look for in a Fine Clarinet 7-2
Testing for Tuning 7-3
Beginning the Tuning Test: How to Test Each Pitch 7-4
What are Tuning Ratios? 7-5
Tuning of the Throat Tones 7-6
Tuning the Third Register 7-7
How to Understand the Results of the Tuning Test 7-8
Some Tuning Faults Common to Many Models 7-8
Unacceptable Tuning Ratios 7-8
Conclusion on Tuning 7-9
Testing for Blowing Resistance 7-9
Effects of the Mouthpiece/Reed Set up on Testing Clarinet Resistance .. 7-10
Benefits of Even Blowing Resistance 7-10
Testing for Response 7-12
The Clarion Register 7-13
Response and Resistance in the Clarion 7-13
Testing for Tone 7-14
The Bottom Line 7-15
FAQ Concerning Clarinets and Clarinet Selection 7-15
Conclusion 7-20

CHAPTER VIII: ALL ABOUT CLARINET MOUTHPIECES

The Mouthpiece and the Elements of Music 8-2
Common Mouthpiece Materials and Tone Quality 8-2
Part of the Mouthpiece 8-2
The Mouthpiece Facing 8-2
The Reed Table 8-4
Concave and Non-Concave Mouthpiece Reed Tables 8-4
Convex Reed Tables 8-4

The Mouthpiece Facing Resistance Curve 8-5
Measuring Mouthpiece Facings 8-5
Asymmetrical Side Rails 8-5
Playing Characteristics of Askew Facings 8-6
Symmetrical Facings 8-8
The Tip Rail 8-8
Tip Opening, Resistance Curves and Reed Strengths 8-8
So, What's the Difference? 8-9
Rail Thickness 8-10
The Mouthpiece Window 8-10
The Mouthpiece Tone Chamber 8-11
The Baffle and Tone Color 8-11
Vices and Virtues Encountered in Baffle Design 8-12
The Side Walls (Chamber Width) 8-12
The Bore 8-13
Possible Bore and Chamber Width Combinations 8-14
Mouthpieces and Tuning: an Important Consideration 8-14
Mouthpiece Length: More about Tuning 8-15
How to Select a Mouthpiece 8-15
Stage One: Clarifying Your Needs 8-15
What Sort of Tone, Tuning and Shape Would You Prefer? 8-15
What Strength Reeds do you Wish to Play? 8-16
Hand-made vs Machine-made mouthpieces 8-16
Stage Two: Examining the Mouthpiece 8-17
Visually Examining the Facing 8-17
Measuring the Mouthpiece 8-17
Using a Model 8-18
Play Testing 8-18
What Materials Should be Used for Testing? 8-18
One Final Consideration 8-19
Your Second Mouthpiece 8-19
Conclusion 8-20

CHAPTER IX: FUNDAMENTALS OF REED BALANCING

Introduction 9-2
Just What's Wrong with Commercial Reeds!?! 9-2
Just What is an Unbalanced Reed? 9-2
Why should the Reed Be Balanced? 9-4
Playing Characteristics of an Unbalanced Reed 9-4

Learning to Test the Reed 9-4
Beginning the Process of Correcting Reed Imbalance 9-4
Basic Reed Resistance 9-5
Reed Response 9-5
Reed Response and Mouthpiece Facings 9-5
Criteria for a Well Balanced Reed 9-7
The Dynamic and Pitch Range Response Tests 9-7
Performing the Dynamic Response Test 9-7
A Word about Biting and the Dynamic Response Test 9-9
Evaluating the Dynamic Response Test 9-9
The Pitch Range Response Test 9-9
Evaluating the Pitch Range Response Test 9-10
A Simplified, Easy to Learn Method of Reed Finishing 9-11
Reed Balancing Made Simple 9-11
What You Will Need for Reed Balancing 9-11
How to Use Your New "Sophisticated" Reed Tools 9-11
Correcting the Response: Balancing the Tip Area 9-12
Adjusting the Resistance 9-12
Final Finishing 9-17
Practicing Your Reed Finishing Techniques 9-17
Clipping the Reed 9-17
New Reeds and Reed Balancing 9-18
Wetting the Reed and Warpage 9-18
Sanding the Flat Side of the Reed 9-19
Reed Placement for Practice and Performance 9-19
Conclusion 9-20

CHAPTER X: CLARINET CARE AND MAINTENANCE

Introduction: The Importance of Clarinet Maintenance 10-2
Clarinet Care: General Remarks 10-2
Care of the Clarinet Key Mechanism 10-2
Cleaning the Key Mechanism 10-4
Care of Key Plating 10-4
Flat Spring and Needle Spring Maintenance 10-5
Pad Care 10-5
Pad Inspection and Compression Testing 10-6
Wood Care 10-7
Oiling the Bore 10-8
How to Oil the Bore 10-8

How Often to Oil the Bore 10-8
Loose Bell Rings 10-9
What Happens if Your Clarinet Cracks? 10-9
Tone Hole Maintenance 10-10
Cleaning the Register Tube 10-10
Cleaning the Mouthpiece 10-11
Cleaning Socket Joints 10-11
Conclusion 10-11

CHAPTER XI: ACCESSORIES FOR THE CLARINET

Introduction 11-2
Barrels 11-2
Adjustable Barrels; Their Use and Abuse 11-4
Tuning Rings 11-5
Bells 11-6
Clarinet Ligatures 11-7
Mouthpiece Caps 11-8
Lip Savers: Their Use and Abuse 11-9
Bore Savers or "Shove Its" 11-9
Clarinet Neck Straps 11-9
Thumb Supports or "Rests" 11-10
Thumb Cushions 11-10
Mouthpiece Cushions 11-10
Swabs 11-11
Reed Clippers 11-12
Reed Storage Methods 11-12
Synthetic Reeds 11-13
Conclusion 11-14

AFTERWORD

Chapter I

TEACHNG THE CLARINET TONE CONCEPT

In this chapter you will learn.....

What students need to help them develop a concept of clarinet tone.

The most common words professionals use to describe clarinet tone.

How to help students begin to hear musical shapes, or tone "photographs" with their ears.

Some outstanding clarinet recordings that will help your students develop their concept of clarinet tone more quickly.

The Two Essential Elements for Teaching Tone Concept

"What should the clarinet sound like?" Posing this question to students and helping them answer it is both essential and fundamental to their development. Think of it this way: imagine a friend has sent you a complicated jig saw puzzle as a gift, but for some reason he failed to include the box that shows how the completely assembled puzzle looks. Trying to assemble the puzzle may already be difficult, but with no point of reference and no picture to study the difficulty of the task increases almost exponentially.

Unfortunately, most young clarinet students find themselves in an analogous position; hearing lots of different pieces of information, being told lots of different things to do, but being given no picture, no clear point of reference which helps them grasp how all those pieces fit together to form a single, complete thing. With no clear idea of what it should be the clarinet remains a largely arcane and even prosaic object for young students. Why? In the preponderance of cases the onus for this common lack must be laid squarely at the feet of the teacher. The next good thing to do in making progress remains obscure to them in large part simply because the teacher has simply passed over the most basic and foundational of all things in teaching: helping the students form a clear standard by which any and all progress can be quantified or measured. Metaphorically one might say the teacher involves his or herself in speaking to the students in detail about each individual tree, but never bothers to show them the forest in which they all belong. What all this means is that time spent helping students picture what clarinet playing really is when all the pieces are properly put together can result in clearer meaning to the instructions they are given and quicken their progress. Here is the locus classicus where the old adage, "a picture is worth a thousand words" is perfectly apropos.

"What should the clarinet sound like?" The astute teacher needs to begin helping his or her students begin piecing together the answer to that question in two ways: with their ears and with the mind; with the faculties of hearing and understanding. Put simply, students need the experience of hearing good clarinet tone (and lots of it!) and then being taught why it is good. Who knows? Hearing fine clarinet tone and understanding with increasing clarity why it is good might also excite them to think that the instrument they hold in their hands can actually do "all that!" in the hands of a great clarinetist and inspire them to follow suit. Let's define each of these tasks a bit more clearly and look at some ways they can be accomplished.

Developing the Auricular Concept: Learning to Listen to Sound
Obviously, if students are to develop fine clarinet tones they must be given examples to hear. With the excellence in recording and the abundance of tape and CD players this should hardly be a problem. (For the teacher who is unfamiliar with clarinet artists a short but excellent list of recordings is provided at the end of this chapter).

Developing an Intellectual Concept of the Tone
Providing students with good clarinet recordings is both essential and necessary, but just hearing recordings is not enough. The teacher must also help them intellectually understand what they should be listening for. This means that they need to be given words which accurately describe each aspect of the tone and indicate what features in the sound are desirable and which are not. Professional clarinetists use common words to describe fine clarinet tone. Some of these words refer to tone color, others to tone shape. Discussing tone color can be problematic and confusing even for professionals. Therefore, it is easier to help young players begin developing their concepts by concentrating on tone shape rather than on tone color.

Teaching the Characteristic Shape of the Clarinet Tone
Some of the words clarinetists use to describe the characteristic shape of the clarinet tone are "centered," "focused," "concentrated," and "well-defined."
It is perhaps best to begin with the word focused since this concept is cross-referenced with the sense of sight. Every child knows when a picture is blurry and when it is clear and this makes it easy for them to distinguish a blurry, uncentered sound from a well-centered, focused one. An easy way to help them make this distinction is to present a few examples of tones, while asking the students to close their eyes and pretend the tones they hear are two different photographs. Ask them which sound "picture" is in focus and which one is blurred.

Once they become comfortable with the idea that they can actually hear shapes with their ears it is easier to get them to hear and appreciate the shape of a professional's tone and begin listening critically to their own. You can continue teaching them to listen to clarinet shape by playing some contrasting examples of clarinet styles. For instance, the style of an old-fashioned Dixieland clarinet player like Johnny Dodds juxtaposed with Harold Wright, Karl Leister or some other great classical clarinetists. It should not be difficult for most students to distinguish between the loose, diffused, unfocused nature of the Dixieland player's tone and the pristine, focused tonal shape that someone like Harold Wright produces.

Once this is done successfully the students can then proceed to listen for differences in examples which are less contrasting. For instance, you might contrast the tones of American clarinetists with those of British players, whose concept of tone is normally somewhat less-focused than that of an American Clarinetist.

At this point you may protest saying there is too much to be done to spend time listening to recordings and examples. No doubt there is a lot to do, but learning to actively and critically listen a little bit each day will actually save time because it will help make better sense of any technical instructions the students receive from you. As the students continue listening to fine clarinet tone they can't help but begin "growing" their own idea of what the clarinet should sound like. As their concepts grow their attention will gradually shift from the question, "What should the clarinet sound like?", to "How can we make the clarinet sound like that?" The following chapters are devoted to helping you give the answer.

A Short List of Clarinet Recordings

The following list is very brief, but it contains a lot of good sounds for your students to soak up.

Harold Wright:
	Brahms Sonatas	Boston Records BR1005 CD
	Weber Concerto in Eb	Boston Records BR 1028 CD
	Shepherd on the Rock	Boston Records BR 1024 CD
	Weber Grand Duo	"

The late Harold Wright was principle of Dallas, National and Boston Symphony Orchestras and was a fixture at the Marlboro Music Festival. Though a great orchestral player he was noted for his sinuous control of the clarinet and his peerless chamber music performances. Many consider his tone, control and phrasing to be ideal.

John Manasse   Weber: Complete Works   XLNT 1004 &18005

John Manasse is presently one of the most sought after clarinetists in the New York City. His recording of Weber's works is widely regarded as of the first rank.

Larry Combs   Bernstein Sonata   Summit 172
    Scriabin and Prokoffiev   Summit 125

Larry Combs is presently principle clarinet in the Chicago Symphony Orchestra, and is considered to be one of the top clarinetists of the latter part of this century.

David Shifrin   Copland Concerto   Angel CDC 49095

David Shifrin is one of the top free lance clarinetists in America and has an international reputation as a recitalist and soloist.

Louis Cahuzac   Hindemith Concerto   EMI ZDCB 55032

Louis Cahuzac was considered the dean of the great French School of clarinet playing. His performance of the Hindmith Concerto when he was in his seventies is still considered a classic. The beauty, power and clarity of Cahuzac's tone and his exemplary legato are qualities any young player would do well to try to incorporate in their own playing.

Robert Marcellus   Mozart Clarinet Concerto   Sony Classics-#62424
Robert Marcellus served as principal clarinetist of the Cleveland Orchestra for many years. His recording of the Mozart Clarinet Concerto is considered among the finest.
Ricardo Morales Trio and Sonata by Rudolph Koch International Classics- #3-7339-2-H1
Ricardo is presently principal clarinet in the New York Metropolitan Opera, a position he won at age 19. Many consider Ricardo to be the most brilliant clarinetist of this generation. He has the rare gift of being equally at home in both orchestral and chamber music settings and is in constant demand as a recitalist, clinician and soloist.

The Caracas Clarinet Quartet
It is always good to let young clarinetists see that the clarinet is ultimately a social instrument and that they can have lots of fun playing clarinet together in ensembles. There is presently a wonderful recording made by the Caracas Clarinet Quartet that is great fun for young clarinetists (and old as well) to listen to. It contains lots of pieces which are rooted in the infectious rhythms and lovely, lyrical folk melodies we have all come to associate with South America. The music will both inspire and excite any young listener. Though this recording is not commonly available in the U.S., at the time of this publication copies can be gotten from Woodwindiana. You can write them at P.O. Box 344, Bloomington, IN 47402-0344, or call or fax them at (812)323-8622. Through the internet you can E-mail them at hklug@indiana.edu No doubt many clarinetists could come up with a short list of recordings which are equally worthy of being added to this list. Care has been taken here to list only a few representative recordings with a stress upon solo and chamber music performances. The reason is simple; chamber music is the context in which the sound can be heard most realistically and intimately and the development of the sound concept is the central purpose of exposing young players to fine clarinet playing.

The International Clarinet Association
The ICA publishes an excellent periodical quarterly. It is full of articles on virtually every sort on the clarinet. The ICA magazine can be helpful in creating enthusiasm among young clarinet students as well as giving them a broader perspective on the instrument they play. The magazine routinely contains the latest information on equipment, up to date information on playing techniques

and research, special interest articles on performers and information about special clarinet events, such as the ICA convention, the Oklahoma Clarinet Symposium and various regional meetings. The ICA can be contacted on the internet at www.clarinet.org/ for information about subscription and other items of interest.
You might also encourage your students to check out their web site and investigate the excellent list of clarinet links the site offers.

In Conclusion

In summary, it is important to note that it is neither arbitrary nor accidental that a whole chapter has been devoted to Tone Concept and how to teach it. Nor is the choice of placing it first a random one. It has this honored place to emphasize that it is neither optional nor ancillary to the process of learning how to play the clarinet. To the contrary, it is both foundational and essential, for in teaching tone concept what is being taught is nothing less than how to listen and what to listen for. Put more precisely, Tone Concept as a subject has been placed at the very head of the book because it is at the very heart of the book, for it is that singular critical technique, that Standard which both monitors and measures the applied techniques; Tone Concept is the Judge, they are the judged; Tone Concept is the plumbline, the are the structures to be plumbed. Tone Concept is therefore qualitatively different than all else that must be learned. To set out teaching students to play without teaching them how to listen what to listen for is to set out dictating to the students' senses while ignoring their sensibilities, which is nothing less than senselessness. To do so is, in fact, to not be teaching at all in any real sense but to be doing something more akin to programming, which is below both the dignity and capability of persons, even, and perhaps most especially, young persons.

Practically speaking, what all this means is that Tone Concept needs to be taught from the very outset of the student's musical experience. Failure to do so makes the task of teaching not less but more time consuming. In contrast, teachers who devote adequate time and energy to helping students learn to listen are giving them the critical tools that will enable them to become their own best teachers. In helping them develope a fine tonal concept the teacher is aiding the students in lifting up their eyes beyond their own halting and reluctant foot steps to see the light at the end of the tunnel. This inner picture of tone once formed, even in the most seminal and rudimentary of ways, enables students to begin running rather than walking, hastening their progress, increasing their enthusiasm, all the while repeatedly saving the teacher the otherwise obligatory and proverbial "thousand words."

Chapter II

THE AIR: BREATHING AND BLOWING CORRECTLY

In this chapter you will learn.....

How to teach students to take a full breath.

Why breath attacks are useful and the two methods of playing them.

What diaphragmatic and compression methods of blowing are and why one works better than the other for playing the clarinet.

How to make the air last longer.

How to help students develop the habit of constantly supporting the tone.

How to teach students to maintain the air stream as they change notes.

How to change dynamics without loss of consistency and stability in tone color, shape and tuning.

PART I
BASIC BREATHING AND BLOWING TECHNIQUES

The Natural Breath
Breathing correctly is as easy as falling asleep... literally! In fact, in a relaxed state of sleep we all breathe correctly. If you observe someone sleeping you will notice that the abdomen gently rises and falls with each breath. The type of breath needed to play the clarinet is exactly the same only more air is taken in.

Though we may breathe correctly while sleeping, most of us breathe less effectively when we are awake. Often the tension and stress that each of us experience each day cause us to do shallow breathing from the chest because our abdominal muscles are contracted so much of the time. Because of this we usually need to help students rediscover what it is like to breathe naturally. The first positive step towards accomplishing this is simply getting them to relax. Relaxation is the first prerequisite to learning practically every aspect of clarinet playing.

The Full Breath
The correct breath is characterized by:
1. An expansion all around the abdomen and lower back area.
2. A corresponding expansion of the chest.

An effective way to teach students what it feels like to take a "full breath" is as follows:
Ask them to:
1. Exhale completely.
2. Bend over so that their upper bodies are now parallel to the floor.
3. Place the palms of their hands on the lower part of their backs.
4. Inhale slowly through the mouth.

When they inhale they will feel an immediate expansion of their rib cage and lower back. This cannot keep from happening because when they are bent over the only possible way to breathe is from the abdomen. Students need to repeatedly practice breathing in this "bent over" position until they feel comfortable and confident about breathing "from the tummy" instead of from the chest and shoulders. Once they are able to do this ask them to see if they can continue to do so while standing or sitting in an erect position.

Breathing this way when they stand or sit may give students the sensation that they are taking air in their chests and their stomachs. (Of course this is not what really happens, but it feels that way). Because of this it might help them to practice taking a full breath in two stages (double breath); first, by filling their tummies and then filling their chests. As the student becomes more comfortable with breathing fully the double breath can be gradually fazed out. For some however, it will always remain a useful technique, especially under performance pressure.

breath from lower stomach and not chest

Example 1: Incorrect and Correct Breathing

A.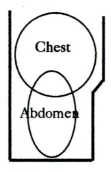

B.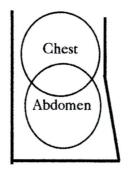

Example "A" represents a shallow breath that only expands the chest. The abdomen remains tight, limiting the amount of air that can be taken in. This kind of breath is common and is often accompanied by shoulders that lift as the breath is taken.

Example "B" represents the full breath. Here both the chest and abdomen expand, while the shoulders remain relaxed. The docility of the stomach muscles permit full distention of the diaphragm which allows the air to fully fill the lungs.

Using the Air: The Two Possible Methods of Expelling the Air

Inhaling correctly is of course only half of the process in clarinet playing and the one most identical to nature. Blowing the air out is another matter. This is usually a technique which must be learned from the ground up. Few do it naturally.

There are only two methods of expelling the air from the body: *The Diaphragmatic Method* and *The Compression Method.* We will also refer to these methods as the "toothpaste tube" and "aerosol can" methods. We do this for two reasons:

1. The way material is contained in and expelled from each of these types of containers corresponds very closely to how the body uses the air in the diaphragmatic and compression methods of blowing.
2. Virtually everyone is familiar with these items and understands how they work.

Relating these common images to the two different ways of blowing usually helps students learn to blow correctly more quickly than all the intellectual explanations and anatomical drawings you can shake a stick at. Why? Because students need to feel what it is like to blow correctly more than they need to intellectually understand how the body actually does it. These images, silly as they may sound, usually help them get the correct "feel" better than technical explanations or drawings.

The Diaphragmatic or "Toothpaste Tube" Method of Blowing

This method of blowing is characterized by a combination of diaphragmatic relaxation and abdominal contraction. After the initial inhalation, the diaphragm is allowed to gradually rises to its relaxed, domed shaped position while the abdominal muscles are used to push the air out, causing the tummy to contract as if were being squeezed like a tube of toothpaste by some invisible hand. "Toothpaste Tube" blowing produces a comparatively broad, slow moving, "warm" stream of air. Most students, even those who take a full breath, treat their bodies like toothpaste tubes when they expel the air. Example 2 shows how the air is expelled with diaphragmatic blowing. The arrows indicate the direction the air is being pushed.

Results of the "Toothpaste Tube" Method

The slow, broad, warm air stream created by this type of blowing is very poorly suited for the clarinet. Here's why:
1. Since the air is low in compression, a higher volume of air is needed to energize the reed than would otherwise be necessary. This means that tones can't be sustained as long as they might be if the air were used differently. In other words, diaphragmatic blowing wastes air!
2. The warm air produces a tone that lacks center, richness and focus. It produces rather, a tone that is broad, "pale," "breathie" and diffused. Such a broad shape has little carrying power. The broad slow air also causes high tones to be unstable, makes them hard to attack securely and causes upper clarion and altissimo tones to be perpetually flat unless the embouchure "bites" the pitch up.
(Most players who use diaphragmatic blowing are also biters out of necessity. More on that in chapter four).

The Educator's Guide to the Clarinet

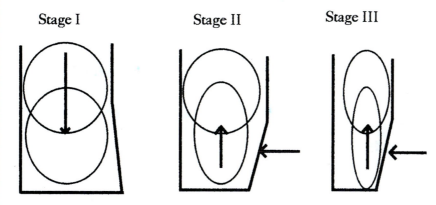

Example 2: Air Depletion in Diaphragmitic Breathing/Blowing

Stage I   Stage II   Stage III

Analysis:
Stage I shows the complete breath (which gives the sensation of filling both chest and abdomen, represented here as two circles).
Stage II represents the contraction of the abdominal muscle as it begins to push the diaphragm upwards and "squeeze" or force the air out of the lungs.
Stage III The air is now virtually depleted, the muscles of the abdomen are completely contracted and the diaphragm is at its highest position in the body, at which point the body will have to quickly relax to reposition itself for stage I.

The Compression or "Aerosol Can" Method of Blowing

In contrast, the second method of blowing is characterized by a combination of full and perpetual diaphragmatic contraction, which necessitates abdominal muscular relaxation. The diaphragm remains fully depressed all the time the air is being expressed, constantly pushing down and out against the abdominal muscles and the lower back. Because of this, the tummy remains distended all the time the breath is being expelled, while the chest area slowly deflates (see ex. 3). Pushing the air down in the body puts a pressure on the abdomen similar to the abdominal pressure felt when lifting a heavy object. Using this method of blowing compresses the air in a way that "squeezing" the air out by an abdominal muscular contraction cannot and causes it to move much faster and with more energy and concentration.

First Steps in Learning Compression Blowing

Try the following method with your students to help them get the feel of what it is like to use the air in this way. They will need a fresh breath, so begin by asking them to blow all the "bad" air out. Next:

1. Ask them to take a full breath. (Make sure their shoulders remain relaxed while the breath is being taken. Also, to help insure they really do have a full breath, you may want to have them use the "double breath" technique we mentioned earlier).
2. If they are sitting, ask them to take a breath and then to direct the air downward, as if they were going to push it straight through the seats of their chairs. When they do this they should feel an outward pressure distending their abdomens, sides and lower backs. (This pressure increase should remind them of how an aerosol can feels all the time!)
3. Next, while maintaining the air pressure in their bodies, ask them to place their index fingers on their lips. (You might even ask them to relax their cheek muscles as well so that the air pressure causes them to bulge out Dizzy Gillespie style. Of course, they will never do this in actual playing and you can bet it will look really silly to them, but it will help you to see that they are actually creating and maintaining the air pressure in their bodies).
4. Finally, ask them to remove their fingers and allow their lips to relax. When they do this if they have maintained their downward pressure the air will instantaneously and forcefully burst out of their mouths.

When playing the clarinet is added to this routine, the tongue's placement on the reed will replace the finger on the lips as the means of holding and releasing the pressurized air. (We will cover the tongue's effects on the air stream thoroughly in chapter four.) Once the tongue releases the air into the clarinet, all that is needed is to maintain the push of air down and against the abdomen. Rather than the tension of abdominal muscular contraction, blowing this way actually causes the expansion, relaxation and distention of the abdominal muscles.

As we have said, this method of blowing compresses the air giving it much greater speed, concentration and energy than the toothpaste tube or diaphragmatic method. In fact, it is so different from toothpaste tube blowing that it is almost misleading to call it a method of blowing at all. It would be more accurate to call it a method of creating and maintaining constant air compression in the body, similar to the compression which a bag piper must maintain in order to keep the drone at a constant volume and pitch level. Most clarinetists find that this method of blowing helps them maintain both consistency of air flow and air pressure with greater ease.

> Example 3: Air Depletion in the Compression or "Aerosol Can" Method of Blowing
>
> Stage I   Stage II   Stage III
>
>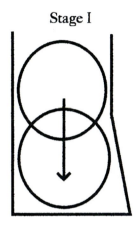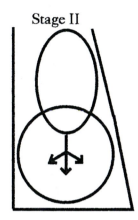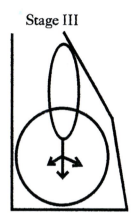
>
> Analysis:
> Stage I is a full breath. (The arrows represent the direction the air is being pushed).
> Stage II shows the depletion of the air filling the upper chest area while the downward blowing pressure keeps the abdomen area filled and distended.
> Stage III represents a further depletion of upper chest air. Notice that the abdomen is still filled. From stage III the player is now ready to relax the downward pushing and take a fresh breath.

The Results of the Compression Method of Blowing

The compression method is ideal for the clarinet. Both tone and tuning are significantly improved by using the air in this way.

Once students learn to blow correctly their relaxation and ease in making the sound usually increases. Another thing they may experience is a sense of having no constriction or impediment between their lower abdomen and the tip of the reed and mouthpiece. They may also have a sense that the pressure in the clarinet and the pressure in the body are somehow equalized and the sound is being magically and mysteriously sustained without any perceivable effort. They may also notice the following:

Chapter II: The Air: Breathing and Blowing Correctly

1. *The air they do take in, because it is compressed, goes a lot further.* (Increased air compression energizes and excites reed vibration with significantly less air volume than the comparatively low compression, "toothpaste tube" method).
2. They may be able to play stronger reeds with ease.
3. Since they get more sound with less air volume students usually note an increased ability to sustain phrases. Passages which previously took two breaths can, in some cases, be played with only a single breath....and with air to spare!

Example 4: Summary of Diaphragmatic and Compression Methods of Blowing.

Air Quality	Compression Method	Diaphragmatic Method
Air Speed	Fast	Slow
Air Volume	Low	High
Air Shape	Small, Dense	Broad, Diffused
Air Temperature	Cold	Warm

[handwritten note: print — works better with high resistance instrument (i.e. oboe)]

The Two Methods of Blowing and Other Wind Instruments

At this point teachers whose primary instruments are not the clarinet and who have been taught the Diaphragmatic Method of blowing, might object. However, the fact is that not all wind instruments work best with the same method of blowing. The determining factor seems to be the inherent resistance of the instrument itself. Higher resistance instruments, such as the oboe, tend to work better with Diaphragmatic Blowing. Lower resistance instruments, such as the clarinet, most definitely work better with Compression Blowing. The difference is clear from each player's attitudes towards the breath: oboists are always trying to get rid of the breath and complain of having too much air, while clarinetists can't seem to get enough, and are always seeking ways to make their air go further. That is where the Compression Method shows its superiority!

What to Play?

The best way to learn how to blow the clarinet correctly is to play long tones and slow intervals. Slow scales are also good as long as fingering the notes does not distract the student from giving full attention to the acts of breathing and blowing. All of the focus needs to be placed upon how the body is working and how the breath being taken in and used.

What to Notice?

Long tone practice is no time to put the brain on cruise control. Quite the contrary. Long tones give the clarinetist the time to do what he or she cannot do while playing complicated technical passages--- pay attention to and closely examine all the facets of tone production which support all those notes and rhythms, most especially the facet of breathing and blowing.

One of the best approaches to long tone practice is to have a set list of things you routinely think about as you sustain long tones and slow intervals. Here are some of the things which should be on that list:

1. Am I creating a constant compression of air in my body by consistently directing the energy of the air down against my abdomen, lower back and sides?
2. Are my abdominal muscles relaxing to make room for the full downward movement of the air and the diaphragm?
3. Am I maintaining a consistent, stable high/back tongue position as I blow? (See chapter 3 for a full summary of the role of the tongue in tone production).
4. How long am I able to sustain a tone on a single breath? What can I do to increase the duration?
5. Am I biting as I sustain tones or does my jaw remain in its proper dropped position?
6. How does the air feel as it flows from my body into the clarinet?

If you are teaching young players you might think of holding weekly contests to see who can sustain a single tone the longest. Doing this once a week might encourage the students to routinely practice that which might otherwise be neglected entirely. Be creative! <u>Any way you can motivate the students to practice breathing/blowing techniques will give them a rich pay off in increased confidence, greater relaxation and improved tone and tuning.</u>

Habitually "Supporting" the Clarinet Tone

Students commonly begin notes with energy only to let the volume quickly drop, causing their tones to sound much like the flame of a match looks; very bright when first struck only to die down quickly. Students need to correct this tendency by using better breath support for the tone to the point that doing so is habitual and automatic.

The first positive step to teaching them to cultivate this habit is to avoid the use of the word "support" altogether. In fact, avoid any terms which are abstract or require too much reasoning. You are the only one who needs to understand how things actually work. Reasoning only gets between them and the act of playing and slows the process of learning, especially in the early stages of their development. Instead, try to get the student's senses, nervous system and muscles to react properly by stimulating their imaginations with familiar action images. You do the thinking while they do the doing.

One of the more effective action images which helps students form the habit of constantly "supporting" the sound is that of blowing up a balloon.

With all this in mind, try teaching the students to properly support the tone by asking them to close their eyes and imagine that their clarinet tone is a balloon. As they play (keeping their eyes closed) ask them to see the balloon getting slowly but steadily larger and larger.

Because of the tendency most students have of dropping the air, the image of a steadily enlarging balloon usually results in the production of a steady, even, full tone, rather than one that actually gets louder and louder. An added advantage of using action images such as this is that you can quickly correct their lack of support with hardly any words at all. Simply looking at them and puffing out your cheeks like a balloon is usually ample reminder to snap them out of the "lazy air stream doldrums."

Simple ideas like this can help students improve the support of sustained tones and long phrases dramatically and help get them on their way to good blowing habits.

The Air and the Fingers

We've all heard about people who can't walk and chew gum at the same time. If we and our students are going to be successful as clarinetists we can't be one of them, at least when we're playing the clarinet. Clarinet playing requires a whole litany of things which must be properly coordinated (not just two). Among the most important of these is that of blowing a steady stream of air while the fingers move to create different notes. It's sort of the musical equivalent of patting your head and rubbing your tummy at the same time.

Many players, not just beginners, imperceptibly "flinch" each time they play a different tone and this causes them to adjust their air stream. This "flinching" may be subtle, but whenever it happens it causes a loss of beauty, smoothness and richness in the phrasing and breaks or weakens the musical line.

[Handwritten margin note: Kids sometimes flinch / shift embrochure when they move notes]

You can help students become aware of how much they are adjusting the air when they finger the clarinet by the following method:
1. *Ask them to play a certain passage. (Keep it simple for starters).*
2. *When they are finished, rotate the mouthpiece around so that the student can control the blowing while you control the fingering.*
3. *Ask them to blow the clarinet while you finger the same passage they just played.*
4. *Next, you can simply finger random notes while they blow. Make sure to play unpredictably so they can't anticipate what you might play and begin reflexively adjusting their air stream or some other part of the tone production system.*

The results of this simple demonstration is usually remarkable. Most students notice an immediate improvement in both tone quality and legato when you, not they, are fingering the clarinet. This little "A-B" comparison is often enough to convince them of how much they are getting in their own way by needlessly adjusting the air stream as they change notes. Once they are convinced, they will need some ways to help them work on the problem.

The Think/Play Exercise: Blowing Through, Not To the Notes

The Think/Play Exercise requires that students think one thing while doing another for the purpose of helping them distinguish between two actions and focus their attention on the one which usually gets the least attention. In the case of air and notes, it's almost always the air that gets the short straw. So the idea is, whenever they are playing the notes, they should make believe they're only playing a long tone. Doing this helps them focus on the breath rather than fingering the notes. Example 5 shows how it works.

The "Think/Play Exercise" can be done alone, with two players or in a group. The object of course, is to help the student concentrate on keeping the air stream as constant as possible, no matter what! If two players or a group are doing it, ask them to listen to those playing the line they are not and to pretend they are playing that instead. Another approach is to have the students turn their mouthpieces around so they can blow the clarinet while another fingers the notes. Group them off in pairs and have partner "A" finger line one on partner "B's" clarinet, while the partner "B" fingers line two on theirs.

Chapter II: The Air: Breathing and Blowing Correctly

This exercise should help the students become aware of the importance of the constancy of air pressure and how it can improve everything they play. It should help them to learn to "blow through the notes, not to the notes." With a little inventiveness you can think up scores of variations on this exercise that can be played individually or collectively by the students, all with the same goal in mind: Achieving constant support of the air while the fingers are moving. The only precaution is to not make the exercises so complicated that attention can't be given to the air stream.

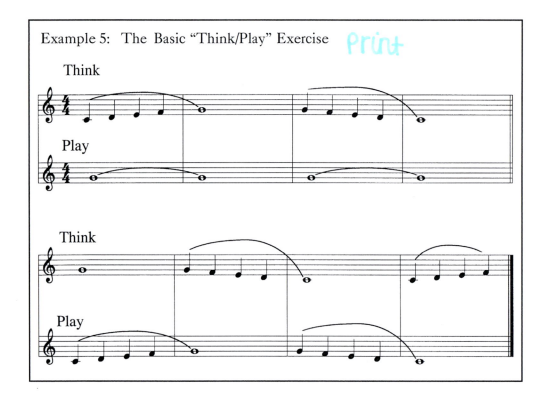

PART II:
ADVANCED BLOWING TECHNIQUES:
PLAYING DYNAMICS

What is Modulation of the Air?

Modulation of the air is an advanced technique and should not be taught until the student is thoroughly grounded in the habit of breathing and blowing correctly. "Modulation of the air" refers to the way the air changes as dynamics change. How well the player makes these changes in the air determines how consistent the color, shape and tuning of the tone will be throughout any dynamic changes.

Air Pressure, Air Volume and Playing Dynamics

Many players blow the clarinet differently when they play softly than when they play loudly. Specifically, they may use compressed air at louder volumes, but switch to "toothpaste tube" air at softer levels. The problem with using different blowing methods is that they produce essentially different qualities of speed, direction and shape in the air. These different qualities in turn, cause the tone color, shape and tuning to change (as the air changes, so does the tone!). This is problematic since the clarinet tone needs to be consistent in color, tuning and shape, even throughout changes in dynamics.

This three-fold consistency in tone can only be accomplished in dynamic changes by using the same *quality* of air stream, no matter how much the quantity may vary. Practically speaking, this means that the student must learn to differentiate between air pressure (quality) and air volume (quantity), learning to keep one constant (pressure) while varying the other (volume). Additionally, air pressure and volume must also be coordinated with what the tongue and embouchure are doing. Here's how to begin learning the technique:

Play a tone at forte and begin tapering it smoothly to piano. As you play softer, incrementally increase pressure on the reed by gently snugging the mouthpiece more firmly against the lips. (If you bite rather than snug the mouthpiece to add pressure to the reed, the color, shape and tuning will all change for the worse, no matter how perfectly you may be blowing: Biters play perpetually sharp! Don't do it!)

The gradual increase in reed pressure compensates for the gradual decrease in air pressure and volume which happens as the sound grows softer. This exchange helps maintain identical shape and color in the sound. The amount of increased snugness that will be needed as you play softer will depend primarily upon how well balanced your reed is : Better balance will require less increase, worse balance will require more. It's that simple.

The Tongue, the Soft Palate and Playing Dynamics

Next, the air and embouchure can be greatly assisted in their labors by both the tongue and the soft palate. Here's how:

Essentially, the tongue must maintain its *high/back*, arched position at <u>all</u> times. *Allowing the tongue to relax and move low and forward as air pressure decreases robs the air of the speed and energy needed to keep the sound healthy, and increases the demands upon the embouchure pressure to maintain the tone.*

The flexible, sensuous soft palate, located in the back half of the roof of the mouth needs to be lifted at all times, similar to the position it assumes when one yawns with the mouth closed. If the muscles of the soft palate relax and do not tighten or contract <u>and</u> there is adequate air pressure from blowing correctly, the soft palate usually lifts "naturally". But as air pressure decreases for softer dynamic levels the temptation is to let the soft palate lower or drop. This temptation needs to be resisted. As the tongue must remain high and back, so the soft palate must always remain in its "blown up", lifted, or "yawning" position, and this, at times, means that the clarinetist needs to consciously think of maintaining the lift. When this happens there is no need to force in some grotesque fashion. A gentle lifting will do. Though as one plays softer the lifting usually needs to increase accordingly. As always, the ear is the final arbiter.

Putting it all Together

Finally, all the while air, embouchure, tongue position and soft palate are coordinating with and counterbalancing one another, the method of blowing (compressed air) must remain unchanged, no matter how soft the sound may become. The only thing which varies is the quantity of air.

Perhaps it might be easier to conceptualize how this is done if you think of the downward pressure put on your lower abdomen as being analogous to the foot pressure applied to an automobile's gas pedal; the more pressure the foot adds, the more gas is fired and the faster the car goes. Similarly, the more forcefully that downward pressure is exerted the louder the sound becomes. However (and here is the critical part), playing softer does not mean that downward pressure ceases altogether. Not at all! The quality of the air must remain just as dense, just as cold, and just as compressed as ever; just less of it! Relaxing the blowing compression and switching to "toothpaste tube method" at any point is tantamount to letting your foot off the gas pedal altogether and beginning to coast. It's a no no.

A good way to help students begin learning how to maintain pressurized air while varying air volume is to:

1. Ask them to blow air through a small opening in their lips as if they were playing "forte." They will be able to hear lots of compressed air rush between the narrow opening of their lips.
2. Ask them to blow the same way, but without pushing the air down and out against their lower abdomens quite so aggressively. They should still hear the same quality of compressed air rushing forcefully through their lips. It should be traveling just as fast and be just as dense. There will just not be as much of it in terms of volume. Put another way, the hissing between their lips will be just as intense, only softer.

In actual playing, the degree of downward pushing needed at any given moment is determined by several factors. These include:
1) The pitch range of the passage
2) The dynamic extreme required.
3) The amount of snugging pressure required to control that particular mouthpiece/reed set up (a well balanced reed makes life a lot easier).
4) The nature of the passage (ie. fast, slow, slurred or articulated).

The ear of course, must ever and always be the final arbiter. What the student should be listening for as the dynamics change are:
1) No color variation in the dynamic change.
2) No shape variation
3) No pitch variation
Only the dynamic should change.

Fluid control of dynamics doesn't just happen. It takes intelligent, deliberate, attentive practice. It takes time and determined effort to learn to coordinate all the means at one's disposal (embouchure snugging, tongue position, subtle changes in the glottis, and the smooth, even modulation of the compressed air) to make seamless, escalator-like dynamic changes a reality. The necessity of the constancy of compressed air and snugging of the mouthpiece/reed wedge cannot be overstressed. The coordination of these two actions are essential to the achievement of pitch, color and shape stability in dynamic changes. If you put your hand on the

Chapter II: The Air: Breathing and Blowing Correctly

tummy of a fine player to check the compression of the air you will find it to be the same no matter how softly or loudly he or she plays. Soft or loud, it's always "aerosol can" air. Learning to blow this way is one of the great secrets of superb clarinet playing. It is the Master Key that opens the door to all the tonal beauty of which the clarinet is capable.

Review of the Relationship between Embouchure Pressure and Air Volume in Playing Dynamics

As we have previously indicated, the relationship of embouchure and air when making dynamic changes is extremely simple: As air volume gradually decreases, embouchure (snugging, <u>not</u> biting) pressure incrementally and proportionately increases; as air volume increases, embouchure pressure decreases. These two expressions of energy must constantly and sensitively counterbalance one another to maintain the integrity of the tone as the dynamics change.

The degree to which embouchure pressure must be increased in dynamic diminuendo depends upon how well the reed/mouthpiece are balanced. The degree to which the embouchure can relax in dynamic crescendos depends upon how well the total clarinet setup itself "holds" the color, shape and pitch. The less the degree of "hold" in the set up, the less the embouchure will be able to relax at louder dynamic levels.

Example 6: Review of the Role of the Various Elements Involved in Playing Dynamics	
Air	gradual decrease in volume
Dynamics	Forte ———————▶ Piano
Embouchure	gradual increase in (snugging) pressure
Tongue	In stable high/back position throughout
Quality of Air	Compression Method of Blowing throughout

Throughout every facit of tone production success is dependent upon how fluidly and seamlessly transference of resistances and energies are made from one part of the tone production system to the other. Ex. 6 shows how the relationship looks.

However, the whole system falls apart if at any time the clarinetist uses jaw closure to apply pressure to the reed. If this happens, the pitch level, tone color and shape will change, no matter how perfectly the blowing mechanism is being maintained. Any increase in embouchure pressure needs to be done by lifting or snugging the mouthpiece and reed more firmly against the lips, as described in chapter IV, *never* by biting!

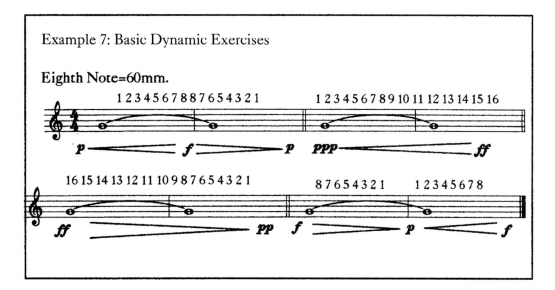

Basic Exercise for Improving Modulation of the Air and Dynamic Control

The exercises in example 7 are the most basic for gaining dynamic control. They need to be practiced on pitches in all registers and they should be made an essential part of the daily practice routine. It is best to intersperse them throughout the practice session, since doing several in a row can be physically taxing.

Notice the numbers above the tones. The number system can be helpful in developing perfectly uniform increases and decreases in dynamic gradations. Obviously, the higher the number, the fuller the sound; the lower the number the softer the sound. The goal is to control the dynamic level on the clarinet as you would the volume dial on a radio.

All dynamic exercises need to be played with a metronome. This will help insure that the swells will be even and in proper proportion. Use of a tuner can also be added to help maintain the integrity of pitch throughout the exercise. (Snugging rather than biting for all necessary embouchure/air exchanges can greatly improve pitch stability).

Breath Attacks: Starting the Sound with the Breath

Beginning the tone by releasing the tongue from the reed is commonly done and commonly taught. However, many great players cultivate the art of making breath attacks. They do so because of the subtle and beautiful musical effects they can create with the technique.

Breath attacks can give "soft", gentle beginnings to notes, as if they appear out of thin air, similar to note beginnings somewhat more natural to the voice or string instruments. Such note beginnings (they really should not be called or thought of as "attacks") can be delightful to hear.

Methods of Beginning Tones with the Breath

Two different methods can be used to begin tones with the breath alone. We will call them the *Decreasing Pressure Method* and the *Increasing Pressure Method*. Their common denominator is that neither uses the tongue in any way to initiate the start of the note. Rather, they approach the beginning of the note from opposite ends of the pressure spectrum.

The Decreasing Pressure Method

This method begins by setting the air pressure and tongue position as if the sound were already being produced, but placing so much embouchure/snugging pressure on the reed that it cannot respond. Since the tongue is not placed on the reed at all in this sort of attack much of its job of helping "hold" the sound back must be reassigned to the embouchure. This means the snugging pressure needed to "hold" the sound will have to be somewhat greater than it would be if the tongue were touching the reed. The sound is begun when the snugging pressure and embouchure muscles relax to the point that the reed can respond as it should to the air column. This method begins the tone in two stages. It may be summarized as follows:

Preparation:
1. Preset the air pressure several moments before the tone begins.
2. Partially "Hold" the air with the throat and the reed with embouchure snugging and firm lip muscles (never biting!!!!).
3. Place the tongue in its proper high/back voicing position.

Release:
4. Coordinate the relaxation of throat and snugging to successfully allow the tone to appear. (In most cases the relaxation of the throat to release the air will begin a moment before the embouchure release. This order of release will help insure that there will be adequate air pressure to set the reed into motion at the needed frequency).

This coordination needs to be practiced repeatedly until enough sensitivity and control is developed to precisely yet gently begin tones in all registers of the instrument at all dynamic levels.

The Increasing Pressure Method

The second method for beginning tones with the air alone is as follows:
1. Form the embouchure, assume the high/back tongue position and bring the mouthpiece to the lips, but do not snug the mouthpiece against them.
2. Blow air gently into the mouthpiece without making any sound. Nothing should be heard except the sound of the air freely going into the clarinet.
3. Simultaneously increase both air volume and snugging until the sound appears.

Either of these two techniques is valid and can effectively produce tones without the use of the tongue. Once they are mastered they will be two of the most expressive and most used tools in the clarinetist's artistic and technical arsenal

Conclusion

The air is the heart of any wind instrument. It forms the foundation upon which all other techniques can properly function. When the air fails in its job, it throws the whole structure of tone production techniques which depend upon it out of whack; nothing else can be as it ought to be or function properly without adequate air pressure. Working on all the other techniques discussed in subsequent chapters is virtually futile if breathing and blowing techniques are not properly developed.

Therefore, it is of utmost importance that considerable time and energy be spent upon teaching students correct breathing/blowing techniques. Once learned, care should be taken to make sure these techniques are maintained by habitual practice. Anyone, beginner or professional, can "fall asleep at the wheel" regarding the air at any time. The only safety net is the persistent and conscious application of correct methods.

Chapter III

THE TONGUE: VOICING THE CLARINET TONE

In this chapter you will learn.....

How the tongue position affects and controls the air column.

How to teach proper tongue position to your students.

How tongue position can dramatically affect the color, shape and tuning of the clarinet tone.

How correct tongue position can significantly improve upper register tuning.

How correct tongue position can assist the embouchure in controlling tuning and pitch.

Some valuable exercises which students can practice to help achieve and maintain correct tongue position.

Introduction

So far we have discussed how to generate the sound by breathing and blowing properly. Now we must turn to the component of tone production which regulates, shapes, directs and channels the energy of the breath: the tongue.

Unfortunately, it seems many fail to appreciate and understand the great influence the tongue has on the sound. Because of this, the tongue is frequently the neglected or forgotten component in tone production pedagogy. Yet, if a pedagogy is to be complete, the tongue's role must not be overlooked.

Essentially, the tongue's regulation of the air flow is analogous to how a nozzle regulates water flowing through a hose. Simply put, the tongue has the sole responsibility of controlling the shape, speed, and direction of the air stream as it flows from the lungs into the clarinet. The common term among clarinetists for this use of the tongue is called *voicing*. The tongue's control and regulation of the air affects every aspect of the tone without exception; tuning, color, shape, response, and volume (dynamics); change the position of the tongue in the mouth and you change the speed, shape and direction of the air; change the speed shape and direction of the air and every aspect of the tone changes with it. Logically, what this means is that tones which are uniform in color, shape and volume can only be achieved through the development of a stable, consistent and correct tongue position. No piece of equipment or embouchure technique can adequately make up for an incorrect and/or unstable tongue position.

How the Tongue Affects the Air

At the top of the oral cavity we find the hard and soft palates. The hard palate is fixed. The soft palate, located in the very back of the roof of the mouth, can move, but a only to a comparatively small degree. At the bottom of the oral cavity we find the tongue. Of the three, the tongue is by far the most mobile and therefore the most able to create significantly smaller or greater distances between it and the roof of the mouth. The air, which emanates from the lungs, must flow through the oral cavity to reach the mouthpiece and reed. When the tongue lifts itself up and back in the mouth it creates a narrowed passage between it and the roof of the mouth called a *venturi*. The venturi speeds up the flow of the air dramatically, just as placing one's thumb partially over the end of a hose concentrates and speeds up the flow of water. The faster, more concentrated air stream caused by the high/back tongue position benefits the clarinet tone in the following ways:

1. clarification of the tone and increased resonance.
2. superior tonal focus.
3. Higher pitch.

4. Elimination of detuning (out of tuneness) in upper clarion (G to high C) and third register tones.

The evil twins of the above virtues are, of course, a fuzzy, unfocused tone, general flatness, flat high tones and "grunts" at the beginning of upper clarion tones. These *always* appear as symptoms when the tongue fails to do its job of properly controlling the air column.

Negative Effects of Poor Tongue Position on the Embouchure

Many teachers have the misguided notion that the problems just mentioned are caused by a weak, loose embouchure. Therefore, it seems to them that the quick and obvious fix is simply to add more embouchure pressure to the reed (biting). While biting does seem to "solve" some of these, it does so only at the expense of creating others which are equally bad if not worse. For that fact, biting as a solution to any clarinet problem is a false solution, something like trading a headache for an upset stomach. Some of the many problems caused by biting includes:

1. The loss or reduction of resonance, depth, flexibility and freedom in the tone.
2. Frequent the cutting of the lower lip.
3. A thinness and brightness in tone, especially in the high register.
4. General sharpness.
5. Decreased embouchure endurance.
6. Decreased reed durability.

If the tongue does its job by voicing the sound properly, there will be no need for such use of the embouchure in such an abusive way and this whole litany of problems and many others can be avoided altogether.

Negative Effects of Poor Tongue Position on the Tone and Tuning

Beginning students may find the concept of a high, back and arched tongue position a bit foreign, even though they place their tongues in this position countless times each day to produce the sound of the consonant "K." Unfortunately, "lazy tongue," that is, a low and forward tongue placement, is very common, even among players who have played for years. Such tongue placement needs to be corrected as soon as possible. The slow, broad, dispersed "warm" air stream it creates causes the following serious problems in tone and tuning:

1. It significantly lowers the general pitch level.
2. It causes both the throat tones and higher tones to be very flat.
3. It tends produces an uncentered, dull, spread, hollow, tone quality.
4. It contributes to instability and insecurity in playing high tones.

5. It makes production of third register tones virtually impossible without excessive biting.
6. It forces the embouchure to compensate by inordinate tightness and biting.

For these reasons and many others, the sooner young players begin to develop a connaturality with the high/back, arched tongue position for the clarinet, the better for all the other systems which contribute to the clarinet's tone.

Beginning to Learn Correct Tongue Placement

Obvious as it is, few of us ever think about the fact that our tongues must be in different places in the mouth to form the various vowel and consonant sounds. Helping students become consciously aware of this is the first step in learning to voice the clarinet tone correctly. Here is a good way to begin:

1. Ask the students to <u>slowly</u> say the vowels A, E, I, O, and U, while noticing the movement of their tongue. They should quickly see how different the tongue placement and movement must be to create each sound.
2. Next, ask them to say the word "key" or "cake." In order to do this they must lift their tongues up and back in the mouth and arch the middle of the tongue. Usually, the middle of the tongue almost touches the roof of the mouth and the sides of the tongue touch the insides of the upper back molars.
3. Finally, ask the students to say the word "kick." and "hold" the "k" position at the end of the word, and... there they have it! (The word "key" may also be used, but holding the last "k" in "kick" helps insure the tongue will be high and back.)

The position the tongue assumes to form the consonate "k" is the correct tongue position for voicing the clarinet tone. It is formed by arching the middle of the tongue back and up to the roof of the mouth, as if you were preparing to say the letter "k" or hiss like a cat .

Relating Aural Concept to Physical Technique

Correct tongue position can and ought to be taught in coordination with teaching students to listen for a focused tone. As young players are trained and conditioned to recognize what a centered tone sounds like, they will begin to demand it of themselves and others, to the point that when they do not hear proper focus, the clarinet tone will simply seem "wrong" to them. Once the connection is made between what the tongue does and what the ears hear, correct tonal concept will help students monitor own tongue positions. In other words, the inner demand for correct tone created by having learned to listen should significantly reduce the need to constantly nag the students about maintaining the proper high/back tongue position; their internalized tone concept will now be doing that job.

> **Example 1: Comparison of Correct and Incorrect Tongue Positions**
>
>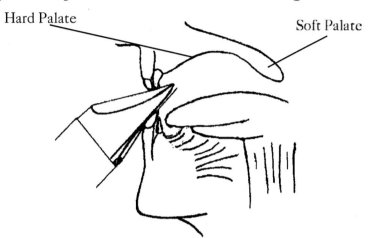
>
> **Incorrect low/forward tongue position:** Notice how great the distance is between the tongue and the roof of the mouth. Also notice how the broad stream of air this position creates is directed only generally toward the front of the mouth and lacks the necessary concentration for keeping the high tones from tuning flat.
>
>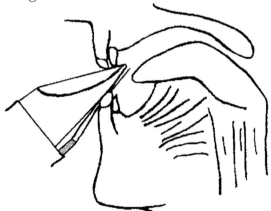
>
> **Correct high/back tongue position:** Notice how the high/back position narrows the passage between the surface of the tongue and the roof of the mouth. Notice also how the air is directed right at the reed, instead of just generally towards the front of the mouth. (Not indicated in the drawing is the lifting of the soft palate that should be done in tone production).

Using a Tuner

A tuner can be useful in helping young players understand just how much the tongue can change the tuning of a tone. They can learn this by playing a sustained tone on the mouthpiece (or mouthpiece and barrel) into an automatic chromatic tuner. The correct placement of the tongue usually produces a sharp concert "C" (or very flat "C#") if the mouthpiece alone is played. If the barrel and mouthpiece are played, the pitch should be concert "F#." As the students blow, ask them to change the position of their tongues from low and forward (the "O" position) to high and back (the "kkkey" or "kickkk" position) while watching the tuner. If they do their job correctly, what they see will be a real eye (and ear) opener for them! Students need to experiment like this to help them understand what a big difference tongue position makes on tuning.

The High "C" Exercise

It is often the habit of young players to unconsciously move their tongues high and back to play high "C" in tune, only to be lax about tongue position when playing tones in or below the staff. Such laxness not only creates inconsistency in pitch (playing flarp...both flat and sharp) and tonal shape, it also results in a loss of richness and presence in the tone (try to use "presence" instead of "projection" to describe the tone's carrying power). Learning the high "C" exercise is beginning of the cure for this problem, for it will quickly help students understand how the maintenance of correct tongue position improves consistency in tone color, shape and tuning throughout the clarinet's range. Here is how it works:

1. Ask the student(s) to play high "C" and lift their tongues until the tuning is at its highest point and the sound at its most focused.
2. Once the "C" is well focused, have the students play a slurred scale from the high "C" down to right hand clarion "C," while keeping the tongue in the high "C" position. Also remind them to keep a steady flow of air as well. (Nothing works without the air!)

Example 2: The High "C" Exercise

Results of the high "C" Exercise

If the students maintain a correct tongue position and a steady air stream the shape, color, and tuning of the notes will automatically match throughout the scale. However, if the air slows and/or the tongue position relaxes, the right hand clarion tones will lose focus and clarity. In fact, any time a note sounds "white," "washed out," flat or unfocused, it is almost always due to "lazy tongue" (a low/forward tongue position combined with an anemic air stream). Correct these two things and the great part of the tone production battle is won! Insist that the students play this exercise repeatedly until they are successful at hearing how the tongue affects the sound and can maintain a correct, stable tongue position throughout.

Extending the High "C" Exercise

Once the student is comfortable with the basic high "C" exercise it can and ought to be extended a varied. The scale can also be varied by beginning on the low "C" with the tongue in its high/back position. Finally, intervals can be introduced, all the while demanding consistency of tongue position while they are being played. Extending the exercise helps the students gradually gain the habit of bringing the tongue up and back whenever they begin to make the clarinet tone. Example 3 contains several exercises based on the high "C" exercise, but don't stop with these. Be inventive and create several pages of them as routine assigned practice. The more often these types of exercises are practiced, the more quickly the high/back tongue position will become second nature.

Example 3: Extended High "C" Exercises for Correctness and Stability in Tongue Position

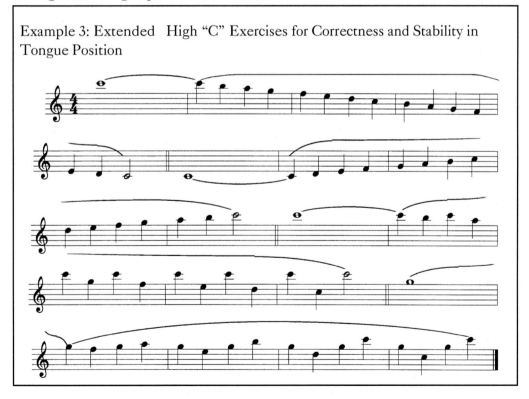

The Tongue and Playing Dynamics

You will perhaps recall that in chapter two we mentioned that some players support the sound with "aerosol can" air when playing at louder dynamic levels, but switch to "toothpaste tube" air as they play increasingly softer. Such a practice is really very detrimental to the sound; as dynamic levels change a consistent pitch, color and shape in the tone can only be achieved if the speed, shape and compression of the air remain constant throughout. In addition, in chapter II we said there should be only two changes in the tone production system while playing dynamics: a) the volume of the air *(but not the compression)* and b) *embouchure pressure (by this we do not mean biting, but the degree of firmness with which the mouthpiece is snugged against the lips)*. Because of its profound effect upon virtually every aspect of the air columc, the tongue also plays a major role in playing dynamics. For example, relaxation of the high/back tongue position while playing a diminuendo has the effect of immediately changing the compression of the air, which, as we said, needs to remain as constant as possible at all times. Such relaxation is the worst thing the tongue can do, especially when air volume decreases to make the sound softer, yet it is commonly done, even by many advanced players. Such a change in the tongue position has the effect of causing the air quality to change from "cold air" to "warm air". This change of air quality will happen even if the player continues to blow correctly, and it effectively ruins the consistency of the tone. Not only will the relaxation of the tongue position cause an instant loss of tonal center and focus in the sound, the decreased energy of the air may also make the player feel the reed is going to stop responding. The player usually reacts to this by adding embouchure pressure incorrectly to the reed (biting) to help regain the center of the sound and to keep the sound sustaining. This method "works" after a fashion, but the tuning, tone color and shape all change for the worse as a result.

There is only one real solution: the tongue must maintain its high/back position at all dynamic levels and most especially at softer levels. Doing so will preserve the needed consistency in color, shape and tuning while minimizing the degree of embouchure/air pressure exchange.

Tongue Position and Properly Voicing the Registers

So far we have talked about keeping the tongue position fixed for both concentration and consistency in air speed. This does not mean that no changes are needed in the tongue position to voice particular areas of the clarinet. Subtle changes in the first third (tip area) of the tongue can be very helpful in properly voicing special areas, especially higher tones. However, it must be stressed that while these subtle changes occur in the tip area of the tongue, the middle of the tongue remains in its high/back position. Think of the tip area of the tongue as independent of the rest of the tongue, like a hinged section that can freely move while the other parts remain stationary and you will have the idea.

As we said, these changes are subtle and are usually found by a combination of relaxation and developing a sensitivity to the different compression each tone sets up in the mouth. With relaxation, correct placement happens almost reflexively and unconsciously. The following exercise demonstrates how subtle movements can make a big difference in the quality and response of the specific tones:

1. Play the "C#" just above the staff
Notice where the tip area of the tongue is placed to make the best sound.
2. Slur to high "D," but make sure to keep the tongue in <u>exactly</u> the same position as it was on the "C#."
You will notice the high "D" is very poor in color.
3. Move the tip area of the tongue slightly higher and lower and see how you can improve the high "D."

If you repeat the first three steps, only starting with high "D," you will notice that the "C#" is very poor when the tip area of the tongue is in the best position for high "D."

Tongue Position and Elimination of Undertones in the Upper Clarion Register

One of the most problematic areas for undertoning is the clarinet's upper clarion register. It is challenging to play these notes without "grunts" at the beginning of the sound. This happens especially, but not only, in articulated passages. It can also happen often while slurring, in soft passages or as a note is being tapered to its softest dynamic levels.

These grunts are usually called "shadowtones" or "undertones." Such tones are actually the low register note that comes out of the same tone hole as the clarion tone. For instance, when you play high "B" the undertone you will hear is first line "E." When you play high "C" the under tone you hear is first space "F" and so on.

Whenever undertones appear they are caused by one or a combination of the following:
1) Too little resistance or poor balance in the reed/mouthpiece set up.
2) The register key pad opening being too great.
3) Failure to set the air pressure before the tone is released (see pg 5-12 ex. 5).

4) Too little resistance in the clarinet bore. (Some clarinet models are much more inclined to "grunt" than others, even when everything is in optimum adjustment).
5) Failure to keep the mouthpiece snugged firmly against the lips.
6) Incorrect low/forward tongue position.
7) Biting.

All of these faults must be corrected if you hope to eliminate undertones.

Learning How to Voice the Upper Clarion

As stated earlier, correct use of the first third of the tongue can help eliminate undertones. But there is no precise, measured formula by which you can calculate where the tongue needs to be placed for each tone. Therefore, success is not gained by consciously having the tongue "memorize" a precise position, but by relaxing the tip of the tongue in such a way that it can sensitively respond to the subtle changes of resistance in the air column created by each pitch. In other words, learning correct placement is similar to learning how to keep your balance on a bicycle: It is something which one must come to feel or sense rather than measure or calculate.

The best way to go about getting the "feel" of where the tongue should be for upper clarion and third register tones is to practice overtone exercises as well as special exercises which we will appropriately dub "Honks and Squeaks."

The Tongue and the Third Register

The back of the tongue is important in playing the third register. Its role is to flatten and move somewhat forward. This has the effect of placing the narrowest part of the venturi further forward in the mouth and closer to the tip of the mouthpiece and reed. As the tongue is pushed forward (but remains high) the air that impacts the reed is increasingly intensified and concentrated, helping the reed to vibrate rapidly enough so that the high tone frequencies can be produced. Learning how to do this is a matter of experimentation for the student; a matter of sensation more than measurement. The thing the student must always strive to do is voice the pitch into sounding correctly rather than biting with the embouchure.

Honks and Squeaks

"Honks and Squeaks" are overtone exercises performed without the normal venting used for each register. Rather, the low register fingering is maintained throughout, while the tongue, glottis and air make the changes necessary to produce the tones.

Example 4 presents a series of "Honks and Squeaks" exercises with instructions. They may sound silly, but practicing them results in an improved ability to play better in tune, with greater security, better accuracy and fewer undertones! In addition to these exercises the student can also learn to practice playing bugle calls. This is done by playing third line B natural and stopping up the bell of the clarinet by placing it on your leg or some other object which closes the end of the bell. When the student blows into a stopped clarinet only a small sound will

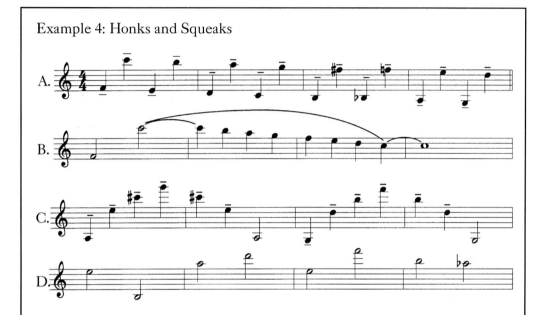

Example 4: Honks and Squeaks

Example A should be played with breath attacks and without using the register key to produce the high pitches. This may be frustrating at first, but with practice the student will learn the differentiation of air and position of the glottis to help produce each pitch. The student should not be allowed to bite to get the higher pitches.

Example B should be played completely without the use of the register key. All the left hand twelfths can be played similarly.

Example C shows all of the overtones being produce while only fingering the low register pitch. The very highest tones will be out of tune without the register key, but that is not the point of the exercise.

Example D tests the student's ability to accurately pick pitches out of the air. Only the low register fingering should be used for each come from the reed. By experimentation with air and voicing (glottis movement) the students will find that they can produce all the pitches of a major triad. Once they can successfully play the triad, ask them to try to play "Taps" or other familiar bugle calls.

In the process of learning these different bugle calls, students will become aware of all the subtle changes which must be made in air placement and the throat to produce the various pitches. It sounds silly (and is a great party "trick") but the skills learned in the process can improve their voicing immensely.

Correct Voicing and Articulation

The tongue is used for articulation as well as for voicing. The question might then come up about how tonguing is affected by voicing correctly.

The answer is: "Very positively." If you refer back to example I on page 3-5, you will notice that when the tongue is lifted high and back its tip is moved closer to the tip of the reed. In contrast, the low/forward tongue position places the tip of the tongue much lower on the reed's surface. When the tongue touches the surface of the reed rather that the tip, the noise from the tongue is clearly and unhappily audible in the tone. It can also cause delays in response, squeaks and undertones.

In articulation the arched middle of the tongue must remain stable, as if its sides were fastened to the inside of the upper molars while only the front third (the tip) of the tongue moves. The reed should be touched at its tip. Any part of the tip area of the tongue can be used to touch the reed; the tip, back of the tip, or wherever is comfortable, as long as the high/back tongue position is retained. This will be covered in more detail later on in chapter five.

Clarinet Tone the Oral Cavity

Many players and teachers are under the impression that the oral cavity is to the reed as the body of a classical guitar is to the vibrating string. However, any corollary in reality to such a notion is not to be found. The body of a guitar resonantes and amplifies the vibrating string, but the oral cavity does not act upon the reed in the same way. No doubt, there is some reciprocal relationship between the response and resonance of certain tones and the configuration of the oral cavity. The soft pallate is most particularly significant in this regard. But even in the case of the soft pallate, the response and resonance is much more strongly related to the air column, its speed and direction, than the resonating of the reed as the guitar body resonates the string. The tone of the clarinet is directly related to the quality of the air in its every aspect; speed, shape, volume, compression and direction. Some will point out that a very large, open oral cavity, formed ostensibly to create "resonance," produces a big sound. In reality, a large oral cavity does not produce a big sound. Rather it produces a broad, hollow, diffused tone which may sound "big" up close, but lacks the concentration needed for any real carrying power. Therefore, such a sound is not only not big at a distance, it is often barely audible. Experience reveals that the clarinet tone's carrying power and presence, its audibility, is not acheived by its perceived size (especially up close), or even its volume (dynamics) but its shape. Specifically, it must have a concentrated, focused shape, and this cannot be produced by anything but a concentrated, focused, highly compressed air column. This reality precludes the whole notion of the necessity of creating a large interior cavity to "resonate" the clarinet tone. Those who have always thought that a big sound requires a large oral cavity would do well to delete the notion from their conceptual hard drives, at least as far as clarinet tone production is concerned.

Conclusion

The point of this chapter has been to show the integral role of the tongue in controlling the volume, speed, shape and direction of the air and as a consequence, the profound effect that it (the tongue) has on every aspect of the tone. Once one understands that _air makes tone, and that which controls the air controls the tone_, one can clearly see the tremendous importance of tongue position in producing a truly characteristic sound. Much of the information in this chapter can be clarified for students only by individual experimentation, which is needed to help him or her develop a connaturality with the concepts presented here. Learning the correct things to do with the tongue is not a matter of precise slide rule measurements which precludes listening. Not at all. Rather, it is a matter of understanding a few basic principles which serve as a guide in the process of making the needed physical adjustments to correct the tone pitch, color and/or shape, listening to the results, making further adjustments until the sound is correct, and then remembering what it feels like at that point. Once that is achieve success is only a matter of consistency, which is attained by consistent and vigorous efforts (a.k.a. practice). The most important idea is simply this: Many players, in their efforts to control tuning, color and shape, are trying to do with the embouchure what should really be done with tongue position. Only once the tongue assumes its proper role can the embouchure truly work correctly and allow the reed greater vibrational amplitude and freedom without the danger of losing the integrity of fine tuning and a well-focused tone. The bottom line is this: learning about and mastering the proper relationship between the embouchure and tongue position is essential if the student is ever to develop a really fine, characteristic clarinet tone.

Chapter IV

HOW TO TEACH CLARINET EMBOUCHURE

In this chapter you will learn.....

Why proper function is more important than the embouchure's cosmetic formation.

How proper function forms the embouchure correctly.

The two possible types of reed control and why one is superior to the other for clarinet playing.

What direct and indirect pressure are and why one is best for clarinet playing.

The paradox of musical tone and how it can help you understand the goals of clarinet embouchure and evaluate the results.

How the parts of the embouchure work, both individually and together, to properly control the reed.

Exercises which help find the proper angle for playing the clarinet and how to find the right amount of mouthpiece to take into the mouth.

How double-lip playing can help permanently solve serious embouchure problems and improve the clarinet tone.

Form and Function in Clarinet Embouchure

In the previous chapter we saw how the tongue controls the air stream to affect color, shape, volume and tuning of the tone. In this chapter we will discuss how the embouchure controls the reed. Most clarinet embouchure pedagogy concentrates almost exclusively on getting the embouchure to look right. However, this is a superficial, "cart-before-the-horse" approach. We say this because the outward appearance of the embouchure is not a cause but an effect of good embouchure. There is an old saying that perfectly expresses the idea: "Form follows function."

In short, the embouchure can look right without working right...and if it doesn't work right, it won't sound right...but it can't work right without sounding right! (Unless, of course, you totally forget to put air into the clarinet).

For this reason, the approach we will take concentrates more on how the embouchure actually works than on merely how it should look. The comparatively small amount of time spent on really learning and understanding correct embouchure functions will yield big and sustained dividends in teaching and problem solving.

The Goal of Embouchure

The real goal of embouchure is to help the reed make the musical tone which ultimately creates the musical phrase. This means that if we are to understand objectivelly how to best control the reed we need to become familiar with a few important things about the nature of musical sound itself.

The Paradox of Tone

Fine musical tone (as distinct from mere noise) is a paradoxical in nature. That is to say, it is made up of elements or qualities which seem to be diametrically opposed to one another; elements which in reality they mysteriously subsist as vibrant complementarities (not contradictories) within the same tone. For example, fine musical tone sounds at once truly free and yet highly controlled, variable yet consistent, liquid yet substantial, richly colored yet transparent and so on. Musicians commonly use certain words to criticize or describe musical tone. Some of these words, such as dull, unclear, thin, unresonant, or inflexible, indicate an absence of freedom in the tone. Others, such as wild, uncentered, undefined, or harsh, indicate an absence of control. In either case, the descriptive words reveal that some element of the paradox regarded as essential to good tone is missing; something which ought to be there, isn't.

The point of this is that the descriptive terms musicians use to describe the qualities of musical tone indicate that the notion of paradox is not something we subjectively or arbitrarily impose on musical tone. It is not even something we find to be a part of musical tone: it *is* musical tone. Without it there is only random noise. We intuitively sense this, whether we consciously know about the paradoxical nature of musical tone or not.

Now, there is a direct connection between how a tone sounds and how it is produced. This means that imbalance in the paradox of sound is directly caused by technical faults in the methods and means used to produce it. In other words, correct tone cannot be produced by incorrect methods and means. Neither can incorrect tone be produced by correct methods and means. It is impossible. Therefore, finding and correcting the faults in the *methods* and *means* of tone production will bring the paradoxical qualities back into proper proportion and relationship and as a consequence, improve the tone.

Obviously, the *means* the clarinetist must use is the clarinet itself. The *method* is how the clarinetist uses the embouchure, tongue and air to generate and control the sound that the reed produces. Let's consider that briefly.

The Relationship of Tone, Reed and Embouchure

The reed is the sole means by which this paradox of musical tone is realized in the clarinet's sound, and the embouchure is the sole agent that directly and constantly acts upon the reed. Therefore, if a fine tone, which is both vibrant and free yet focused and well controlled is our goal, the embouchure must receive the reed in such a way that the reed can vibrate in both a controlled yet free manner.

This may sound like a kind of double talk, but it is not. It is something of a riddle to be sure; a mystery to be solved, no doubt. But it isn't double talk. Nor does the solution involve a logical contradiction (that would be no solution at all). There is a logical solution to this dilemma, but there are several steps we need to take before we solve it. Let's begin those steps by looking at the various parts of the embouchure to better understand how they work.

Parts of the Embouchure

The embouchure is made up of the lip muscles and chin muscles, supported by the jaw and teeth. Let's examine each of these and see how they work, both individually and together, to control the reed properly.

The Two Possible Methods of Controlling the Reed

As we discuss each element of the embouchure, keep in mind that there are ultimately only two possible methods of controlling the reed's vibrations. We will term these methods the *Clamp-Style Embouchure* and the *Friction-Style Embouchure.*

The *Clamp-Style* Embouchure gains control of the reed by using upward jaw closure to directly press the reed to the mouthpiece facing (this is commonly referred to as biting). The Friction-Style Embouchure controls the reed by snugging the mouthpiece/reed wedge into the fixed, stable opening created by the lips, teeth and jaw. As we will see, the Friction-Style Embouchure produces vastly superior results in every respect.

The Jaw (and lower teeth)

A great many clarinetists use the closing action of the jaw to clamp or press the reed to the mouthpiece facing in order to control the tuning and the shape of the sound. This viselike jaw closure is commonly called biting, and it is the worst possible thing for clarinet tone. Yet, it is probably the most common tone production fault among clarinetists of all age and skill levels. It would not be an exaggeration to say biting is an epidemic throughout the clarinet playing community.

Rather than biting, the jaw and lower teeth need to function exclusively as a support for the lips, chin and face muscles. The jaw does this by simply dropping open and positioning itself forward enough so that the lower teeth are even with the upper teeth (similar to the way the jaw would move if you tried to blow a feather off the end of your nose). The open/forward placement of the jaw creates a kind of platform to receive the reed. Once the jaw does this, its job is over. It simply remains there in "neutral" so to speak. It should never close, reset itself after the mouthpiece is inserted, or move in any significant way; a stable, open/forward jaw position is essential to correct embouchure.

When the jaw works correctly it creates a fixed slot or window. This opening is called the Embouchure's *Tonal Window*. (As we will soon see, the wedging of the mouthpiece into the fixed opening, rather than the clamping of the jaw, is the best means of creating the needed pressure and resistance to control the reed).

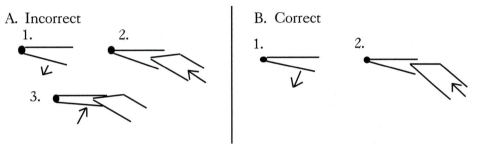

Example 1: Correct and Incorrect Jaw Useage

A: Incorrect useage is a three step process: 1. The jaw and mouth open to receive the mouthpiece and reed. 2. The mouthpiece is inserted. 3. The jaw closes on the mouthpiece (bites) in order to control the reed's vibrations.

B. Correct useage of the jaw is only a two step process. 1. The jaw drops open, creating a fixed aperture. 2. The mouthpiece/reed wedge is inserted into the aperture created by the jaw and lips, while the jaw remains stationary. Reed control is gained as the reed is snugged more firmly against the lips.

The bottom line is simply this: to be of maximum effectiveness in controlling the reed, the jaw need do no more than remain passively stationary in its fixed aperture, neither opening nor closing. In fact, to do otherwise would actually do harm to the tone in one way or another.

The friction, no-bite method of reed control rightly casts the jaw in a supporting role. But biting makes the jaw the star of the show, and as we have already said, this is the most destructive thing that can possibly be done to the sound, with the possible exception of poor breath support. Because it is so prevalent, before we go on, we really need to look closely at the technique of biting and its effect on the tone.

Biting: What it is and its Effect on Tone

Biting is the upward closing action of the jaw (See ex. 1). Biting is done to press the reed to the resistance curve of the mouthpiece in order to gain control over the pitch and shape of the sound. There are many problems created by this method of reed control. Here are some of them. Perhaps you will recognize one or two:

1. *Biting causes the pitch to tend towards sharpness.*

2. *Biting gives a bright, thin, shrill quality to higher tones.*

3. *Biting causes inflexibility in tuning.*

4. *Biting causes a generally pinched, tight tone.*

5. *Biting causes a loss of depth and resonance in the tone.*

6. *Biting cuts the lower lip.*

7. *Biting increases tension throughout the face, the body and the hands.*

8. *Biting causes incorrect use of the chin muscles.*

9. *Biting prohibits proper muscular development of the lips.*

10. *Biting makes reeds sound bad and significantly shortens their playing life as well.*

More could be said, but this short list should be enough to demonstrate that biting needs to be avoided at all costs.

The Lips

Both upper and lower lips are actually part of a single muscle called the *orbicular muscle*. The lips, not the jaw, need to act upon and control the reed. In doing so they should never squeeze or constrict the reed. Rather, they have two simple functions: to seal (the air) and to cushion (the reed).

How do the lips control the reed without squeezing and constricting it in some way? They control the reed simply by firmly resisting and cushioning the upward, inward snugging movement of the mouthpiece/reed wedge. In short, all they do is "hold their ground" as the mouthpiece is inserted into the opening created by the jaw and the lips. This "passive" resistance the lips give the mouthpiece/reed wedge is all that is necessary to control the reed.

The Lower Lip

The lower lip must not "give in" to the inward force of the mouthpiece, by allowing itself to be pushed into the mouth and collapsing over the lower teeth. Rather, it needs to be firm, using the teeth only as a support structure while resisting and cushioning the mouthpiece/reed wedge. If this is done, you will find that the red of the lip will be positioned more in front of the teeth than over them. Therefore, when you face yourself in a mirror or examine one of your students while playing, you should be able to see a generous amount of the red of the lips on either side of the reed. If not you almost certainly have too much lip over the lower teeth. Allowing a large amount of lower lip to go over the lower teeth will significantly reduce resonance and impede the response of the high register.

Example 2: Correct Amount of Lower Lip

Notice in the example, despite the natural thinness of the players lips, it is not difficult to see a generous amount of lower lip while he is playing. Normally, if the lower lip can't be seen when students are playing they have much too much over their teeth. The give away is a small, dull tone, lacking resonance and depth and an unresponsive high register.

The Upper Lip

The upper lip also needs to firmly cushion the inward movement of the mouthpiece. Any and all the energy exerted downward from the top lip needs to be directed away from the middle of the upper lip and concentrated at the corners of the mouth. Sometimes clarinetists refer to this use of the upper lip as "side pressure." This aids in sealing the air stream and helps prevent downward (squeezing) pressure from being applied by the middle of the upper lip and upper teeth. Pulling the muscles of the upper lip down at the corners also helps the jaw to maintain its' dropped, relaxed position and reduces the temptation to bite.

Example 3: Upper Lip Side Pressure

Upper lip Side Pressure helps eliminate downward pressure in the middle of the lip, which would close the reed. Arrows indicate the energy of the upper lip being directed towards the corners of the mouth which is represented by the oval.

The Chin Muscles

Cosmetically, the chin muscles are usually described as stretching down, causing the chin to form a point. Sometimes this is called a "flat chin" because of how the chin muscles pull so tautly against the bone structure of the jaw. Pulling the chin muscles down helps prevent the lower lip from being pushed over the lower teeth and into the mouth as a result of the mouthpiece's inward/upward movement. Here's how: When the chin muscles stretch down they pull the lower lip down with them. This causes the lower lip to end up more in front of than over the lower teeth. The *"down and out"* movement of the lower lip is used to resist the *"up and in"* movement of the mouthpiece/reed wedge. The oppositional actions of the lower lip and the mouthpiece/reed wedge are what create the needed friction to control the reed. (Don't forget, all the time this is going on, the jaw simply remains in its "neutral" open/forward position).

The Upper Teeth

Like the lower teeth, the upper teeth serve as a structural support for the upper lip. One thing that helps students learn to do this is to ask them to think of pulling their teeth slightly apart while their lips remain in contact with the mouthpiece and reed. Doing this helps counteract the closing/biting tendency of the jaw and upper teeth; something which should never be done for any reason. Vertical closure of the embouchure always hurts the sound in some way!

Example 4: Four Commonly Seen Cosmetic Embouchure Formations

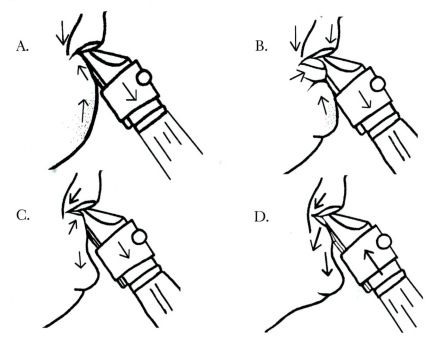

Analysis:

Above are four examples of commonly seen embouchure profiles. It is important to note the arrows, since they indicate the direction embouchure energy is being exerted, which both forms the embouchure and determines how the reed can vibrate.

Example A shows the chin bunched with no lower lip visible. This sort of embouchure damps reed vibration to such an extent that the sound is very dull, soft and lacking in resonance. Such damping makes the production of upper clarion and altissimo tones almost impossible.

Example B shows the lower lip bulging as it presses into the reed. High register tones will probably come out, but will sound wild and harsh. Since the bunched chin is also an indication of a low/forward tongue position the upper tones will probably be flat. The commonly unstable tones of the clarinet (throat A, clarion A and high E) will probably have the tendency to crack.

Example C shows the embouchure of an inventive student. He has learned to pull the chin down to satisfy the teacher, but is still biting. The biting causes the pushing of the lower lip into the reed, which can be seen by the subtle (and sometimes "not-so-subtle") bulging of the lower lip.

Example D shows the embouchure functioning and looking correctly.

The Right Hand Thumb

So far we have talked so much about eliminating jaw and teeth pressure on the reed that it might be easy to get the impression that no pressure should be added to the reed, but this is hardly the case. Pressure *must* be added to the reed to achieve the needed control to shape its vibrations. We avoid biting pressure not because pressure in itself is bad but because the *kind* of pressure that the jaw and teeth create is bad. The problem is not pressure but *biting* pressure.

In the Friction-Style, no-bite system, the thing most responsible for adding pressure to the reed is the right hand thumb. Strange as it may seem, the right hand thumb is critical to the whole equation of reed control because it is the sole energy source that keeps the mouthpiece and reed firmly snugged against the lips.

This lifting may be greater at times (such as when playing softly and/or in the upper register) or less at others (such as when playing in the low register or at louder dynamics). But no matter what, the thumb always needs to be lifting to some degree. The thumb should never let the mouthpiece fall away or simply float loosely in the lips.

Besides controlling the reed, the lifting action of the thumb can promote good habits and relaxation in other seemingly unrelated areas of playing. For instance, it is helpful in eliminating the unspoken fear many young students have of dropping the clarinet, or of the mouthpiece leaving the mouth. This fear usually manifests itself in two ways:

1. The students use the biting, clamping action of the jaw as a means of "holding" the clarinet.

2. They use their fingers to grip and hold on to the clarinet.

Of course, the embouchure should never be used to hold the clarinet, and the fingers should only be used to play the notes, not to hold the clarinet. When the thumb does its job correctly both embouchure and fingers do their jobs better and more easily. Psychologically, it can be helpful to students to frequently use the phrase, "Thumbs up!" to remind them to maintain the snugging, lifting action of the thumb. An elastic clarinet neck strap can also help the thumb in maintaining the needed lifting of the clarinet. And finally, it can also be helpful to refer to the device the thumb uses to hold the clarinet as the "thumb support" rather than "thumb rest."

The Tongue

The tongue is obviously no more a part of the embouchure than the right hand thumb, but we must mention it here because of how it relates to the chin muscles. This relationship is simple: next to the jaw, the tongue exerts the greatest influence upon the chin's formation! Here's how:

When the tongue assumes its proper *high/back "kick"* position described in chapter three, the chin tends to automatically stretch down into the cosmetically classic *"point."* In fact, in the majority of cases, chin formation problems are directly related to a poor tongue position. Correcting the tongue position is often the quickest way of getting the chin muscles to work correctly. It is not impossible, but it is certainly highly unnatural for the chin to bunch up while the tongue is in the high/back position. So much so, that when a student maintains a correct tongue position virtually nothing needs to be said about the chin. It just happens correctly.

The Throat

Many have the idea that a good tone requires clarinetists to force the muscles of their throats open in some grotesque fashion. This is simply untrue. Opening the throat is a process of relaxation which results in an inner expansion due only to the pressure the air column creates in the lungs, throat and oral cavity.

Begin having students learn to open their throats by asking them to place their fingers on the Adam's apple and say "aaaa." While they are saying "aaaa" ask them to move the Adam's apple lower. The sound of the "aaaa" will instantly deepen and become more resonant (this is the way radio announcers are trained to speak). Once they can do this ask them to play open "G" and move the Adam's apple into the low position as they play. The same thing will happen to the sound of the "G" as happened to their voice.

Of course, students don't need to be distracted by worrying about their Adam's apples while they are trying to learn the basics of tone production. Therefore, it is probably best *not* to begin working on such exercises until they have a solid grasp of all the other tone production techniques. Exactly when the student should be taught anything about the throat is a judgment call only you as the teacher can make.

How to Find the Best Angle for Playing the Clarinet

The clarinet needs to be held at a more acute angle than most other woodwinds, such as the oboe or saxophone. This more acute angle allows the reed to vibrate more freely and fully on the resistance curve of the mouthpiece.

Basically, it might be said that the clarinet should be held at about a thirty-five degree angle, but this is only a generalization. Since everyone has a different bite, the best angle for one will not be the best for another. There is no "one size fits all", ubiquitous playing angle. A good rule of thumb to follow is that the more overbite the student has, the more acute the angle will be. The less overbite, the greater the angle will be. (Students with underbites, with hardly any exception, should simply not play the clarinet at all.) The best angle can almost always be found for your students by the following method:

1. With their heads erect and looking straight forward, ask each student to play a tone while holding the clarinet out at around 60 degrees from their bodies.

2. While playing, ask them to gradually reduce the angle by pulling the clarinet closer and closer to their bodies. (Make sure their heads remain stationary and erect--see example 5).

As each student pulls the clarinet closer you will hear the sound getting clearer and more resonant, but after a certain point the sound will begin to lose resonance and take on a choked sound. The degree of angle at which the sound is most resonant and clear is the best playing angle. Ask the students to repeat this exercise several times until they can readily feel and hear the difference.

Friction-Style Embouchure, Clamp-Style Embouchure, Reed Vibration and the Paradox of Musical Tone

Now that we have discussed each element of the embouchure and understand better how each works, we are ready to understand how the Friction-Style, no-bite approach to reed control actually affects the reed's vibrations and to better understand why it is superior to biting. This means we need to recall what was said earlier in the chapter about the paradox of musical tone. Specifically, we said that in order for this paradox to be realized in the tone itself the embouchure needs to receive the reed in such a way that it will vibrate in both a controlled yet free way. Here is how the Friction-Style Embouchure fills the bill:

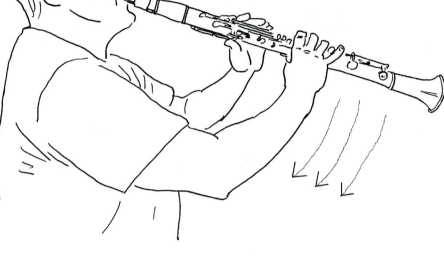

Example 5: Finding the Best Playing Angle

Arrows indicate the direction that the clarinet is slowly moved while a long tone is being played. The point where the sound becomes clearest, most resonant and free is the best angle for that specific student to play the clarinet.

As the reed/mouthpiece wedge is snugged against the lips and into the opening created by the embouchure, two things happen simultaneously:

1. The lip pressure on the reed's surface is increased. This increase creates the needed control over the shape of the tone.

2. At the same time, the tip of the reed is snugged into the mouth, past the point of greatest pressure and resistance. The fact that the tip moves well past the pressure point means it can remain open, and be free to instantly respond to the air column.

Therefore, the single action of snugging maximizes both control and freedom, and this is what makes the Friction-Style Embouchure the superior method for the production of clarinet tone.

While the Friction-Style Embouchure *simultaneously* optimizes both control and freedom, the biting method can only optimize one at the expense of the other. For example, when the viselike action of the jaw presses the reed directly on to the mouthpiece's resistance curve to gain control two negative things happen:

1. The tip of the reed is closed down at the tip of the mouthpiece and cannot vibrate and respond freely.

2. The reed's ability to vibrate as fully as it might on the full length of the mouthpiece's resistance curve is seriously inhibited. This results in a loss of depth, resonance and flexibility in the tone.

If the player opens the jaw in an attempt to regain the loss of freedom, depth and response, control of the reed (and the sound) is lost and the sound loses its center. Therefore, lack of jaw pressure works no better than jaw pressure to effectively produce the sound. Clearly, the problem is not too much or too little jaw pressure, but the use of jaw pressure altogether to control the reed.

From this scenario we can see that the real problem with the technique of biting is that it is utterly incapable of fully realizing and optimizing the full possibilities of both freedom and control in the sound simultaneously. The best it can do is walk an acoustical tight rope which achieves a kind of mediocrity in each. This fact alone should be reason enough to do everything possible to avoid, prevent and eliminate use of this cripplingly limited and yet epidemically common approach to reed control. Failure to do so will unavoidably stunt both technical and artistic development of the clarinetist somewhere along the line.

Example 6: Comparison of Stresses Created by Direct and Indirect Pressure.

Direct   Indirect

The directional stresses in the first mouthpiece (direct pressure) pinches the reed closed and prevent it from vibrating fully on the facing curve. The directional stress shown in the second mouthpiece (indirect) gives the reed much more vibrational amplitude and enables the tip to remain open. The directional arrow on the mouthpiece indicates that the stress is really being created by the snugging of the mouthpiece and not any active exertion by embouchure. The embouchure only passively resists the motion of the mouthpiece by remaining stationary.

Example 7:

Summary Comparison of Friction and Clamp-Style Embouchures and Their Effects on Reed Vibration

Method of reed control:

Friction-Style Embouchure: Snugging of the mouthpiece/reed wedge into the fixed opening of the embouchure (embouchure tone window).

Clamp-Style Embouchure: Jaw closure to press the reed to the mouthpiece resistance curve.

Type of pressure added to the reed:

Friction-Style Embouchure: Indirect or oblique reed pressure.

Clamp-Style Embouchure: Direct reed pressure.

Results of these types of pressure:

Indirect: Adds pressure to the reed without pinching the reed tip closed, and allows the reed to vibrate fully along the mouthpiece's resistance curve, creating both depth and flexibility in the tone.

Direct: Adds pressure which prevents the reed from vibrating as fully as it might on the mouthpiece's resistance curve, and pinches the reed closed at the tip.

Effect on the vibration of the reed's tip:

Friction-Style Embouchure: Tip is snugged well past the pressure point and remains open to respond and vibrate freely to the air stream.

Clamp-Style Embouchure: Direct pressure closes the tip on the resistance curve, reducing its vibrational amplitude.

Effect of each method on embouchure development:

Friction-Style Embouchure: Encourages correct development of lip, chin and facial muscles as the means of cushioning and supporting the reed.

Clamp-Style Embouchure: Closing action of the jaw sets itself in opposition to the proper movement of chin and lip muscles. The reed is controlled by the jaw and lower teeth, while the lower lip acts only as a shim between the teeth and the reed. As a consequence, little or no muscular development of the lips takes place, while chin muscles join the upward pressure of the jaw by bunching and pushing into the reed.

Chapter IV: How to Teach Clarinet Embouchure

Example 8: Exercises for Finding Correct Amount of Mouthpiece to Snug.

A.

See if you can play exercise "A" with a stable, even color, dynamic and shape, and without moving the embouchure or clarinet at all.

B.

Try exercise "B" at soft dynamic levels as well as fuller levels. If you can play this exercise softly and the tones remain stable and don't crack, it indicates you have snugged the correct amount of mouthpiece in your mouth.

C.

See if you can play these octaves without the higher ones being louder and sticking out. Try to keep them all at the same dynamic level.

Each of these exercises is designed to help you "find" the best amount of mouthpiece to snug into your mouth. The tones "A" and "E" are stressed because they are unstable tones on the clarinet. Playing them without loss of control or focus is a strong indicator that you have the correct amount of mouthpiece.

The "A's" are particularly important. For instance, if there is too much mouthpiece snugged into the mouth, the throat "A" will be unstable and tend to spread. If there is not enough mouthpiece snugged, the high "A" will not speak. (Make sure that you do this test with the best fingering for high "A" and with a well balanced reed. The high "A" will not respond well if there are any problems with equipment, tongue position or air. So, when you do this exercise, make sure you have your "check list" out).

How much Mouthpiece Should be Snugged?

Too much or too little mouthpiece in the mouth can cause problems with tone, response and control. So it's important to find just how much mouthpiece needs to be wedged into the mouth. This can be done with the following method. (It is similar to how you found the right angle for playing).

1. Create the Embouchure Tonal Window by dropping the jaw.

2. Place a small amount of the mouthpiece very loosely into the mouth. While blowing, begin slowly snugging. The tone will sound flat, "airy" and unfocused at first. Then, as you snug in more, you will hear the sound getting clearer, more centered and higher in pitch.

After a certain point, however, you will hear the focus and clarity begin to deteriorate, even to the point of squeaking or the tone cracking. When this happens it means you have gone past the best place for control and sound. The point where the sound is clearest and most focused and the tuning is the highest, just before it begins to spread and deteriorate, is the amount you need to snug for most normal playing, and no more!

Another method of telling whether you have the right amount of mouthpiece is to play the exercises in example 8. If you can play these exercises securely, without instability, spreading, cracking or producing "ghost tones" or undertones on the upper clarion notes, you have the proper amount of mouthpiece snugged. Learning to find that point is like learning to keep your balance on a bicycle: It is more a matter of feeling or sensing than of applying some precise, "one size fits all" measurement. You know when you get it right, because it works!

This approach to finding the best point for reed control shows how flexible the embouchure needs to be. Setting an arbitrary amount for how much mouthpiece should be taken in gives the erroneous impression that the embouchure sets itself into the mouthpiece and reed, and also that the embouchure is fixed, rigid and set like granite or concrete.

The embouchure certainly should be firm, but it is also needs to be flexible. Keith Stein, in his excellent book "The Art of Clarinet Playing," speaks of "playing the sound of the clarinet where you find it." Snugging to find the best amount is a good expression of the application of this concept, and with it you can adapt quickly to most any reasonable reed/mouthpiece set up and begin getting the best out of it almost immediately.

Trouble Shooting and Teaching Tips

Success with this friction-style, no-bite embouchure depends upon four things:

1) keeping the jaw down.

2) keeping the red of the lips firm.

3) keeping the tongue in the high/back position.

4) keeping the reed and mouthpiece properly snugged against the cushion-like firmness of the lips.

Almost every possible problem is caused by a failure to maintain one or more of these tone production disciplines. Here are a few tips to help you, as a teacher, see if these things are being done and to help your students make any needed corrections.

Teaching Tips For Embouchure

Try to make sure there is no repositioning or resetting of the jaw whatsoever after the mouthpiece has been snugged. Watch the student carefully as he or she inserts the mouthpiece. If he or she does no more than open the mouth and snug the mouthpiece, all is well. However, if the student repositions or resets the jaw, the student is biting. This should be corrected immediately.

A few teaching commands which can be effective in preventing students from resetting of the jaw are: "Form it first" (in reference to formation of the Embouchure Tone Window), or "Bring the mouthpiece up to you, don't reach out for it." This can help the student understand that although the embouchure opens to receive the mouthpiece, it never closes around it.

It may also be helpful to ask the student to stand with his/her back and head against a wall. Ask the student to form the Embouchure Tone Window. While the head and body remain in contact with the wall, insert the mouthpiece into the Tone Window. This can help the student understand the concept of bringing the mouthpiece to the face, rather than the mouth reaching out for and enclosing around the mouthpiece. Another thing which can be helpful is to ask your students to keep a small mirror on their stands at home so that they can periodically check the embouchure formation as they practice. Make sure you tell them what things they need to be looking for.

Use of a mirror in the class can be effective as well. A beautician's mirror, which shows front and both side angles can be very helpful in getting the students to attain a fine cosmetic embouchure. Of course it goes without saying that the student should try to achieve a good looking embouchure by means of correct embouchure functions rather than in lieu of them.

Teaching Tips for the Tongue

The high tongue position raises the pitch and brings the shape into the characteristic "point of focus." This means that the true characteristic shape of the clarinet sound is more onion shaped, or pear shaped, than round. Sometimes the point of the sound shape can be described as looking like the top of a Dairy Queen ice cream cone.

Lowering of the pitch or a loss of center or "point" in the shape of the sound can only mean one of two things. Either the thumb is no longer maintaining proper snugging, or the tongue has gotten lazy and is no longer maintaining a correct high/back position. Looking at the student and hissing like a cat or making a "kkkkk" sound can remind him or her to get the tongue back in the correct high/back position.

Teaching Tips for the Thumb

The thumb is simple. As we just mentioned, if the loss of center or focus becomes a problem it can only be a low tongue position or relaxed, lazy thumb. Try the phrase "Thumbs up!" If that doesn't completely cure the problem, then suspect that the tongue position is incorrect as well.

Teaching Tips for the Lower Lip and Chin

Cosmetically, the flesh directly below the red of the lower lip should be pulled down tautly against the bone structure of the jaw in a very dressy fashion (see ex. 4). There should also be some red of the lower lip showing even if the student's lips are very thin. If you see bunching or bulging of the lower lip and/or the face and chin muscles just below the lower lip, or if you cannot see any red of the lower lip, the student is biting.

Obviously, the student needs to be told to pull the chin muscles down, flat against the chin and keep the lower lip from being pushed over the teeth. But failure in the chin, lip and muscles just below the red of the lower lip is almost always accompanied by and even caused by some failure in the jaw and/or tongue as well. Making sure the jaw and snugging techniques are functioning properly and that the high/back tongue position is maintained will often cure the lower lip and chin problems. It is worth restating that it is very unnatural to bunch the chin muscles while maintaining a high/back tongue position.

How to Check for Biting

A good way to see if students are biting is to grasp the barrel while they are playing and try to pull the mouthpiece out of their mouth. The mouthpiece should come out easily as soon as the force of your pulling overcomes the lifting of their thumb.

If there is difficulty in extracting the mouthpiece, it's almost certain that the student is biting. It is not uncommon to go through an entire clarinet section without being able to pull the mouthpiece out of a single one of the player's mouths without difficulty. Such is the nature of the viselike, death grip many young players have on the mouthpiece and reed. No wonder so many clarinet sections sound the way they do! Sections of players who persist in playing this way have no hope of ever making a fine sound, either individually or as a group.

Another, less direct way to check for "lock jaw" is to ask the students to totally relax the lifting of the right hand thumb. The relaxation of the thumb should cause the clarinet to *immediately* fall from their mouth. If this happens correctly ask them then to restore the sound by lifting the clarinet up with the right hand thumb. Doing this over and over again while they are producing the tone can help them realize they don't need to clamp with the jaw to make the sound happen.

The Educator's Guide to the Clarinet 4-21

(what we did in class)
How to Teach a Beginner the Friction-Style Embouchure

Beginners can start learning a friction style embouchure at the very git go, before the onset of bad habits. Of course, the whole process needs to avoid any detailed explanations. Instead, concentrate almost completely on positive action images and simple, one-step instructions. Here is one approach that is usually effective.

1) With only the mouthpiece and barrel assembled, ask the students to open their mouths and put the tip of the mouthpiece between their lips, pretending it is a soda straw. (You might ask them to "sip" some air through the mouthpiece to complete the soda straw image).

2) Next ask them to blow air (without letting their cheeks puff out) through the mouthpiece while holding the mouthpiece loosely in the lips. (Some may blow hard enough to start making some sort of noise).

3) While they are blowing take the barrel in your hand and snug the mouthpiece firmly against their lips. In most cases, the tone will instantly appear full, clear, fairly well focused in shape, and higher in pitch.

4) Repeat this several times until the students notice the sound improvement and get an idea of how it feels.

5) Once they get the hang of it, ask the students to do the snugging of the mouthpiece themselves, reminding them to make their lips firm whenever they feel the mouthpiece snugging up against their lips.

6) Next they can try making the sound appear and disappear by snugging the mouthpiece and then relaxing the snugging. This will help them realize that the energy to initiate the sound comes from the snugging of the mouthpiece, not the clamping of the jaw.

7) Ask them to listen for the moment when the sound becomes the clearest and most focused. Also, ask them to listen for the instant the sound becomes less focused as they snug the mouthpiece. When this happens they have snugged too much mouthpiece.

8) Have them snugging and listening critically until they can relate how the air and embouchure feel when the sound is best and clearest to the ear and how it sounds and feels to go too far with the snugging.

Work on these exercises until the students feel comfortable making the sound and can sustain a steady, clear sound for ten or fifteen seconds. You might offer a prize each day to the student who can hold a steady tone the longest.

Adding the Tongue Position

Once they become comfortable and confident in making the sound (usually about a week of practice), you can start teaching them the high/back tongue position. Begin by asking them to put their tongues in a low/forward position by saying "oooooooooo" (while the mouthpiece is being held loosely), and then move their tongues in the high/back "hhhhheeeee" position as they snug the mouthpiece. Have them say "ooooohhheeeee" several times without the mouthpiece in their mouths so they can feel what the tongue should be doing more easily.

The high/back position should bring the pitch up even higher and improve the focus and clarity of the tone as well. You will also notice an improvement in the chin formation when the tongue is correct. Generally, it's best to say little or nothing about the chin until the tongue position is added to the embouchure formula.

Use of the Tuner in the Development of Correct Embouchure and Tongue Position

Once the students have the snugging action and high tongue position technique down, ask each of them to play a sustained note on the mouthpiece or the mouthpiece and barrel into a tuner. If the mouthpiece is used they should produce a slightly sharp concert "C." If the barrel is used they should be able to play a concert "F#." If they are flat when they start the pitch, make sure they raise the tuning by either snugging or using a higher tongue position rather than by biting.

Once they can do this, ask them to sustain the correct pitch very steadily for several beats. Looking at the tuner as they play can be extremely helpful in correct tone production development, and will give the students some visual evidence to buttress what they hear and feel.

Embouchure Development and Equipment

We will devote several chapters to equipment and its relationship to playing technique. Here we need to stress only that a poor reed/mouthpiece combination can limit endurance and cause the development of poor tone production habits. Most importantly, your students need to play on well balanced reeds as much as possible. Good habits and good equipment form the positive cycle that breaks the vicious one of poor habits and poor equipment.

PART II:
PLAYING FRENCH EMBOUCHURE, OR DOUBLE-LIP

In an article from "The Clarinet" in the 1970's master clarinet pedagogue, Keith Stein, stated that 75% of clarinetists played with an incorrect, biting style of embouchure. This is a very conservative estimate, to say the least.

Why do so many players bite? There are probably several reasons. Perhaps it's done for security. Perhaps because of tension. Perhaps it is because of poor breath support forcing the use of more embouchure pressure. Perhaps they were never presented with a viable alternative method. Or perhaps biting is common because since our earliest years we just reflexively and habitually bit anything that was put into our mouths.

Whatever the reasons, many clarinetists whose playing has suffered from the negative effects of biting seek a way out of their bad habits. Most find double-lip to be a very effective remedy for their tone production problems.

Fallacies and Factoids about Double-Lip Technique

Unfortunately, there are many who could benefit from double-lip technique, but never think of trying it because they have been exposed to so much erroneous information about it. Here are a few of the many fallacies and factoids concerning double-lip:

1. Double-lip playing requires a softer reed: This is not true. Many double-lip players actually play harder reeds than most single-lip players. Double-lip does, however, require a well balanced reed. (And so should single-lip playing).

2. Double-lip players don't have the endurance of single lip players: The opposite is probably true. Once the technique is developed, the clarinetist can play without tiring.

3. Double-lip produces a smaller sound and less volume: This, again, is simply untrue. In fact, those who switch to double-lip often find that they can actually play louder than before without loss of tone quality, tuning or shape.

4. Double-lip produces a spread sound. This is not true, but it could be that some educators get this impression by hearing their beginners play while holding the clarinet loosely like a recorder. However, this is hardly a way to judge a technique. In order to fairly judge a technique (or anything else for that fact) you need to look at the results garnered by those who do the technique best and most correctly, not those who have no technique at all!

5. Double-lip is difficult and painful to learn. Again, this is not true. The pain many who first try the technique may experience is usually caused by not doing it correctly. Double-lip is a very sensitive gauge for many things, and it will certainly tell you very quickly just how much you are biting.

6. Double-lip takes years to master. Wrong. Some students take to it like the proverbial duck takes to water. Usually those who find it difficult are simply not performing the technique correctly, but continue to bite or retain other bad habits.

7. Double-lip is a no-pressure embouchure. Actually, in the double-lip system lots of pressure is applied to the reed. It just doesn't come from the clamping action of the jaw. It comes from snugging of the mouthpiece against the lips.

Positive Benefits of Double-Lip Technique

As we said, many players, especially those who learned to play by biting, turn to double-lip for help in solving their tone problems. Once they do, they not only find their tone is better, but many other things improve as well. Here are some benefits that are often instantly apparent:

1. An improved legato: Intervals have a seamless connection.

2. More tonal depth and resonance: The reed is no longer being strangled by the clutching action of the jaw and so is free to vibrate more fully along the curve of the mouthpiece facing.

3. More flexible tuning: Since the pitch is no longer controlled by the clamp action of the jaw, the clarinetist can be much more flexible with the pitch without losing the integrity of the tone center.

4. A more even tone color throughout the range of the clarinet.

5. A more secure response and richer, fuller high tones.

6. A more responsive, lively articulation.

7. Greater relaxation in the jaw and facial muscles.

All these advantages and more await the player who will give double-lip a fair try.

Double-Lip as a Corrective for Poor Embouchure Habits

Dr. Lee Gibson, professor emeritus of clarinet at the University of North Texas and one of America's best known clarinet teachers, wrote the following remarkable statement in his article on Embouchure and Air Column in "The Clarinet," Vol. 4 No. 2.

"I am fond of saying that there will be nothing wrong with one's clarinet embouchure which cannot be cured by practicing with the double-lip embouchure, regardless of whether it may or may not be used in public performance. I myself am a switcher: I always practice with the double-lip, while performing with it for part of my professional playing."

Some young players develop poor reed control habits that seem all but impossible to break. Double-lip is often the only technique that will enable these players to effectively break their bad habits without either them or the teacher having a nervous breakdown in the process.

All the things we admire about a fine embouchure; the flat, pointed chin and face muscles pulled against the bone structure; all of these things happen more easily and naturally with double-lip technique in most every case.

Therefore, when all else fails, many teachers find double-lip to be very useful in putting developing players on the right track. Once the problems are corrected and the student's embouchure is working properly, he or she may want to return to single-lip playing, while retaining double-lip as a practice technique to "keep them honest" about biting.

Learning Double-Lip

If you've played single-lip for several years, the first thing you will need to learn is that double-lip is not just single-lip with the upper lip under. Theoretically, that *should* be the only difference. But the reality is that most single-lip players bite to control the reed. This will never do for double-lip playing (and it shouldn't for single-lip either). For a single-lip player, not biting is a moral imperative, but for a double-lip player it is an absolute physical necessity. That is, unless you enjoy feeling sharp pains shooting through your upper lip while you're trying to make lovely music and produce a beautiful tone.

Therefore, if double-lip is to be comfortable, the player must learn to control the reed by the friction-style, indirect method described earlier in this chapter. The closing, cutting action of the upper and lower teeth common to so much single-lip playing must be eliminated if double-lip is to be played with comfort (see ex. 6).

Double-lip fosters good muscular development in the lips, but this muscular development is not caused by exchanging the clamping action of the jaw for the squeezing action of the lips. Not at all. This development comes from the lip's cushioning action as a response to the mouthpiece's inward thrust. In this way the lips imitate the jaw (when properly used) by simply creating a fixed window and nothing more. The lips, like the jaw, are passive, resisting the motion of the mouthpiece, but not moving themselves. As one clarinetist from the nineteenth century loved to say, "The reed rests in a bed of roses." This language is perhaps a bit too flowery for today, but his point is clear: The lips should never squeeze the mouthpiece! If more control is needed, the right hand thumb simply snug the mouthpiece a bit more firmly against the lips.

Double-Lip and the Soft Palate

The soft palate is locate in the back half of the roof of the mouth. What most teachers and players call playing with an "open throat" is, in reality, not the throat at all, but the soft palate being lifted high and back, as if one were mildly yawning with the mouth closed. Lifting the soft palate enhances resonance and tonal beauty and is *essential* in playing at softer dynamic levels. Usually, young players who get bright, tight sounds, and have difficulty playing the high register or at soft dynamic levels are playing with a tight, closed down soft palate. One of the greatest of the many natural benefits of tucking the upper lip under the upper teeth is that of the automatic lifting of the soft palate, making it almost impossible to play with what many players (erroneously) refer to as a "closed throat".

Initial Problems Learning Double-Lip and Their Solutions

Endurance can be a problem for the novice. You may have been playing for years, but your upper lip is a rank beginner. It is a muscle, and it needs time to develop. You can set yourself back two days for every one that you overdo it. Here are a few suggestions which will help prevent this from happening:

1. Rest the bell of the clarinet on your knee or knees.

2. Make sure the reeds you play are very well-balanced. Unbalanced reeds tend to spread the sound and be undependable in response unless you add lots of embouchure pressure (bite). This can wear anyone out.

3. Play slowly at first; long tones, slow scales and arpeggios, beautiful legato melodies. This will help you appreciate the increased freedom, flexibility and the improved legato and tonal depth double-lip affords the sound.

4. Avoid playing too much in the upper registers for a few weeks. Wait until you have developed enough lip muscles to absorb the increased snugging sometimes needed for higher playing.

5. Rest frequently. Don't worry about playing quantity. Rather, concentrate on playing quality and try to play correctly all of the time you are playing. You might try playing for a minute and resting for a minute, until your endurance builds. You will be surprised at how quickly the energy and strength of the lips are restored after only a few moments rest.

You will probably find the most problematic tones are those which have fewest fingers closing the tone holes. These notes are likely to feel a bit unstable and shakey at first. High "C" especially can be a problem. The remedy is to finger high "C" in the normal way, but to add the third ring finger of the left hand and open the side key Eb/Bb key as well. This fingering is not only very well in tune, but it is also a bit more rounder, fuller and darker than the usual fingering. True, it is impractical to use in rapid passages, but it is perfect for legato playing and whenever you must slur smoothly to or from high "C", whether you are playing double-lip or not.

Double-Lip and Finger Technique

Double-lip makes you more sensitive to the qualitative aspect of your finger technique. Many players are very heavy handed, slapping the keys and having a lot of gripping tension on the tone holes. Of course, the fingers should never close and grip on the tone holes. They should only rest on the tone holes. Closing a tone hole should be a relaxation, rather than an exertion of muscle tension. Such heavy-handed playing causes instability in the embouchure, especially if you are not properly "snugged up."

Double-lip will force relaxation and the use of a lighter finger technique. But after all, this is something the majority of clarinetists need to do just about as much as not biting. Playing double-lip simply makes *both* a matter of necessity.

Switching

It is not uncommon to find players who alternate between double and single-lip. For example, many military band clarinetists switch, playing double-lip in concert and single-lip when marching. Many symphony players also use both, playing technical passages single-lip, while using double-lip for more lyrical passages which require beauty of tone, flexibility, sensitive dynamic control and faultless legato. You may be a bit unsure of the idea of switching at first, but almost everyone who tries it finds it very workable. There is little tendency to confuse the two styles of embouchure and most players find that switching back and forth is glitchless. A final advantage which may encourage the reluctant to give switching a serious try is that using one method for even a short time in performance actually constitutes giving the other a rest, making performance endurance less of a problem.

Double-Lip and its Effect on Single-Lip

All the good things in embouchure and tone are more easily and naturally achieved with double-lip. Once the "double-lip feel" is experienced its transference to single-lip playing results in the reduction or complete elimination of biting, a more open, flexible, ringing tone and better interval connections. In short, learning double-lip does nothing but improve the clarinetist's approach to the mechanics of single-lip embouchure.

Double-Lip and Articulation

An important benefit of double-lip is an improvement in the quality of articulation. Most players find that articulated notes usually have more life and presence as well as "ping" and "ring." They also note that staccato tones are fuller and "meatier." The cause of these improvements is simply the reed's ability to vibrate more freely and fully along the resistance curve of the mouthpiece and to respond more quickly and freely at the tip.

How Much Lip Should be Tucked Under the Upper Teeth?

What determines how much upper lip needs to be tucked under the upper teeth is comfort. Some people have long upper lips and short upper teeth. They would tend to be comfortable with more lip under than persons with short upper lips and longer upper teeth. The only danger in either case is taking so much lip under that it damps and dulls the tone, creates resistance and prevents the high tones from responding.

Some Pit Falls to Avoid

There are a few problems that routinely crop up in learning double-lip. The first of these is the failure of the right hand thumb to consistently lift enough to maintain snugness of the mouthpiece and reed snug against the lips. The second is dropping the head or holding the clarinet out so that the student is blowing straight into the clarinet. (The angle of the clarinet should be the same, whether you are playing double or single-lip).

Finally, holding the clarinet out, off the knees can get tiring. For this reason, most of the playing time should be spent with the clarinet supported by the knee or knees. If a sustained bell "B" must be played the bell can be lifted to increase the clarity and presence of the tone.

Double-Lip and Younger Players

Two questions that might be asked at this point are, *"If double-lip gives so many advantages, is it possible to start younger players with double-lip? And if so, is it advantageous to so do?"* The fact is, there is nothing whatsoever that would prevent most young players from successfully playing double-lip right at the outset. In fact, most who begin this way have little problem overcoming the usual and otherwise ubiquitous temptation to bite. As a consequence, they almost always produce freer, clearer, fuller, and more pleasant sounding tones. Just as importantly, double-lip enables most students to achieve both cosmetically and mechanically superior embouchures more naturally, easily and quickly. The primary task of the teacher in the process is to make sure that the mouthpiece remains snugged firmly against the student's lips at all times, for there is a tendency for younger students to let the lifting of the thumb relax, which causes the pitch to sag and the tone to become uncentered and flabby. Secondarily, but just as critically, the teacher needs to make sure that the jaw stays down and the tongue remains high and back. Once the student learns to be consistent with these three habits, he or she will pass over many of the difficulties related to tone production that commonly frustrate beginning and intermediate clarinetists (not to mention many advanced and professional clarinetists who, unfortunately, were improperly taught and never learned how to control the reed without biting).

Finally it must be said to the skeptical that the opinions expressed here are not unique to this author. Many of the most respected and experienced teachers, even those who play single-lip, agree that correct embouchure mechanics are, in fact, easier to achieve for most students by playing double-lip. And that when and if they switch to single-lip, all the good habits learned by use of double-lip transfer over automatically in most every case. In other words, the student's approach to single-lip can be nothing but benefited and enhanced by learning to play double-lip at the outset. The smart money says, "Try it. Odds are good you'll like it." You'll never know until you do.

Conclusion

In summary, it can be said that diligently working to master proper embouchure functions may require considerable effort from the student (and patient but firm persistence from the teacher). But the treasury of technical and artistic rewards is more than worth it. Hearing a great clarinetist who has mastered these techniques should be enough to inspire both beginning and advanced players to spare no effort to attain mastery and perfection of correct embouchure techniques. Next, it is obvious that no two embouchures will ever *look* exactly alike. Therefore, basing an embouchure pedagogy strictly on cosmetics *alone* can be both deceptive and misleading and the musical results disappointing. There are many cases when an embouchure may look right (especially to the untrained eye) but is, in reality, malfunctioning in some critical and fundamental way, making it impossible for the student to produce a beautiful, free, flexible and resonant tone. Further, the vise-like action of the jaw, which would *seem* to be the most natural and logical way to control the reed, turns out, after close analysis, to be seriously flawed and limited in both its technical and musical results. By contrast, the more passive, receptive method of reed control, accomplished by dropping the jaw to form a fixed window or framework with the lips and teeth into which the mouthpiece/reed wedge can be snugged, fully satisfies the demands of musical tone by optimizing the vibrational mechanics of the reed. Boldly put, this writer believes that, when all is said and done, there is *objectively* only one best method of reed control, which has been clearly demonstrated by the evidence presented in this chapter. Proper embouchure functioning, and *not* cosmetics, is the common denominator and ultimate criteria for success or failure in clarinet embouchure development. In the end, it is a combination of the teacher's thorough understanding of how the embouchure actually functions to enable the reed to produce musical tone along with his or her unwavering insistence upon the correct application of these functions by the student which ultimately yields the ideal technical and musical results, each and every time. The bottom line is simple: Despite the unique differences of each person's facial features, all embouchures must *function* in the same way if both tonal freedom and control are to be optimized as they must be if a truly beautiful musical tone is to be achieved.

SUMMARY OUTLINE OF TONE PRODUCTION TECHNIQUES

Putting it All Together

This section briefly summarizes and reviews the material presented in all the chapters up to this point. It can be used for quick reference, and may be helpful in gaining an overview of the most salient concepts of correct blowing, voicing and clarinet embouchure. The teacher may find that step-by-step presentation of how to begin the sound on pages SO-3 and SO-4 to be especially useful in teaching beginners to make their first sounds.

Teaching the Tone Concept

Students need to develop a concept of clarinet tone. This concept is instilled in them by two things:

1. Having them listen to recordings of great clarinet players. (If this is not done consciously the standard for tone will be unconsciously formed by the way their peers sound).

2. Giving the students words and descriptions which help them understand what they are hearing and why it is good. Here are some descriptive words, both good and bad, which help draw their attention to different qualities in the tone:

Freedom

The following words are commonly used to describe the good qualities of freedom in the tone: **Resonant or "Ringing", Rich, Vibrant, Flexible.**

The following words are commonly used to describe the negative qualities that appear in tonal freedom: **Shrill, Harsh, Bright, Metallic, Uncentered, Wild, Diffused, Hollow.**

Control

The following words are commonly used to describe the good qualities of control:

Centered, Focused, Dense, Well-Defined.

The following words are commonly used to describe the negative qualities of control when sufficient freedom is lacking: **Tight, Pinched, Small, Thin, Inflexible, Dull, Choked.**

A Short Discussion on Tonal Shape

A more complete idea of clarinet tonal shape can be instilled in players as they mature by using three-dimensional images. The word "roundness" often comes up as a descriptive word. If this is used, make sure that they understand you are speaking of the roundness of a ball, not the roundness of a two-dimensional circle.

Perhaps an even better descriptive image is "pear-shaped." The pear shape should give the student the idea that the clarinet tone is not only three-dimensional like the rubber ball, but also has a point of density or focus from which the tone emanates or grows. Be sure to point out to the student that the top and bottom of the pear shape are created by distinctly different elements of the tone production system. Specifically, the jaw, remaining dropped in the "O" position creates the "body" of the pear, while the high/back placement of the tongue focuses the air in such a way that it forms the top, pointed part of the pear.

In other words, the depth of the tone and the center of the tone are caused by distinctly different components of the tone production system.

The truly characteristic shape of the clarinet tone is a diphthong "oe" or "ue" shape. Both of these vowel shapes, being simultaneously present, cause the tone to "spin", and make it more "interesting" to listen to than the comparative blandness of plain vowel sounds.

Concise Summary of the Elements of The Tone Production System and How They Work

Two elements function together to generate the clarinet tone: the air column and the reed.

Two elements function together to control the clarinet tone: *the tongue and the embouchure. The tongue controls the air column, and the embouchure controls the reed.*

The Air Stream and Tongue

The air stream needs to be highly compressed. The best type of air for the clarinet is sometimes described as "cold air." What this means is that the air stream must be a small, narrow, concentrated, fast moving stream, rather than slow, broad and diffused. This type of air column is produced by the combination of two things:

1. Blowing compressed, or "aerosol can" air: This is done by taking a full breath and then pushing the air down at all times. This keeps the abdomen distended while the chest gradually deflates. The downward pushing both causes and maintains a constant compression of the air in the body. This sort of air stream is essential if the tone color, shape and volume are to be consistent.

2. The tongue is used to "voice" the sound. It does this by controlling the shape, speed and direction of the air stream. In order to assist the blowing mechanism in creating the fast, cold stream of air, the tongue needs to be positioned high and back in the mouth, in an arched position, as if you were <u>about</u> to pronounce the word "cake" or "key." The middle of the tongue should be very close to the roof of the mouth and the insides of the back upper molars should be felt by either side of the tongue.

This high/back position creates a narrow passage between the surface of the tongue and the roof of the mouth called a **venturi.** This venturi acts upon the air stream like the nozzle on a garden hose when it is adjusted at its smallest opening; it speeds up and concentrates the stream dramatically.

The Embouchure: Controlling the Reed

The embouchure should act upon the reed in such a way that it can vibrate in both a controlled and free way. The best way to begin learning this is to:

1. Open the teeth slightly, as if you were holding a soda straw in your mouth and sipping a chocolate malt (or the flavor of your choice). To do this, the jaw must open as if you were saying the vowel "O" (as in "go").

2. Place the tip of the mouthpiece/reed wedge between the lips very loosely and begin to blow air into the clarinet. You should hear the air passing freely through the clarinet, but without any tone. If the air is not passing completely freely through the clarinet, it means that there is embouchure/jaw pressure being added to the reed. If that is the case, begin again at step one and make sure the jaw does not close <u>in any way</u> on the mouthpiece as it is inserted into the embouchure opening created by the lips.

3. Increase the air so that tone appears, but do not increase any pressure on the reed or move the jaw in any way. The tone will be very flat at this point.

4. With the jaw remaining in its downward, "O" open position, firm the red of the lips, and with the right hand thumb, lift the clarinet and snug the mouthpiece/ reed wedge firmly against the lips, while simultaneously moving the tongue from the "O" position to the high/back "Key" position (notice that tongue's high/back movement will automatically cause the chin to stretch down into the classic cosmetic "point"). This simultaneous action of thumb and tongue might be easily coordinated by telling the student to think, "Thumb's up, Tongue's up!"

Example 9: Thumb/Tongue Rudimentary Voicing Exercise

Tongue: low/fwd.....&...... high/bk................low/fwd....................high/bk............
Soft Palate: dwn/fwd.....up/back................down/fwd.................up/back............

"oooooooooooooeeeeeeeeeeeeeeeoooooooooooooooeeeeeeeeeeeee

Thumb's down........Thumb's up..........Thumb's down......Thumb's up....
Jaw down "O"..
Flat pitch...............High pitch.............Flat pitch.............High pitch......

The Thumb/Tongue coordination exercise should aid the student in learning that biting is not needed to raise the pitch and/or center the sound. Have the student repeat this coordination exercise until it is second nature and they will always automatically center the sound in this manner. Begin the exercise with air flowing freely through the clarinet, but without producing a tone. Then increase the air until the flat open "G" appears. If the open "G" is not flat when it appears, the student is biting. One of the major points of the exercise is to get the thumb to raise the pitch by snugging, rather than have the jaw do it by biting.

Results of the Proper Coordination of Tongue, Air and Embouchure

If these four steps are done correctly, you will notice the tone will grow simultaneously louder, clearer, fuller, more centered and higher in tuning. If at a certain point the sound begins to spread and lower in pitch, it simply means you've:

a) snugged too much mouthpiece in your mouth.

b) failed to keep the lips firm and/or have allowed them to be pushed over the teeth and into the mouth by the movement of the mouthpiece/reed wedge.

c) moved the jaw too open or failed to keep the tongue position high and back and the soft palate properly lifted or "blown up".

The Educator's Guide to the Clarinet

print

CLARINET TONE PRODUCTION AT A GLANCE

JAW
The jaw should open and move slightly forward to create the embouchure "tone window." Once in position the jaw must remain completely stationary. It must not close on the reed to control the sound; this is biting and ruins the tone quality.

TONGUE
The tongue primarily determines the tuning and focus of the tone by controlling the shape, speed and direction of the air stream. It does this by arching its middle high and back in the mouth, similar to when one forms the letter "k". The high/back position creates a narrow passage, or venturi, which both speeds and concentrates the air column.

LIPS
Both upper and lower lips are used to cushion and resist the mouthpiece/reed wedge, as it is snugged into the mouth. Most of both lips should be easily visible, rather than being pushed over the teeth and into the mouth by the mouthpieces inward movement. Corners of the mouth need only follow the natural movement back caused by the combined energies of the taut chin and the high/back voicing of the tongue.

SOFT PALLATE
The flexible, balloon-like soft pallate, located in the back part of the roof of the mouth, needs to remain lifted at all times, as if one were mildly yawning with the mouth closed.

MOUTHPIECE
The mouthpiece/reed wedge is snugged firmly against the lips and into the mouth by the right hand thumb to gain control of the reed, and help the tongue raise the pitch and focus the sound.

THROAT
The throat remains relaxed at all times, neither forcing open nor contracting.

SHOULDERS
The shoulders and upper body remain relaxed throughout the breathing and blowing process.

AIR COLUMN
The air stream is compressed and concentrated by the constant downward push of the diaphragm. This creates an "aerosol can" effect in the quality of the air column, increasing both the speed and focus of the air.

CHIN
The chin is pulled down flat and taut against the jaw bone, forming a point. This has the effect of pulling the lower lip down, helping it to resist the upward/inward movement of mouthpiece/reed wedge. This resistance of the lower lip helps create the friction needed to control the reed. Finally, the tongue's high/back voicing position helps the chin achieve its characteristic taut, flat, pointed appearance.

Chapter V

HOW TO TEACH ARTICULATION

In this chapter you will learn.....

Where the tongue should touch the reed and where the reed should touch the tongue.

How maintaining correct voicing can improve tonguing technique.

The best syllable to use for tonguing on the clarinet and why.

How the tongue should move and how to best relate the concept to students.

How air and embouchure affect tonguing.

Different styles of tonguing and some helpful ways of teaching them.

A method for teaching beginners to tongue.

What "Stop, or Rebound Tonguing" is and how and when it should be used.

A method of teaching students to begin tones with the tongue.

How to develop speed, once correct tonguing methods are learned.

Introduction

Teaching tonguing can be a perplexing and frustrating matter for both teacher and student. The primary reason for this is that successful tonguing, most especially in regard to the quality and security of articulated tones, requires the presence of a relatively high degree of perfection in the foundational aspects of tone production: embouchure, air and voicing. It is not uncommon to find that even some advanced players admit to having what they think is a tonguing problem. Often they are both surprised and shocked to find that they really don't have a tonguing problem---what they, in reality, do have is an "everything-else-problem"! That is, one or another of their tone production techniques has been improperly developed and is negatively affecting their ability to tongue well.

Those who teach need to be aware that, in their concentration on learning how to tongue, younger players commonly fail to maintain proper tone production habits. They let their air columns decompress, their tongue positions drop and their embouchures tighten; just the very opposite of what ought to be done! Considering this, the question quite naturally arises, "When should tonguing be introduced?" Not surprisingly, there is no consensus among teachers on this matter. The right time must be a judgment call by the teacher. This, however, does not mean that one is altogether bereft of any clear criteria for such a judgment. Specifically, it can be objectively said that tonguing should be not introduced until adequate time has been spent on air, tongue position (voicing) and embouchure development so that correct application of these techniques are well on their way to being second nature. (It is especially critical to maintain constant air pressure, for both tongue motion and tone quality are greatly dependant upon the air.) If these foundational techniques are shaky they will tumble like a house of cards the moment tonguing is added to the mix. If this happens more time still needs to be spent on foundationals and tonguing put off till sometime later. Finally, it needs to be said that the reed/mouthpiece set up will affect speed, quality and security in tonguing. If the reed is poorly balanced, tongued attacks on high tones at softer dynamics can be treacherous and insecure, to say the least.

Tongue Placement on the Reed

What part of the tongue and reed should come into contact with one another? Years ago the stock answer to this question would have been that the tip of the tongue must touch the tip of the reed. But this, in reality, is like saying everyone should wear the same size shoes. It just isn't possible. The critical question is not which part of the tongue should touch the reed, but which part of the reed the tongue should touch. The reed needs to be touched as close to its tip as possible and, in most tonguing styles, as lightly as possible.

Many very fine clarinetists touch the reed with the tip of their tongue, others touch somewhere further back. Some clarinetists even contact the reed with the underside of their tongue. Others use different parts of the tongue for different speeds and styles. A small number even anchor tongue with some success. There is no doubt that tip-to-tip is most ideal, but if doing so is an impossibility, don't despair. Success is still possible.

One thing is for sure, a large mass of tongue contacting the area of the reed's surface below the tip causes several problems and needs to be avoided. Among these problems are a percussive sound at the beginning of the tone, a sluggish, delayed response, severe undertoning of the upper clarion and third register tones, and instability in pitch due to jaw movement during the tongue action.

"Off-the-Reed-Tonguing": What it is and How to Recognize it

Many times a student's first attempt at tonguing results in a series of squeaks and squawks. Now, to students, the worst thing is not failing to learn how to tongue correctly. The worst thing is being embarrassed in front of their peers by squeaking. Because of this fear, a few squeaks are often all it takes to discourage many of them from making any further attempts to touch the reed with the tongue at all.

But students are inventive. They realize they must not only protect themselves from embarrassment, but satisfy the teacher's expectations in some way as well. Therefore, they often try to "simulate" tongued attacks by touching the tongue to the area of the gums just *behind* the reed and mouthpiece, rather than the reed itself. In short, they begin to develop what is called "off-the-reed-tonguing."

This would be a wonderfully inventive maneuver on the their behalves were it not for the fact that off-the-reed-tonguing has major faults:
1. It causes a woody, dull, percussive noise before the beginning of each tone.
2. Tones above the staff are almost impossible to begin, and if they do speak at all, the attack usually sounds terrible.

The teacher's job is to listen for the "thuddy," percussive sound off-the-reed-tonguing causes, and give the students who do it the special attention they need to overcome the habit. As we have already mentioned, the problem is often nothing more than the fear of squeaking in front of their peers which discourages them from learning to tongue on the reed.

Such squeaking is usually caused by one or two things:
1. Too much tongue or tongue pressure on the reed.
2. Little or no air pressure present at the beginning of the tone.

Often, simply letting the student know that squeaking commonly happens when you first try to tongue, and that it can take a little time to coordinate the air and learn how to use the tongue so that squeaking doesn't happen, is all that is needed to put the student back on the right path.

The critical thing for the teacher is early detection, for once the student ingrains this habit through weeks and weeks of repetition, breaking them of it can be a real chore.

Tongue Position in Tonguing

As we said, all the other elements of tone production need to be especially perfect in tongued passages, and this especially includes the tongue's role in voicing the tone. The classic high/back arched tongue position is actually helpful in tonguing, because it lifts the tongue up in the mouth so that it can more easily touch the tip of the reed. This can be seen by comparing the tongue positions in example 1 on page 3-5.

Those who play with a low/forward tongue position invariably strike the reed well below the tip. Such a technique (if it can be called a technique) not only interrupts the reed's vibration, but also inhibits vibration, and the tongue noise (a kind of "thunk") is clearly audible in the tone. Lifting the tongue properly helps eliminate this problem as well.

The Proper Tonguing Syllable for the Clarinet

Different wind instruments successfully use a variety of syllables for articulation. The clarinet is not as pluralistic in this regard. During articulated passages, the high/back tongue position needs to be maintained. Syllables such as "ta" and "da" cause the tongue position to drop, slowing the air, causing excessive tongue movement and directing tongue placement below the tip area of the reed.

For this reason, the safest syllable to work with is that of "Tee" or "Dee," since the "e" syllable in each of these helps keep the tongue position high.

Motion of the Tongue

The motion of the tongue should be limited to the tip area (first third) of the tongue, while the middle of the tongue remains stationary in its arched, high/back position, and the sides of the tongue maintain contact with the insides of the upper molars. The tonguing motion itself should be an economical up and down rather than a back and forth motion.

It is usually not difficult to get students to feel this type of action in the tongue if you get them to softly whisper the syllable "tee" or "dee" in a continuous repetition. By *whispering* rather than *saying* "tee," the tongue will economize its movement just as it should in the actual act of articulating tones on the clarinet. Whispering will also help eliminate any jaw motion the student might be tempted to add.

The Embouchure in Tonguing

Our usual response to tackling any new task is one of increased tension. When this new task is tonguing, the tension often expresses itself in the form of increased embouchure pressure (biting). Biting is never good, but because it so seriously inhibits the reed's ability to speak, the temptation to bite needs to be particularly avoided in articulated passages. A firm, but non-constricting embouchure and a jaw which remains fixed in its "O" dropped position and does not close or clamp on the reed are all that is needed. If pressure does need to be added to the reed for soft, high tongued passages, it should be added by snugging the mouthpiece more firmly against the lips rather than clamping the reed with the viselike action of the jaw. (Please see the section on Embouchure for more detailed information on the role of the jaw in tone production).

The Chin in Tonguing

There should be no visible external movement in the chin or jaw during tonguing. The chin should be as stable in tonguing as in sustained playing. So much so, that if someone were watching you play, but could not hear you, they would be unable to tell whether you were tonguing or playing legato.

The Air and Tonguing

No matter how good the other techniques are, nothing happens without adequate air pressure. It is often the habit of young players to drop the air pressure when they begin learning to tongue. This needs to be nipped in the bud by always reminding the student of how important it is to blow with steadiness and consistency. "Blow through the notes, not to the notes," can often be a meaningful and effective exhortation. "Don't forget to keep making the balloon larger while you are tonguing!" can be another.

An analogy that most young players understand readily is that of a water tap. The tap acts as a valve, releasing and shutting off the water, but even when the tap is closed, the water pressure remains constant, ready to force the water out of the tap as soon as it is opened the least bit.

The tongue, of course, is analogous to the tap, the air compares to the water, and the pressure (which makes everything work) relates to the proper blowing technique (aerosol can air).

Just as the water pressure continues when the tap is closed, so must the air pressure continue when the tongue is on the reed and no sound is being produced. Thus, sound or no sound, the student must have the sensation of blowing just as constantly as if he or she were holding a single sustained tone.

Failure to do this results in what is commonly called "huffing and puffing." That is, the student stops the blowing pressure each time a tone ends. This means, he or she must reset the blowing for the next note. This can:
1. Cause notes to respond late.
2. Cause the next tone to be a different color and volume.
3. Cause some higher, less stable tones to crack, squeak or break up to a higher overtone.

These faults are good reasons to avoid developing the "huffing and puffing" habit.

Beginning Efforts at Tonguing

There are several ways of teaching students to tongue. What ever method you settle on, always begin by reminding them that it is the air which is responsible for the tone, and that their tongues are only used to momentarily interrupt the reed's vibration. Therefore, above all things, they must maintain constant support of the tone with the air, or nothing will work right at all.

Having said that, here is a step by step approach to teaching tonguing which is usually effective:

1. First, ask the students to repeatedly <u>whisper</u>, "tee tee tee tee tee." Ask them to notice the way their tongues work as they whisper the syllables.
2. Ask them to produce a sustained tone by using the air only. This means they will need to use the syllable "heeeee" to begin the tone.
3. While they are sustaining the tone, ask them to repeatedly "whisper" the syllable "tee" or "dee" in the exact same way they did without the clarinet. They should then be blowing continuously while whispering "teeteeteeteeteetee". The sound should be continuous, with only a gentle "bump" of the sound as the whispering action of the tongue lightly brushes and quickly withdraws from the tip of the reed.

Some Things to Watch and Listen For in the Student's Initial Efforts at Tonguing

While the students are playing watch for:
1. Jaw motion.
2. Bunching chins.
3. Excessive movement in the throat.
Also listen for:
1. Tongue noise accompanying the articulated tone.

Jaw motion and throat movement are indications that the whole tongue is moving to articulate, rather than just the tip area. Tongue noise is an indicator that the student is touching the reed too hard and on its surface, rather than lightly at the tip. If the students are really doing the whispering action of the tongue and using the syllable "tee" none of these things should occur.

What to do Next?

Each day for several weeks ask the students to repeat the three-step exercise described above, always tonguing only on a single tone. Strictly keeping this routine each day will help them to concentrate on tonguing, blowing and listening. There will be plenty of time later for the fancy stuff.

ADVANCED TONGUING TECHNIQUES

Once the basic act of tonguing is sufficiently mastered and the students have gained some confidence, they need to learn how to coordinate the tongue and air to create different effects commonly indicated in music.

In presenting these styles, it can be useful to show students just how the shape of the sound "looks." Being able to actually see the shape of the sound can be very helpful to young students who are as yet unaccustomed to the idea of "seeing" shapes with their ears. Drawings can help them make the transition from a visual to an audial orientation more easily.

Here are some of the most basic styles they need to learn and their shapes:

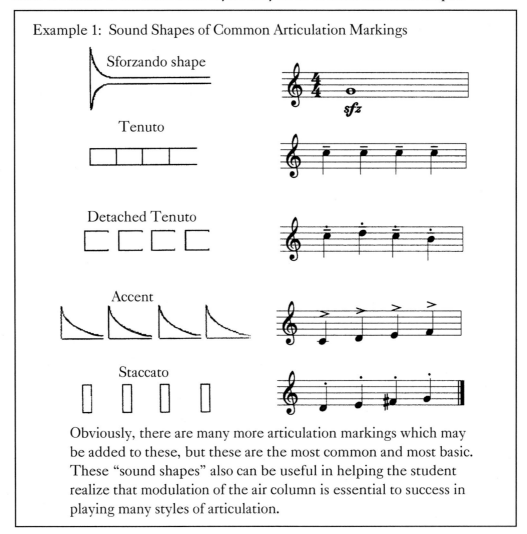

Example 1: Sound Shapes of Common Articulation Markings

Obviously, there are many more articulation markings which may be added to these, but these are the most common and most basic. These "sound shapes" also can be useful in helping the student realize that modulation of the air column is essential to success in playing many styles of articulation.

Stop or "Rebound" Tonguing

One style of articulation which is almost unique to the clarinet (though saxophonists use the same technique) is called "Stop Tonguing." With this technique the tongue not only begins the tone but ends it as well. It does this by placing the tongue back on the reed, as if the tongue were saying teeeeeeeet. That is, the tongue leaves the reed and then rebounds back on it. Stop tonguing gives the end of the note an abrupt cut off which clearly defines its ending to the ear. Example 2 shows how to begin developing this technique.

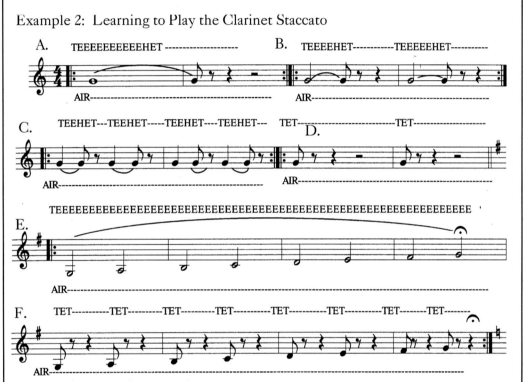

Example 2: Learning to Play the Clarinet Staccato

Explanation: The above exercises are designed to help the student learn to play a true staccato (stop tonguing) by a step-by-step process. Notice the air pressure is maintained continuously throughout each exercise, whether the tone is actually being sounded or not.

Notice the note values in exercises A through D become progressively shorter, but the actual tongue action is identical throughout. The goal, of course, is to be able to end the tones of exercise D abruptly with the tongue.

Notice in exercises E and F that the air pressure is constant in both. Only the action of the tongue differs.

Finally, note the use of the syllables "te or tet" to help maintain the high/back tongue position.

When to Use Stop Tonguing

The technique of ending or "clipping" tones by abruptly stopping the reed's vibration with the tongue has many more uses than just playing staccato passages. For instance, it is used to cut or clip the last slurred note before a staccato. This is done because staccato tones are not only short, they are also separate. Therefore, if a tone is to be a true staccato, it must be both preceded and followed by a silence separating it from the tones on either side of it. If the last slurred tone is not cut short, there will be no silence before the staccato tone (see ex. 3).

Example 3: Clipping Slurred Tone in Mixed Articulation

Written

Sounds

Explanation: Notice the slurred note before the first staccato is always ended abruptly in order that the first staccato tone may be preceeded as well as followed by silence. Such a laconic style of articulation may seem a bit harsh, but application of the technique in rapid passages creates a cleanness and clarity which can be achieved by no other means. The faster the articulation, the more effective stop tonguing and clipping slurred notes becomes.

Despite the great value of this style of articulation and the perfect clarity it gives to rapid articulation, it is certainly possible to go over board in its use. A good rule of thumb is that articulation techniques are meant to serve music, not vice versa. Therefore, the smart money is on letting the musical taste and interpretive insight as well as particular playing conditions dictate the use of any specific technique, rather than blindly (or deafly) "plugging in" this or that technique automatically---we are meant to be artists, not trained monkeys.

Stop tonguing is an advanced exercise and should not be done until embouchure, air and tongue position are all fairly well established and working well together, and the student is being successful at basic tonguing techniques.

How to Play Tongued Attacks

Players of all skill levels find playing attacks challenging. The greatest difficulty is that of playing articulated tones in the higher register at soft dynamic levels. Success in doing so requires not only perfection in tone production techniques, but an excellent reed/mouthpiece set up as well. Here we will only concentrate upon the playing techniques.

There are four things which players need to do when playing tongued attacks.
1. Keep the jaw in its dropped position.
2. Keep the mouthpiece and reed well snugged.
3. Have the air column "up and running" well before the tongue withdraws from the reed to begin the sound.
4. Make sure the tongue is in contact with the reed at its very tip, not pressing the reed closed, but only blocking the air from entering the opening between the reed and mouthpiece tip. Pressing the reed completely closed on the mouthpiece with the tongue can cause all sorts of problems. These include delays in response, undertoning and, of course, audible tongue noise at the very inception of the sound.

Often young players try to begin notes without preparation of the air, and the results are uniformly disastrous. This is most especially true in the upper register, where tones crack up very easily unless there is adequate air pressure to stabilize them at their very inception. (The great majority of the cracked tones and squeaks in the upper register are caused by *too little* air pressure being used to initiate the tone rather than *too much*)! Students must be taught to prepare the air, and to be "set" with their embouchure, as if the tone were already being produced, long before the sound actually begins.

The "set" position before the release of the tone can be taught very effectively by use of the technique of stop tonguing. Here's how:

1. Have the students play the stop tongue exercise "A" in example 2. The very instant they end the whole note with the tongue tell them to "freeze" right where they are: The tongue should be on the reed, the air pressure up, the jaw down, the mouthpiece and reed properly snugged and the embouchure completely formed. From that "set position" they are now perfectly poised to <u>successfully</u> begin a tone with a tongue release.

2. Have them do this several times so that they have ample opportunity to notice precisely where their tongue, air and embouchure are the instant the long tone is ended.

3. Next, ask them to assume this position without first beginning and ending a long tone. This will be their "set" position from which the tongue can then withdraw from the reed, releasing the air into the clarinet. Have them memorize this routine and practice it daily.

Remind them often that any purposeful action requires careful, thoughtful preparation. A good and familiar example of this is a baseball player preparing to hit. He goes through a routine that properly prepares him to concentrate on the ball and swing the bat. Initiating tones on the clarinet requires a similar purposeful routine and concentration (see example 4).

Example 4: Routine for Initiating Tongued Attacks

	SET			RELEASE
1. Full Breath.	2. Tongue on Reed.	3. Form Embouchure and Snug Mouthpiece.	4. Begin Pressurized Blowing.	5. Withdraw the Tongue from the Reed to Begin the Tone.

Once the students are familiar with each of the steps in the "Set and Release" they need to practice them repeatedly until the whole routine becomes second-nature. The only material needed to practice "set and release" are separate tones in all registers. These tones may be long or short, but each should be preceded by silence. The student should practice them at all possible dynamic markings. Here are a few samples of the kind of material they can use which may be helpful in developing the skill:

Developing Speed

Once the student gains comfort in the basic technique of tonguing, the issue of speed begins to enter the picture. Speed is gained by daily, systematic practice with a metronome, thoughtful experimentation and a good method to record progress.

As the students begin to work on increasing tonguing speed, they will find that speed alone is not the whole issue. The factors of both speed and duration must be taken into account. For instance, a student may find that he can tongue sixteenth notes at 116 beats per minute for nine beats, sixteenths at 120 beats per minute for four beats and sixteenths at 132 beats per minute for only a beat and a half.

All this data needs to be recorded. The student's next task is to work on tonguing each day in an attempt to extend the duration of each of these tonguing speeds. In the midst of the student's efforts to improve, there are a few things which you as the teacher can remind the student of: economy of tongue motion, using only the tip area of the tongue, always "tonguing on the air," and keeping the jaw stable. The rest of it is up to the determination of the student to develop the tongue muscle by regular practice, disciplined work with a metronome and accurate record keeping. It goes without saying that some students have naturally faster tongues than others. But this does not mean that most every student can't significantly improve the speed of their tonguing with intelligently directed, daily practice. This is where record keeping can be a source of encouragement. With it the student can see real progress over several months of work.

Tonguing on the Fingers

Coordination of fingers and tongue is an added challenge. The biggest problem is caused by trying to move the fingers to the next note the very instant the tongue releases the sound. The fingers always need to anticipate and work an instant ahead of the tongue's release. Example 6 shows how this can be practiced slowly. The challenge is to increase the speed and retain the coordination and clarity of the passage.

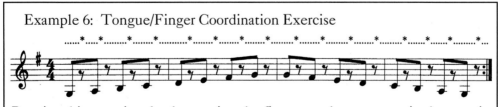

Example 6: Tongue/Finger Coordination Exercise

Practice this exercise slowly, moving the fingers to the next tone in the rests in between tongued releases, as the asterisks indicate.

Conclusion

As we mentioned at the beginning of the chapter, tonguing as a technique is highly dependent upon all of the other elements of tone production. When the air, jaw, embouchure and tongue position do their respective tasks properly, the job of the tongue is made much simpler.

Variability in equipment adds yet another fly to the articulation ointment. Poorly responding reeds can negatively affect both the qualitative and quantitative aspects of articulation, making them considerably more difficult. A clarinet which varies in its blowing resistance from one area to another can also negatively effect progress in articulation, and so on. In short, success and comfort in tonguing demands the best from every other facet of the clarinet, both mechanical and acoustical. Evenness of resistance is an especially valuable feature in equipment. Though poor equipment may be a reason for difficulty, it should never be an excuse. The more perfectly students master the techniques presented in this and the other chapters, the more capable they will be at getting the best from any set up they might have to play.

However, in the early stages of learning and developing correct tone production mechanics the student needs the very best equipment possible in order to facilitate his or her efforts. It is just as encumbent upon the teacher to make sure that this is provided as it is that the teacher give good instruction, most especially since most young students cannot tell good equipment from bad, except in the broadest, m ost primitive sense of the word. It is the teacher's knowledge and skill regarding good equipment that will stand between the student and frustration, and may even make the difference between success and failure.

All in all, the task of articulation may seem initially daunting to the student, and understandably so. Remind them that, though challenging, it is by no means an impossible goal, and one not without rewards and satisfactions. Remind them also, that persistence on their parts is the real key to developing first class articulation techniques. If they work correctly daily, it will happen sooner than they expect.

Chapter VI

TECHNIQUE: FINGER FUNDAMENTALS

In this chapter you will learn.....

How the fingers should cover the tone holes and what he natural hand-position should be.

The job of each finger and how it should be performed.

How repair condition affects finger technique.

The correct motion of the index finger for playing the throat tones.

How to develop independence of the pinkies and why it is critical for good technique.

How the left hand thumb is "sneaky," and how to correct its tendency toward certain bad habits.

What the touchpoint system is and how it can improve both the quality and quantity of your student's techniques.

How to play over the middle break smoothly.

How to develop a legato finger technique.

How to "grow" a traditional technique.

Introduction: The Quantitative and Qualitative Aspects of Technique

As the title implies, this chapter is not so much about the notes as the fingers which must play them and the habits they need to cultivate in order to function with both efficiency and relaxation. Each finger must do very different things, as well as coordinate in various ways with one another. The better we understand each finger's job and its relationship to the whole hand, the better we will be able to teach finger technique, and solve any problems which may arise. The philosophy of technique behind this sort of thinking may be stated in the following way:

The qualitative dimension of technique has a direct and profound bearing upon the quantitative dimension. In other words, an undisciplined technique, characterized by wasted motion and tension will slow and even completely arrest the clarinetist's technical development (practice doesn't make perfect; only perfect practice makes perfect). Essentially, each bad habit is like a heavy rock in the pocket of a runner; in order to run faster, he must stop and take the time to empty his pockets. The key to developing a clarinet technique is to build it in such a way that students never pick up any "rocks" in the first place. Only such an approach will insure their steady progress by means of, rather than in spite of, the finger habits they acquire.

In addition to the stunting effect poor finger habits and tension have on technical development, they can also damage the hands and fingers themselves. Playing with perpetual tension may eventually cause serious and even permanent medical problems, many of which can be avoided if relaxation and efficient finger habits are taught and practiced at the very outset.

Let us now begin to examine the work of each finger in detail, keeping in mind that the quantitative aspects of technique can best and most quickly be achieved by the development of the qualitative aspects.

THE HANDS: GENERAL COMMENTS

The Natural Hand Position and Relaxation

If you hang your hands at your sides, you will notice that the fingers naturally curve. This natural, relaxed curve should be transferred to the clarinet. When this is done, the tone holes will be covered with the rounded area near the finger tips rather than with the flatter area lower on the top finger joint.

In order to retain the curvature of the fingers while playing, the motion used to open and close tone holes must be made by moving only the lowest finger joint at the knuckles. Opening the tone holes by straightening the fingers requires excessive motion and reduces tone emission. In addition, whenever the fingers straighten, tension is present, and tension results in paralysis of the hand by degrees, seriously limiting technique and stunting technical development.

Students should be advised to practice often in front of a mirror in order to see the proximity of the fingers to the keys, and how the fingers are moving. They will be amazed at what they see in terms of wasted motion, straightness of the fingers and miscoordinations.

Relaxation when playing doesn't just happen. It is achieved by conscious and deliberate effort. It must be practiced all the time everything else is being practiced. Whenever tension creeps in it tends to spread. Therefore, vigilance is always necessary. For this reason, make sure that you remind students to take care to relax their forearms and shoulders as well the hands and fingers.

How the Fingers Should Close the Tone Holes

Closure of the tone holes should be an act of controlled relaxation, not of tension.
A simple exercise can demonstrate the proper action of the fingers:
1. Place your hands with the palms down on a desk top. Make sure the fingers are curved, so that you are touching the surface of the desk with the finger tips.
2. Now, while retaining the finger's curve, lift them from the desk top, one at a time, then let them completely relax and fall to the desk top.
Notice that in order to lift the finger and retain its curve, the lifting motion must come from the lowest finger joint, at the knuckle. (As an experiment, you can lift the fingers a second time by straightening them, just to demonstrate how much wasted motion there is in this approach).

That's really all there is to it. Correct action of the fingers is nothing more than a controlled relaxation. Gripping, squeezing or popping the fingers hard on the tone holes is a waste of energy, a source of tension, and presents a serious impediment to developing technical facility. All the fingers need to do is lift, relax, lift, relax. The weight of the finger should be enough to adequately cover the tone hole.

Finger Action and the Repair Condition of the Clarinet

If the clarinet is not properly adjusted, the fingers will not be able to work correctly. Here are some of the important things to look for in the clarinet's adjustment:

1. All ring heights need to be adjusted so that the pads close well, without any need for the fingers to squeeze on the rings. If the ring heights are too low the pad will not close, if they are too high, the fingers cannot close.
2. The pads need to be well seated. A poorly seated pad will require squeezing to make the tone respond, forcing the fingers into bad habits, and creating tension in the hands and throughout the body.
3. Spring tensions need to be strong enough to keep the pads firmly closed, but not so strong that the fingers must press hard to operate them.

THE LEFT HAND

The Left Hand Index Finger

The left index finger has three tasks. The first and most obvious one is closing the top finger hole. The second is playing throat Ab. The third is playing throat A.

In order to make a smooth connection from the E or F# to throat A, the index finger must learn to perform a rolling, or rocking motion. Many students will try to make the index hop from F# to A, but this causes open G to appear as an unwanted, ungraceful "grace note" or "blip" in between. Ask the student to play the following exercise while watching the left hand in a mirror.

Example No. 1: The Rocking Motion of the Left Index Finger

Play this exercise very slowly, and make note of the following things:
1. Be sure that the index finger does the motion of rocking, rather than moving the whole hand, wrist or even arm to play throat A.
2. Be sure that the other fingers of the left hand are not pulled out of place, but remain close to the body of the clarinet and immediately over their respective tone holes.
3. Keep the left hand pinky in constant contact with the low C#/G# key, resting on it whenever it is not depressing it.

The index must also play throat Ab and the chromatic combination Ab to A. It does this by depressing the Ab key with the second joint of the index finger. At this point the first and second joint will form a straight line. The A is then played by simply crooking or bending the top joint, while the second joint and the rest of the hand and the wrist remain completely stationary. Any movement of the hands, wrists or arms to play Ab to A is a waste of motion and should be eliminated.

Example 2: Correct Motion for Playing Throat G# to A

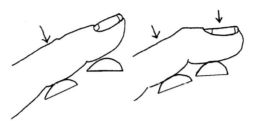

All the time this motion is being learned, make sure that the left hand thumb remains in contact with the thumb ring and register key, rather than moving out of position and placing itself on the body of the clarinet below the thumb hole. Also, make sure that the other fingers of the left hand remain directly over their respective tone holes, with the little finger resting upon either the low C#/G# or the left hand E-B lever on the right hand joint. Finally, make sure the hand and the wrist remain completely stationary, unaffected by the motion of the index finger.

Example 3: Exercise for G#-A Finger Motion

Everything mentioned in example 2 applies here as well: elimination of all wrist and hand motion and keeping the fingers in proper position over their tone holes are essential. Also make sure the thumb remains in contact with the tip of register key lever at <u>all</u> times, and the l.h. pinky remains in contact with the C#/G# key. This exercise should be practiced in front of a mirror. Ask the students to play very slowly, always striving for perfect finger action. Remember, the object of this exercise and all the other exercises in this chapter is the development of correct technique, not just to be able to play the notes by any and every means.

The Left Hand Thumb

The left hand thumb has two duties: to cover the thumb hole and to open the register key. The thumb needs to be positioned so that it can cover the thumb hole while remaining in constant contact with the tip of the register key. Students with double-jointed thumbs will find this relatively easy to do (this is one instance in which a double-jointed finger is not a liability). When throat Bb is played, make sure that the student uses a rocking, rather than hopping, motion to open the register key, and that the thumb *completely* clears the thumb ring in the process. Any remaining contact will partially close the ring, which will also partially close the pad directly under the throat A lever. This makes the throat Bb sound dull and flat. Slow practice in front of a mirror is very helpful in learning how full clearance of the thumb ring feels.

Finally, teachers need to be aware that the left-hand thumb is the sneakiest of all the fingers! Some students habitually place it on the body of the clarinet just below the thumb ring when not in use. Students usually do this from a need to "balance" the clarinet out of the fear it may fall out of their hands. Absurd! This habit needs to be caught as early as possible and nipped in the bud. Otherwise, it may be extremely difficult to break.

Example 4: Two Left Hand Thumb Exercises

These two little exercises can be used to help develop the proper motion of the thumb for two functions:
1. Tipping open the register key while keeping the thumb hole covered.
2. Lifting the thumb so that it completely clears both the thumb hole and thumb ring!
Important: Make sure that the other fingers retain their correct playing positions and remain close to the body of the clarinet all the while these exercises are being performed. (For more specifics see Touchpoint System on pg. 6-10).

The Left and Right Hand Middle Fingers

Only a small amount of observation is required to make one think that the clarinet mechanism was not designed for human hands. As proof of this, the role the left and right hand middle fingers play might be exhibits A and B since they are strongest of all the fingers, and yet the only two with the singular task of closing one tone hole. What else can you say!?!

The Left Hand Ring Finger

The left hand ring finger operates the third finger hole as well as the chromatic Eb/Bb. Its work is pretty straightforward. Only two brief comments need to be made. First, sometimes the chromatic Eb/Bb key needs to be adjusted far enough away from the middle ring key so that it can be depressed without crowding the middle finger, but not so far away that there is danger of the ring finger bumping it accidentally when closing the third finger hole. Second, whenever the ring finger must play chromatic Eb/Bb, make sure that its motion does not pull the left hand pinky out of its touchpoint position on the C#/G# key. It may take some practice to stretch the single tendon these fingers share to the point that the little finger can remain comfortably in place as the ring finger plays chromatic Eb/Bb.

The Role of the Left and Right Hand Pinkies

Though they are the weakest and smallest of all fingers, each pinky is assigned four levers, and must cover the widest range of motion. The action of the pinkies is just the opposite of the other fingers. They do not only close tone holes, but open them by pressing on levers controlled by springs. This means the pinkies need to exert just enough energy to overcome the lever's spring tension, and open the tone hole. All the pinky needs to do to close the lever-opened tone hole is relax and allow the spring tension to overcome it. When this is done correctly the pinky should end up resting on the key. *Therefore, there are only two parts to the pinkie's action: squeeze and relax.* The only reason to lift the pinky from the key it has depressed is to move it to another, or to return to a touchpoint. (We will discuss touchpoints and their value later in the chapter).

Developing Independence of the Pinkies

The pinkies have the disadvantage of sharing a single tendon with the ring fingers. Usually, this means that whenever the ring fingers do something, the pinkies *naturally* want to follow along. Natural though it may be, such "tagalong" behavior needs to be eliminated. This can be done by having students work a bit each day on exercises which will promote the independence of the ring and pinky fingers. The earlier these exercises are begun, the better. Example 5 presents several basic exercises for the development of independence of the pinkies. Mastering these is essential to the successful use of the touchpoint system, which we will introduce immediately after we have completed our analysis of each finger function.

Example 5: Left Hand Pinky Independence Exercises

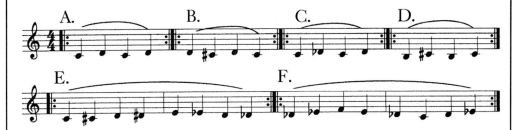

The motion of the pinky throughout these exercises should be only that of "squeeze, relax, squeeze, relax."
*In exercise A make sure the pinky rests on the C# key all the time the ring finger plays C to D.
*Begin exercise B with the pinky resting on the C# key.
*In exercises C and D the pinky should never lose contact with the C# key.
*Throughout exercises E and F the pinky should remain in constant contact with the C#/Db key.

Example 6: Right Hand Pinky Independence Exercises

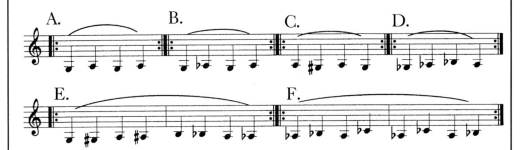

All that was said of the left hand pinky in example 5 holds true for the operation of the right hand pinky in example 6. The object of each exercise is, of course, to foster independence of the pinky and the ring finger. This is done by having the pinky to press on the levers to open or close a tone hole, and to otherwise relax and rest on the lever, no matter what else the other fingers are doing. Both exercises 5 and 6 are fundamental to clarinet finger technique and form the basis upon which the touchpoint system can be developed.

THE RIGHT HAND

The Right Hand Index Finger
The right hand index finger has two jobs, one simple the other more complex. The first is closing the first finger hole of the right hand. The second is playing the four side trill keys on the left hand joint. The index finger only needs to rock back a small amount to open the Eb/Bb and F#/C# side trill keys. However, it will need to actually reach out of normal playing position to operate the top two trill keys. This means the index finger has to stretch further than any other finger. As it does so, care needs to be taken to insure that the remaining fingers of the right hand aren't pulled out of position. Maintaining R.H. pinky contact with the F/C key can help the whole hand retain good position while the index stretches to the B or C trill keys.

The Right Hand Middle Finger
See page 6-6.

The Right Hand Ring Finger
This finger has two functions; to cover the third right hand finger hole and to depress the B/F# chromatic key lever. These operations are fairly straightforward. The only thing which may be a problem is pushing the rings down in the process of depressing the B/F# lever. This is only a problem when the B/F# lever is used to correct the detuning tendencies of certain third register tones such as F and F# above the staff.

There are two solutions to solve this little dilemma. The first involves bending the B/F# lever up and adding a thicker cork under it to prevent excess venting of the pad. Doing this makes the lever, even when fully depressed, somewhat higher than the undepressed ring keys. The second involves simply learning to depress the B/F# lever nearer the brace of the rings, well away from the rings themselves. Most players take the latter option since it's not all that hard to do and just requires a little thought and attention.

The Right Hand Thumb
There are two problems we have to consider regarding the thumb. First, the right hand thumb carries a lot of weight, and because of this it is often subject to a lot of pain. Second, because of the proximity of the thumb to other fingers of the right hand (the "pinch" factor) tension can easily spread throughout the hand. Let's look at some solutions to each of these problems.

There are several solutions to the weight the thumb must carry. The most obvious, common and practical ones are:
a) Allow the knees to bear part of the clarinet's weight when sitting.
b) Use an elastic neck strap, which will help with the necessary lifting.

The elastic neck strap does more than take the weight off the thumb, it also aids the thumb in the lifting it must do to help snug the mouthpiece and center the tone.

Unfortunately the solutions to the "pinch factor" are not as simple or straightforward. Actually, there is no one completely satisfactory solution, and a combination usually ends up working best for most players.

First, an adjustable thumb rest can allow higher thumb placement on the body of the clarinet, out of proximity of finger closure which causes tension. However, moving the thumb up can make the clarinet feel a bit out of balance to some clarinetists. This is understandable, since the thumb naturally falls somewhere in between the index and middle finger.

If the player prefers to retain a natural thumb placement but still wants to avoid the pinch factor, the best solution is to open the right hand up by building up the body of the clarinet directly below the thumb rest. This solution is a bit of trouble, but it offers the best of both worlds; the correct, natural placement of thumb, index and middle fingers and the reduction of tension by means of opening up the hand.

Perhaps a "thumb saddle" used in combination with an elastic neck strap may offer the most complete solution to the thumb problem, since their combined use would open the hand and take the weight off the thumb at the same time.

Now that we have discussed the operations of the fingers, let's turn our attention to a system which is consistent with these habits, and one which will help develop and reinforce them.

The Touchpoint System: The Sure Cure for "Flyaway Fingers"
Students typically move their fingers excessively, waving them in the air, far from the tone holes they must cover at a moment's notice. What to do?

It is hard to think about all the fingers at once. Fortunately, that is not necessary. Thinking about and keeping track of four fingers will suffice; the two pinky fingers, left hand index finger, and the left hand thumb. We do this by practicing the Touchpoint System. Here's how it works.

1. The left hand thumb must maintain contact with the top of the thumb ring and tip of the register key.

2. The second joint of the left hand index finger should maintain contact with the throat Ab key as much as possible.

3. The little fingers must maintain contact with one of the four keys each operates (which of the four levers is designated as the touchpoint at any given time depends upon the context of the musical passage).

The Pinkies in the Touchpoint System

Each finger must remain in contact with its assigned key, either by pressing it or resting upon it. The pinkies are the most critical. Simply keeping each pinky in contact with its touchpoint key will remarkably reduce excessive movement of all the other fingers and keep them closer to their respective tone holes.

As we just mentioned, each pinky controls four levers. This means that the key designated as the touchpoint must vary according to the technical context. *But there should always be a touchpoint!* Some touchpoints are obvious. For instance, the touchpoints for the C or G scale should be the left hand E-B lever and the right hand F-C lever. For an F scale the touchpoints should be the left hand C#-G# lever and the right hand F-C lever. For D and A scales the touchpoints should be the left hand E-B lever and the right hand F#-C# lever, and so on.

Plotting touchpoints is not an absolute science. The best touchpoint may not be clear in every case. There may even be instances of pure ambiguity when the criteria of a coin toss is good as any to decide which key should be used. Whenever this happens, the important thing is to decide upon a touchpoint and be consistent in its use. The critical thing is that the touchpoint system be used in some way as the basis for technical formation and a way of disciplining and econmizing finger technique. Exercise no. 7 shows how the pinky touchpoints for a chromatic scale may be plotted out.

Finally, obviously, the application of the touchpoint system needs to be enlarged and expanded from the isolated exercises needed for initial development of the skill to every thing the student plays.

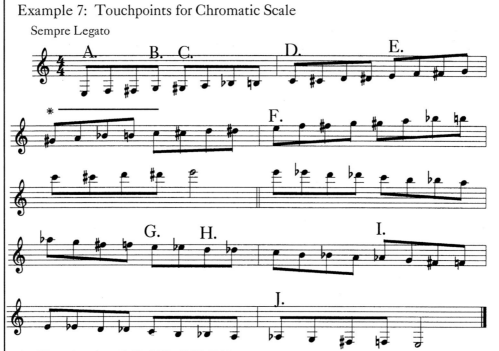

Example 7: Touchpoints for Chromatic Scale

A: Touchpoints LH: E/B, RH: F/C.
B: RH Touchpoint changes to G#.
C: LH Touchpoint changes to C#/G#.
D: RH Touchpoint changes to F/C.
E: LH Touchpoint changes to E/B.
*: Entire right hand closes.
F: LH Touchpoint C#/G#, RH Touchpoint Ab/Eb.
G: LH Touchpoint changes to F#/C#.
H: RH Touchpoint changes to F/C.
I: LH Touchpoint changes to C#/G#, RH changes to Ab/Eb.
J: LH Touchpoint changes to F#/C#.

Notice that throughout the exercise, the position of the pinkies is always being anticipated, usually placing it on its next key several beats before the time it must be used. The preparation of the fingers is a central concept in this approach to technique and technical development: If you wait to go to a place until you <u>must</u> be there, you will always be late. Preparation eliminates this fault. Example 7 needs to be practiced extremely slowly until the pinky preparations and right hand closure over the break are automatic. Only then should speed be added to the technical equation.

Complex Combinations

Along with touchpoints and finger preparation, students need to work on those combinations which require the coordination of two or more fingers. Example 8 contains the most common of these.

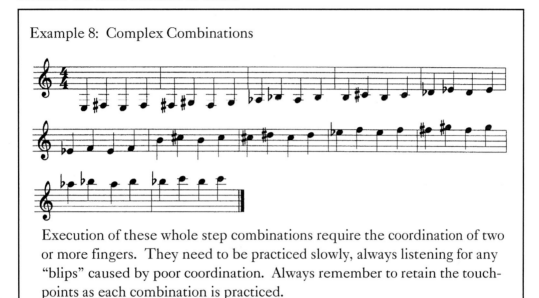

Example 8: Complex Combinations

Execution of these whole step combinations require the coordination of two or more fingers. They need to be practiced slowly, always listening for any "blips" caused by poor coordination. Always remember to retain the touchpoints as each combination is practiced.

"Growing" a Traditional Technique

Rome wasn't built in a day, and neither is a fine technique. Learning technique is not unlike learning a language. It takes time, and it is usually done in bits and pieces; first words, then phrases and then whole sentences. One of the most valuable ways to help students build a traditional technique right from the beginning is to systematically introduce them to scale and arpeggio patterns in small fragments, always insisting upon clean playing and retaining the Touchpoints as the top priority. Example 9 shows one of the most effective and painless ways of presenting traditional material in "digestible" fragments.

Published Material for Technical Development

There are lots of books on the market for young players. One of the best presentations of the basics is in the Scales and Arpeggios book of the James Collis Series, published by Henri Elkan. This text has a beautifully clear presentation of all major and minor scales, as well as other common patterns, the mastery of which is essential for the student's fundamental technical development.

> Example 9: Basic Technical Exercises which Should be Played in All Possible Keys
>
>
>
> This exercise should be transposed into all keys, both major and minor, as well as into different octaves. A scale a week will take the student through all possible major keys in only three months. Then the routine can be repeated, taking three scales a week for the easy keys, and two a week for the more difficult ones. Emphasis should always be placed on playing the patterns using the Touchpoint System.
> It is essential that students learn to always practice good fingers habits along with the note patterns they learn. Always emphasize that if a passage cannot be played without retaining good finger habits, it really cannot really be played.

Another excellent book is the Daily Studies, Book I, by Kalmen Opperman, published by M. Baron Company. Though this is a book for professionals, the creative teacher will find it practical and useful in a variety of ways.

Playing Over the Middle Break

Many young players initially have difficulty playing over the middle break. Sometimes they think it's because the tones over the break are hard to blow, but the real difficulty is usually caused by improperly covering the tone holes. This problem can be partially avoided by having as many fingers as possible cover as many tone holes as possible, as early as possible. Students should be taught that all the fingers of the right hand can close as early as open G. They should also be taught to retain closure of the right hand when a passage begins in the right hand clarion, goes briefly into the throat tone area, and then immediately returns to the right hand clarion register. It can also be useful to have the students mark the right hand closure on their music, just as we have at the beginning of line two of the chromatic scale in example 7.

Example 10: Middle Break Exercises

Sempre Legato

Here are some sample exercises for the middle break. There is no reason to lift the right hand in any of these exercises, except for the last one, as indicated by the asterisks, but even then the right hand F/C key can remain depressed. Notice that playing the break not only requires that the right hand stay down, but the rocking techniques of the left hand thumb and index finger must also be correctly done. Such added complications are all the more reasons for practicing these passages slowly and meticulously in front of a mirror!

Legato Finger Technique: Learning How to Softly Place the Fingers

Many students play with lots of tension, slapping and gripping the tone holes in a kind of death grip. Example 11 presents a simple exercise which will help students overcome this tendency. This exercise can also become the basis of teaching legato finger technique to more advanced students. It should be transposed and practiced in several keys.

Example 11: Legato Finger Exercise

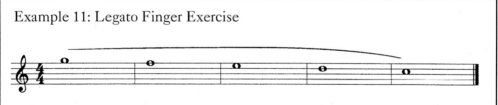

Practicing this little study will help students to see how unnecessary it is to slap and squeeze when covering the tone holes. It should be played so that each finger takes the entire four beats of the measure to complete its closure. For instance, the index finger of the right hand should begin its closing motion from the first beat of the first measure, and take the entire four beats to finally close on beat one of measure two. The finger should retain the same closing speed throughout. The tendency, of course, is to get anxious and grab at the tone hole just before closure.

Finger Technique and the Third Register

The third register of the clarinet presents a variety of challenges to finger technique. First of all, when clarinets are not even in blowing resistance from the upper clarion to the third register, response can be a problem. Clarinetists have traditionally solved this problem by the technique of half-holing. In half-holing, the left hand index finger rolls toward the bell, opening the top half of the first finger tone hole. This technique improves the response of third register tones approached from the upper clarion register. Once the high tone responds, the index finger needs to be rolled completely off the tone hole.

Another solution to many high register response problems is the use of alternate fingerings, many of which respond much better than the standard fingerings. Their only disadvantage is that they are not always as convenient to get to, but this is rarely a problem in legato passages, where smooth connections and predictable responses are most critical and rapid technical execution is not an issue.

The clarinet offers the clarinetist a wide range of fingering choices for the third register, providing workable solutions for almost every technical problem. In addition, many of these fingerings are better sounds than the standard fingering, and should be used routinely in exposed passages where tone quality is critical.

For those who decide to delve into this area of alternate fingerings, we recommend <u>Clarinet Fingerings: A Comprehensive Guide for the Performer and Educator</u> by the author of this present text. It has widely been acknowledged as the standard work on this subject for almost a decade and a half. The book contains over two-hundred fingerings for the third register, offers numerous solutions to technical problems and includes a thorough analysis of each fingering's tuning, response, timbral and resistance characteristics. The book can also be useful in finding the best fingering for exposed unisons when the various brands of clarinets used in a section don't produce the same tuning results with the standard fingering.

Conclusion

Obviously, a complete survey of clarinet finger technique is beyond both the scope and purpose of this present book. Rather, our purpose here has been a modest, yet essential and often neglected one: To define and explain the correct finger habits and techniques unique to the clarinet; habits which should permeate the clarinetist's whole approach to technical development and find thoroughgoing and persistent application in all daily practice.

The techniques we have described here are often challenging even to advanced players. Yet, in their most basic forms, they can and should be presented to beginning clarinetists at the earliest possible time in their technical development, for if good playing habits aren't consciously and purposely formed, bad ones will be unconsciously and randomly formed right from the git go.

Correct finger techniques and habits are, in fact, simpler to learn in early stages of development than later, when, as we have already mentioned, learning correct, efficient technical habits usually entails going against years of unconsciously practicing bad habits. These bad habits, once deeply ingrained in the body and mind of the clarinetist, cannot help but compound the difficulties and frustrations in learning to play correctly. In contrast, with consistent practice of economy of finger motion, natural finger curvature, the touchpoint system and relaxation, the student can begin building a firm technical foundation very early on. This will prevent the need for any "back tracking" later to correct bad habits formed by years of careless, undisciplined playing.

The standard complaint to the approach to technical development presented here is that there is no time for such detailed and specific work; that too much else needs to be done. To such objections we offer the following observation: what seems to be the slow way is, in the long run, found to be the fast way. Ironically, the seeming fast way invaribly turns out to be the impossible way; impossible in that it puts a strict governor or limitation upon the student's ability to increase the quantitative aspects of technical development, while concomitantly bearing the sour fruit of crudeness and lack of refinement in the technique one has, usually by sheer brute force, been able to amass. (Stressing qualitative technical development is ultimately about working smarter, not harder.)

Taking the time to "grow" the qualitative aspects of technique, and emphasize their importance to young clarinetists will ensure years of continued and steady growth with no need to undo what is being presently done at some future time. Aphoristically one might say, make the qualitative dimensions of technique a priority in your teaching and they will become priorities to your students as well, and the quantitative aspects will take care of themselves.

PART II:
THE CLARINET AND CLARINET EQUIPMENT

INTRODUCTION

Things have never been better for the clarinetist in terms of the wide spread availability of excellent equipment. But things have perhaps never been so confusing either. Along with the fine products, there are others which fall somewhat short of what is actually needed, and some products are even detrimental to the development of correct playing techniques and help perpetuate poor playing habits.

How can you know which is which? How can you cut through the conflicting claims and counter claims of competing manufacturers, as well as individual artisans and craftsmen? The best and most effective way is by setting clear standards and developing objective tests to help you judge the quality of each piece of equipment. Armed with these tools, you can enter into the world of clarinets and clarinet equipment confident that you will be able to understand each new piece of equipment and decide how it may or not be of value to you or your students.

The Goal of Fine Equipment

The primary goal of fine equipment is to help you play music with greater freedom, ease, security and beauty. We call equipment which does this well "Acoustically Efficient." Acoustical Efficiency is related to the Mechanical Efficiency of your playing techniques in the following way: The more acoustically efficient your equipment is, the more mechanically efficient you can be with your playing techniques. Or more practically stated, a piece of equipment is good to the degree it allows you to play low, high, loud and soft with a minimum of embouchure/air pressure exchange.

Think of it this way: The parts of your body are adaptable. The clarinet set up you have at any given moment is not. The embouchure, air and tongue are *active and variable,* while the clarinet set up is *fixed* and *passive.*

Now the more regular and uniform the fixed/passive elements are the fewer changes will be needed from the active/variable elements to achieve the full range of musical and technical effects. In short, the more acoustically efficient your equipment is, the more mechanically efficient your playing techniques can be. No matter how you care to describe it good equipment should provide you with greater relaxation, security and confidence in actual performance, an increased ability to play the clarinet as fluidly and unselfconsciously as speaking words and the freedom to put most of your intellectual and physical energies into musical interpretation, rather than being constantly preoccupied with controlling the more primitive and rudimentary elements of playing.

More About Acoustical and Mechanical Efficiency

Efficiency, expressed both mechanically in playing techniques and acoustically in the clarinet itself, is the Unifying Principle of clarinet playing. It is true that absolute perfection in mechanics and acoustics is impossible to realize. But this does not mean they are useless, impractical or merely theoretical concepts. To the contrary, they are extremely practical because they alone provide the standards which rightly guide development and objectively measure progress. In short, they show you where you are, where you've been and where you need to go. The more perfectly and clearly you conceive of and understand mechanical and acoustical efficiency and how they relate one to another, the more quickly you can begin perfecting them and objectively raise the level of your playing.

Remember, there are only two ways to approach the clarinet. You either adapt to the imperfections of equipment (and acquire or perpetuate lots of bad playing habits in the process) or choose equipment which helps you play correctly. The latter is an infinitely better choice.

Equipment and Artistic Preference

Man does not live by bread alone, and analogously, if that man (or woman) happens to be a clarinetist he or she can't live by acoustical efficiency alone (which is not precisely the same as saying that one can live without it). More precisely, equipment needs to give you both artistic satisfaction as well as acoustical efficiency. It does this when it satisfies your performance needs and personal tastes for tone color, shape, and flexibility. Though the technical and the aesthetic are two distinctly different qualities, in reality they are related to one another as the soul is to the body, being united and virtually indistinguishable in the "real life" of actual performance. Therefore, when all is said and done, with rare exceptions, you will find that the most acoustically efficient clarinet set-ups are usually the most artistically satisfying ones as well.

Reasonable and Unreasonable Expectations Concerning Equipment

Exactly what should you reasonably expect from equipment? Some have the erroneous idea that they can find some piece of equipment that will make them great or solve their problems exclusive of working out technical deficiencies and correcting poor playing habits. Approaching the search for appropriate equipment with such an erroneous and unreasonable expectation is bound to result in dissatisfaction, frustration and perhaps even disillusionment. Those who take such an approach often become cynical and skeptical about equipment as a result.

If you were playing with bad habits before you purchased a certain piece of equipment, you will probably be playing with the same bad habits after you buy it and still be getting the same negative results to one or another degree. No piece of equipment will provide the improvements you hope to experience unless you also strive to correct your playing faults.

What, then, is the true relationship between playing techniques and equipment? Good equipment will not substitute for correct playing techniques, but it can facilitate them. On the other hand, poor equipment will virtually force you into playing inefficiently and incorrectly. Therefore, the relationship of equipment and playing techniques is not one of either/or, but of both/and. You must have both good playing techniques and correctly made, acoustically efficient equipment to experience high degrees of technical ease and freedom of musical expression.

This means in their search for equipment the clarinetist is confronted with the old proverbial Catch 22: Without good equipment they can't develop correct playing techniques, but without correct playing techniques they can't distinguish good equipment from bad. Obviously, if the vicious cycle of poor equipment and bad playing habits is to be broken, something outside the system has to intervene and begin a positive process. This is where a competent clarinet teacher comes in, one who is well versed with both playing techniques and equipment issues. Without his or her intimate knowledge of both playing techniques and fine equipment, the students may become frustrated to one degree or another, blame themselves and lose their enthusiasm and heart for playing altogether.

Your Attitude

Finally, a word needs to be said about the attitude with which you undertake your search for equipment. Critical testing is more than looking for faults. In fact, that should actually be a secondary, almost de facto process. Critical testing must begin with appreciation of the virtues and strengths of the thing being tested. Therefore, approach the equipment with this initial thought: "From all that I know and the objective standards which I have clearly formulated, what is this piece of equipment good for?"

Asking this question does two important things. First, it helps you begin with a positive attitude of appreciation, and this always creates an openness to discovery and learning. Second, implicit in the thought is the realistic understanding that there is no absolutely absolute, perfectly perfect piece of equipment that is best in each and every playing situation for all time. Any given piece of equipment is good only inasfar as it helps you realize your particular playing goals with greater ease and perfection. These goals will probably change as you develop technically and grow artistically. The whole process is both creative and dynamic, and as development and growth take place, your equipment needs may also change as well.

However, any change that is made should be an objective one, made for clearly understood reasons, and not simply a desperation move arbitrarily made out of a vague and restless discontent. That is a sure way to put yourself into a state of vertigo and confusion regarding equipment. The only way to avoid such frustration is to do as we have already recommended in this section: Develop a clear understanding of your performance needs, come to understand how each piece of equipment works and learn how to evaluate it. The information in Part II of this book is devoted to help you do just that!

Introducing the Clarinet: Basic Basics

In part two we will embark on a study of the clarinet itself. Therefore, before we proceed to more detailed information we need to learn a little about its nomenclature and a few general things about its musical, technical and acoustical peculiarities.

Parts of the Clarinet
The clarinet has five parts: *The mouthpiece, the barrel, the upper left hand joint, the lower right hand joint and the bell.* We will study each of these parts in the remainder of the book and some will even have whole chapters devoted to them.

Pitch Range of the Clarinet
The clarinet's range spans almost four octaves, from written "E" below the staff to the second written "C" above the staff. Below you can see the three registers of the clarinet, the special area called the throat tones and the pitch range included in each.

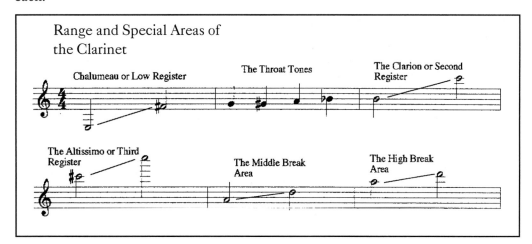

The Throat Tones
Unlike any other woodwind, the clarinet overblows twelfths instead of octaves. This means the clarinet needs a special set of tones to bridge the gap between the first and second registers. These tones, located in the throat of the instrument connect the chalumeau and clarion registers. They are called the "Throat Tones" and require some special finger techniques to facilitate technical execution, as well as some special fingering combinations to make them sound as well as the other tones of the clarinet.

Tuning and the Throat Tones

The throat tones are very sensitive to tuning and are affected more than the other tones to changes in the length of the bore. For example, if pulling the barrel lowers the rest of the clarinet by six cents, the same adjustment can lower the throat tones ten or more cents. Conversely, if an adjustment raises the rest of the clarinet six cents, it can raise the throat tones ten or more cents. Pulling the barrel a large amount can cause the throat tones to sink as much as fifteen to twenty cents lower than the rest of the clarinet! Use of a barrel which is excessively short or long will invariably throw the throat tones unmanageably out of tune with the rest of the clarinet. Therefore, the sensitivity of the throat tones to tuning limits the range of barrel lengths which can be used and still have the hope of the clarinet playing in tune with itself. If the use of such a barrel is really deemed necessary and no other solution exists once all is said and done, the only other choice is to physically retune the throat tones by either adding material to the tone holes to lower the pitches or enlarging the tone hole diameters to raise them.

The Throat Tones and Timbre

Clarinetists try to improve the timbre of the throat tones by using special fingerings called "Throat Tone Resonance Fingerings." Whenever the clarinetist uses the term "resonance fingerings" he is referring to these additional tone hole combinations added to the throat tones. The addition of these special combinations to the standard throat tone fingerings increases the depth and resonance of the tone, and also makes playing the middle break more secure and smooth as well. Here are the most basic resonance combinations clarinetists commonly use. (For more combinations see the author's book, <u>Clarinet Fingerings: A Guide for the Performer and Educator</u>).

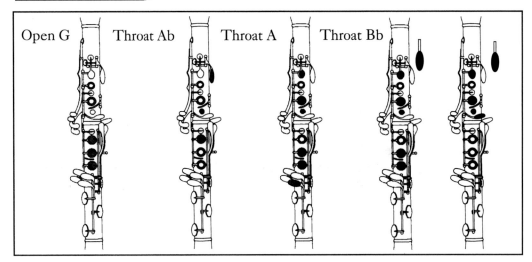

Most manufacturers tune the throat tones a bit higher than the rest of the clarinet for three reasons:
1. It enables clarinetists to pull the barrel to tune the rest of the tones without causing the throat tones to sag unmanageable flat.
2. It enables clarinetists to add resonance fingerings to the throat tones without the tuning going flat.
3. The throat tones are among the most flexible tones of the clarinet (especially in tuning down)...with the notable exception of throat Bb.

The Throat Bb
Throat Bb is the poorest tone on the clarinet. Its color and resistance problems stem from the fact that the same key used to produce the third line Bb (the register key) is also used to vent all the second register pitches. This means the tone hole is a compromise. It's not as small as it should be to function perfectly as a register key, and not nearly as large as it should be to produce a beautiful Bb.

Clarinetists cope with this problem in several ways. First, they use resonance fingerings on the throat Bb whenever they must play it as a sustained note. If they can't use a resonance fingering, they will often resort to using the second side trill key, which also produces Bb, and a very good one in every respect. The reason it isn't used all the time is that it is awkward to get to. Therefore, it can only be used in nontechnical passages, and even then not always without some difficulty and awkwardness.

The Break Areas
The clarinet has two parts of its range called "break areas." They are the middle register and high register breaks. These are referred to as "breaks" because they are areas of transition from one register to another. Clarinetists constantly work to make passages in these areas sound as smooth and seamless in response as passages which don't cross from one register to another.

Pitch Tendencies of the Clarinet
The clarinet tone is best voiced almost at the top of its tuning potential. It is this type of voicing which creates its characteristic "centered" tone. Though some tones and areas of the clarinet are more flexible than others, generally speaking, the clarinet is the least flexible of the woodwinds in its ability to adjust the tuning of a tone while preserving the integrity of shape and color. But no matter where the pitch lies on the instrument, the clarinetist can always shade a pitch down more easily than raise it. "Lipping the pitch up" for a whole performance is

a difficult, fatiguing and even painful experience, usually resulting in a sore lip, a frustrated conductor and an even more frustrated clarinetist.

The clarinet tends to go flatter as the sound grows louder, and sharper as the sound grows softer. Of course, the challenge confronting the clarinetist is to minimize these changes and produce tones which are pitch, color and shape stable as the dynamics change. The clarinetist does this by means of both playing techniques and the choices of equipment he or she makes.

The Bore of the Clarinet

The bore of the clarinet determines resistance, tuning and response and affects tone color, shape and flexibility as well. The bore of most clarinets can be divided into three parts. The first is the reversing cone which begins at the top of the left hand joint and tapers to around the throat A key. The second section extends from throat A in the left hand to low Ab in the right hand, is cylindrical in shape and makes up about five eighths of the total bore of the left and right hands of the clarinet. This section is often referred to as the "central cylinder." The third section is a gradual flare which begins around the low Ab tone hole and extends to the bell. This flare then continues to the end of the bell. The degree of flare sharply increases as it nears the bell. The primary reason for the flare is to help correct the natural tuning spread between the first and second register tones found at the lower end of the clarinet. However, the nature of this flare also has a strong influence on the tone, flexibility, resistance and response of the clarinet.

The Clarinet's Bore Dimensions and What They Mean

Whenever the bore dimension of a clarinet is given the number usually refers to the diameter of the central cylinder. In the past clarinets have been made in both large and small bores, though the last half of the twentieth century has seen a strong preference for smaller bore clarinets. Presently, clarinets are made in bore diameters ranging from 14.5 to 15.00 millimeters in diameter.

It is common for educators to assume that large and small bores have the same effect on clarinet tone as large and small bores have on brass instruments. <u>This is completely untrue!!!</u> A small bore clarinet can have just as much flexibility and can produce just as much sound as any large bore clarinet. The differences small and large bores make is not detected in resistance and flexibility but primarily in tuning ratios and tonal shape.

The central cylinder determines the tuning relationships of the various registers, and dictates where tone holes must be placed, their sizes and how much fraising, or undercutting they will require to bring the various registers in tune with one another. The smaller the bore diameter of the central cylinder, the more undercutting there will need to be to properly tune the clarinet. However, objectively speaking, small bore clarinets can be brought to a much higher degree of tuning perfection than larger bore clarinets, and that is perhaps the singular reason they have increased in popularity, while the large bore clarinets have fallen into increasing disfavor with the possible exception of clarinetists who play dixieland jazz.

The Undercutting and Placement of Tone Holes

Many of the tone holes are undercut, or flared at the bottom. Undercutting is primarily used to adjust the tuning relationships of the different pitches of the clarinet's various registers which emanate from the same tone hole. However, undercutting also has other beneficial affects. It can increase tonal flexibility and clarity, decrease resistance and also mellow the sound a bit. Each tone hole location is determined by several factors, including tuning, flexibility, color, response and resistance. The placement of each individual tone hole must also take into account the response, resistance, color, shape and flexibility characteristics of the tones produced by the all other tone holes. If the tone hole placement design results in resistance variabilities from note to note, even if those variabilities may seem, relatively speaking, subtle or negligible, performance ease and security will be adversely affected, perhaps even severely, depending upon just how imperfect the design and/or the manufacturer's execution of that design may be.

Tuning the Clarinet for Performance

The issue of clarinet tuning is not all bad news. The clarinet may be less flexible on individual tones than other woodwinds, but it has more ways to adjust its tuning. The goal of tuning the clarinet is two fold. First, the clarinet needs to be generally well in tune. Second it needs to be well in tune with itself. To best way to do this is to begin by tuning the clarinet on open "G" (concert "F") by pulling the barrel. Next, tune the written "G" an octave higher by pulling the right hand joint in the middle of the clarinet. Tuning this way effectively gets the clarinet generally down to pitch without causing either the throat tones to be too flat, or the right hand clarion "C" and "D" to be too sharp in relation to the rest of the clarinet. We will go over tuning in more detail later, but this, in a nut shell, is how to go about tuning most models of clarinets for performance or practice.

That's pretty much it for the basic basics. Now that you know the range of the clarinet, something about the peculiarities in tuning and tone color, its pitch tendencies, its bore dimensions and generally how to tune it, you are ready to begin learning about the clarinet and its accessories in greater detail.

Chapter VII

HOW TO TEST AND SELECT CLARINETS

In this chapter you will learn.....

How to test the clarinet for tuning.

What tuning ratios are and why it is important to know the ratios of a clarinet you are considering purchasing.

How to test the clarinet for evenness of tone color.

How to test for stability of shape and color in the tone.

How to test the clarinet for evenness of response.

Why the best clarinet for the professional is not always the best for the beginning or advancing player.

How evaluating and clarifying your own playing needs can help you discover which clarinet may be best for you.

Introduction

The importance of having the right instrument cannot be overstated. Therefore, you need to learn how to test clarinets so you can make intelligent choices for yourself and your students. This means learning to look at a clarinet's playing qualities instead of its label and paying more attention to how each clarinet sounds and feels than to the status quo. Your goal is simple: selecting an instrument which will be truly right for your needs or the needs of your students on the basis of how it plays, not who plays it.

This chapter will give you the information you need to thoroughly test every aspect of a clarinet. The tests in each section are designed to help you learn as much as you can about the clarinet very quickly, so that you can make an intelligent decision based on more than an initial attraction you may have toward a single feature of a particular instrument. Once you've gone through all the tests you should have a balanced and complete understanding of how a particular clarinet plays.

Such testing may seem a bit calculated and not quite in the spirit of excitement one understandably feels at the prospect of buying a new instrument. But the relationship of the performer and the instrument is very much like a marriage. The more you know about each other before the wedding, the better chance you have of not being disappointed afterward. Therefore, these tests are meant to insure that the relationship you have with your next clarinet will be a long and happy one, filled with the joy of making music together rather than frustration.

Playing Features to Look for in a Fine Clarinet

Truly fine clarinets have certain outstanding playing features. These are:
1. Accurate yet reasonably flexible tuning.
2. An even blowing resistance throughout all registers and all dynamic levels.
3. A fine, well-balanced tone that is shape stable, pitch stable and color stable in dynamic changes, and which suits your particular playing needs and tastes.

Regarding these three features, even blowing resistance is by far the most important; the quality whose perfection is categorically non-negotiable. Why? Simply because the highest meaning of the clarinet, it's Final Cause, so to speak, is that of a *music phrasing machine.* And since the phrase is directly dependent upon the perfection of the air, even blowing resistance is the one feature which cannot be compromised without serious damage to the whole essence and ultimate meaning of the clarinet. None the less, all of these features should be found in an outstanding clarinet and the better, more carefully and sensitively you test for these qualities, the better chance you have of selecting an instrument which will give you the satisfaction you seek. Having said that, let's see what sort of information you need and what tests you should perform to help you get the a clear, objective picture of each clarinet you test.

A few bits of advice about testing before you proceed:

1. Test slowly. Take your time. Haste may cause you to miss some important things.

2. Try to detach yourself from the excitement of purchasing a new clarinet, and try to be as objective as possible in performing and evaluating the playing tests.

3. Use a tuner. You may have a great ear, but a tuner as an objective reference point is always helpful.

4. If possible, bring a friend to help you listen.

5. Play each exercise slowly several times if need be, listening carefully and taking care to note any adjustments you need to make to create the qualities in tone, tuning and response you desire. The better and more dependably the clarinet does everything, the less you have to work and the freer you will be to forget about the clarinet in performance and simply concentrate on making beautiful, expressive music.

Having said that, let's begin to consider the first of the three criteria listed above: tuning.

Testing for Tuning

Tuning is critical. The clarinet which cannot be played well in tune is nothing but a liability, no matter how well it may play or sound. If you are to get an accurate idea of the tuning of a clarinet, certain conditions must be met. They are as follows:

1. Test in a room that is not too hot or cold.

Temperatures between 68 to 72 degrees Fahrenheit will be acceptable. Avoid temperature extremes in either direction, since they give a very distorted picture of how a clarinet tunes, and can cause the general pitch of a clarinet to vary drastically. For instance, a clarinet which plays fifteen or more cents flat in a cold room will also play fifteen, twenty or more cents sharp in a very warm room.

2. Warm up the clarinet well. (At least five minutes of playing is needed to do this properly).

3. Once the clarinet is warmed up, tune the clarinet in the following manner:

a) Tune open "G" by pulling at the barrel.

b) Tune clarion "G" by pulling out at the middle of the clarinet.

This procedure will do two things:
a) It will tune the clarinet to the general pitch level you wish to test at (ie... A=440 Hz).
b) It will help the clarinet play better in tune with itself.

Beginning the Tuning Tests: How to Test Each Pitch

Having said that, now let's learn how to accurately test each pitch. You may have perhaps noticed that when you first begin a note the pitch rises somewhat, and then after you hold it for a few seconds, the pitch falls and stabilizes at a certain level. This initial rise of the pitch cannot be completely eliminated even by the finest players. The important thing to remember is this: The stabilizing level of the sustained pitch is the correct tuning of the note.

Therefore, in order to get an accurate idea of how a given note tunes, use the following procedure:

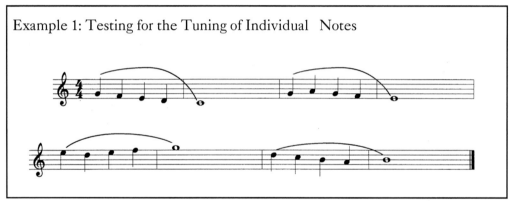

Example 1: Testing for the Tuning of Individual Notes

In example I you will notice that each tone being tested is preceded by four tones. The preceding notes give the pitch level of the clarinet time to settle after the initial attack. So when you arrive at the note to be tested you will instantly get an accurate idea of how it tunes in the context of actual playing.

Slow scales and arpeggios should also be played in several keys, carefully noting any significant deviations of tones within each scale and any specific areas of the clarinet's range where groups of tones seem to be similarly out of tune. If you have several clarinets to test and your time is limited play a slow chromatic scale or simply a "C" scale followed by a "Db" scale, and all of the tones you need to check will be covered. Arpeggios from C major to E major also cover all pitches. Remember to play slowly.

What are Tuning Ratios?

The clarinet overblows twelfths. Tuning ratios refer to how well each twelfth tunes. We get the tuning ratio by measuring the distance between the two tones of the twelfth in cents. For instance, the twelfth interval low "A" and clarion "E" are produced by the same tone hole. If the low "A" plays five cents sharp and the clarion "E" is five cents flat, it means that these two tones are not only five cents away from being in tune, but they are five cents off in opposite directions. This means they are ten cents away from each other, so we say their ratio spread is ten cents. If the low "C" is three cents sharp and the clarion "G" is six cents sharp, we say their tuning spread is only three cents.

Knowing the ratio spread is essential if you want to know just how correctable the tuning ratios of a clarinet might be. For instance, the first twelfth (A-E) cannot be corrected, since perfecting the "A" would make the "E" worse, and vice versa. The second twelfth (C-G) is very correctable, since correcting the "C" will also improve the "G."

No clarinet has perfect twelfths, but some are much better than others. Some of the recently designed models are amazingly close to perfect.

Example II shows how best to test the twelfths for tuning. After warming up the clarinet and tuning the clarinet as we described on page 7-3, play the following passages according to instructions.

Example 2: Testing Twelfths

Every twelfth on the clarinet should be tested like the ones in example 2 above. Make sure you always play slowly and without any adjustment of your playing techniques. The object is to see how the clarinet tunes, not how much you can adjust.

The Tuning of the Throat Tones

Once you've tested the twelfths throughout the left and right hands of the clarinet, you need to consider the area of the clarinet called the throat tones. These tones are not called throat tones because you do something weird or special with your throat when you play them, but because they are located in the "throat" of the clarinet. These tones include open "G" through third line "Bb."

Their high placement on the bore affects their tone color. Because of this, professional clarinetists add special combinations of fingers below these tone holes to make them color and resonate with the depth of other tones of the clarinet. These special combinations are called *resonance fingerings.*

It is probably best to test the tuning of the throat tones both with and without resonance fingerings. Most manufacturers tune the throat tones a bit higher than the rest of the tones of the clarinet for two reasons:
1. These tones are usually played with resonance fingerings which lowers them somewhat in pitch.
2. The throat tones are more sensitive to changes in barrel length, going flatter than the rest of the clarinet when even the barrel is pulled to lower the clarinet's tuning.

If you like a particular clarinet, but the throat tones seem problematic, it should be no cause for alarm. Most problems with throat tone tuning can be quite easily and quickly corrected by a skilled clarinet specialist. Since there are no other pitches which come out of their respective tone holes, they can be tuned perfectly, without any detrimental effects in other areas of the clarinet.

If you find that the throat tone tuning is a problem on several clarinets of the same model you might look elsewhere than the clarinet for the reason. Throat tone tuning problems can be caused by the mouthpiece. The mouthpiece affects the tuning of the throat tones more than any of the other pitches on the clarinet. If the mouthpiece is extreme in dimensions, it can cause the throat tones to be either very sharp or very flat to the rest of the clarinet. If the problem is severe, but you really love that particular clarinet, it may require a change of mouthpieces or barrels to play it.

Tuning of the Third Register

The third register can be a problem in tuning on some models. For instance, the high "F" and "F#" are commonly quite flat, and sometimes the high "E" as well. High "D" on the other hand, can be quite sharp on the same model of clarinet.

That's the bad news. The good news is that in many recently designed clarinets these notes have been corrected and tune virtually perfectly. Here is a good test for evaluating the tuning ratios in all three registers:

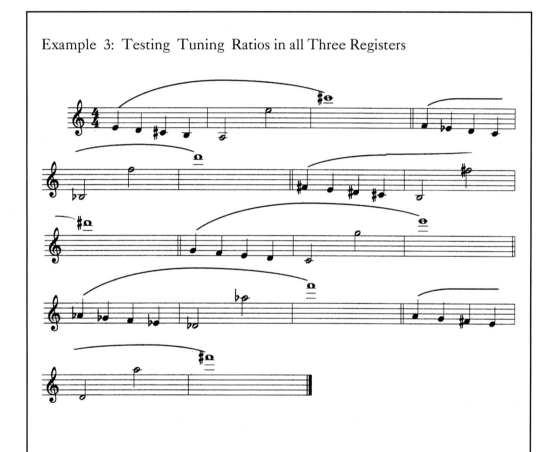

Example 3: Testing Tuning Ratios in all Three Registers

It is probably best to use the standard high tone fingerings in your testing. Whatever the results, keep in mind that there are solutions to practically every upper register tuning problem because each tone can be fingered in so many different ways. This, however, does not excuse significant tuning problems in the third register. The "natural" fingerings should be very, very good.

How to Understand the Results of the Tuning Test

We live in a world of only relative perfections and clarinets are no exception. If you are inexperienced at testing tuning of clarinets, you may be shocked or even mildly outraged to find that no clarinet you test produces every note perfectly in tune. Some are not even remotely close.

But as you test through different models and brands, you may be comforted to find that some tune decidedly better than others. Therefore, your choice is not between perfect and imperfectly tuned clarinets, but between imperfect ones. So as part of your task, you will need to understand how much detuning (out of tuneness) is acceptable and *where* it is acceptable.

Some Tuning Faults Common to Many Models

There is almost always a ratio spread between the twelfths on either end of the clarinet. So, low "E" and third line "B," low "F" and fourth space "C," and low "G" and fourth line "D" will almost certainly have some degree of ratio spread. In the same way there will often, but not always, be a ratio spread between thumb "F" and high "C," first line "E" and high "B." Sometimes, there is also a spread between low "D" and clarion "A," and low "C" and clarion "G."

Some of the newer models have acoustical designs which have remarkably reduced the ratio spread in the right hand tones and have altogether eliminated the ratio spread in the left hand tones. Thus, the tuning of the clarinet has been significantly improved in the last few decades, and many older, better known models have actually been significantly superseded, though, at the date of this printing the general market is yet to acknowledge these improvements on any significant scale.

Unacceptable Tuning Ratios

A few generations ago right hand sharpness in the low register was epidemic. With the advent and popularization of the small bore clarinet (14.6 to 14.7 mm. bore) this tendency toward sharp right hand tones was corrected to a great degree. Many newly designed models have eliminated even the slightest hint of the problem and offer the performer both a chalumeau (low register) and clarion register which is virtually perfectly in tune.

The reason right hand, low register sharpness is such a problem is that there is no cure for it. As we described earlier with the "A" to "E" twelfth, you can't fix one without making the other worse than it already is. But this is no solution at all. So, it's probably better to avoid the problem altogether by choosing one of the many small bore clarinet models available with truer ratios.

Here's how to test for right hand sharpness:

Example 4: Testing for Low Register Sharpness

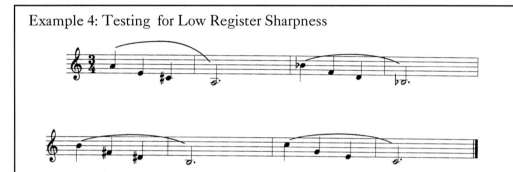

Try these passages at all dynamic levels to see if the sharpness of the lower pitches rise significantly as you play softer. The tuning of an acoustically poorly designed clarinet will be noticeably unstable in dynamic changes, with the pitch sagging flat in the louder dynamics, and sailing sharper in the softer dynamics. In contrast, an excellent clarinet will be very stable in tuning at all dynamic levels.

Conclusion on Tuning

You will find that there are no perfectly tuned clarinets. However, some are much better than others and this is the sort of clarinet you should be looking for. Taking the time to do the needed testing will be well worth the trouble and save you the trouble of future performance problems.

Testing for Blowing Resistance

There are two questions the player needs to ask about clarinet resistance in the selection process. The first is critical : <u>Is the blowing resistance even throughout?</u>

The second question, while important, is much less critical: <u>Is the clarinet characteristically free blowing or resistant?</u>

Effects of the Mouthpiece/Reed Set up on Testing Clarinet Resistance

Before we continue discussing resistance and how to test for it, a word needs to be said about the mouthpiece/reed set up you use to test clarinets, especially in regard to resistance. If the set up you have is resistant, you will tend to prefer freer blowing clarinets. If the set up is free blowing, you will tend to prefer clarinets with more resistance and "hold" in the sound. There is no right and wrong here, but it is something to be aware of, since it will most definitely influence your choice and color your perception. Because of that, you might want to bring several reeds along with you which are well balanced, but which have different blowing resistance characteristics.

Many clarinetists prefer clarinets with more inherent resistance, because they like to play a more flexible mouthpiece/reed set up without enduring the negative consequences of brightness, thinness and loss of center in the tone. Other clarinetists prefer freer blowing clarinets, and create the resistance needed to maintain good color and shape in the tone with the mouthpiece, reed and embouchure.

Generally, the freer the clarinet is, the more you will have to labor to control the sound, while more resistant clarinets contain the tone shape and tuning better and allow for greater freedom and flexibility in embouchure. Again, there is no right or wrong here. Each approach has its virtues and limitations. Which you prefer is a matter of your taste, temperament and particular performance needs. Simply being aware of the options is a help in deciding.

Benefits of Even Blowing Resistance

Whether free blowing or resistant, the clarinet needs to be as even as possible. Even blowing resistance provides the following playing benefits:
1. It makes the clarinet predictable in response, and therefore easier to control.
2. It helps make the clarinet even in tone color and uniform in tone shape.
3. It makes the clarinet dependable and secure in attacks and articulation.
4. It simplifies and facilitates legato playing.
5. It provides technical security, and enables one to concentrate more on musical expression and less on controlling the instrument.
6. It increases the number of playable reeds.
7. It demands less changes in embouchure, air and tongue position for control and security in response.

In short, clarinets with even blowing resistance are like a good friend. They are easy to get along with and a joy to be around. The importance of selecting a clarinet with even blowing resistance cannot possibly be over stressed.

The following musical examples should help you determine how evenly a particular clarinet plays, and how matched or uniform the blowing resistance is throughout its registers.

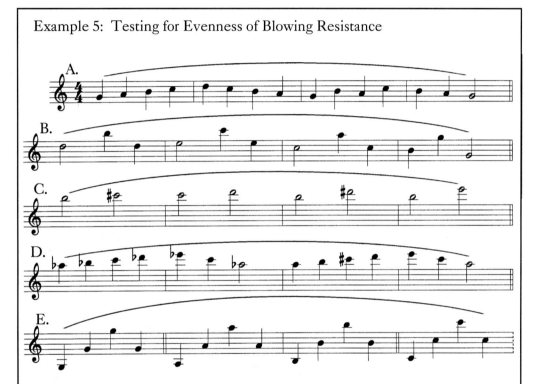

Example 5: Testing for Evenness of Blowing Resistance

Use example "A" to test how evenly the clarinet plays over the middle register break. Try not to adjust your air and embouchure pressure as you play. Listen for any sluggishness in the speaking of the notes over the break, as well as for changes in tone color.
Use example "B" to test the evenness of blowing resistance within the clarion register. Again, keep your air and embouchure constant and listen to how well the tones connect, if their tone colors and shapes match and if they match in dynamics.
Use examples "C" and "D" to test for evenness of resistance over the high register break.
Use example "E" to test for even blowing resistance in octaves. If the resistance is even, the connections should be smooth and the dynamic level constant without embouchure or air presure adjustment.

Testing for Response

Clarinets not only need to tune and sound well, they need to respond well. Response is almost completely controlled by blowing resistance. If resistance from note to note and register to register is steady and consistent, the response will be even, secure and predictable. Such clarinets have great playability and are nothing but fun to play.

One the other hand, the more resistance varies in a clarinet, the more uneven and unpredictable the clarinet will be in response. Clarinets which are uneven in blowing resistance can be nightmares to control.

Finally, the general resistance of a clarinet will also determine how agile and efficient the response is. The more freely a clarinet blows, the less agile and efficient it is, the more resistant the clarinet is, the more agile and efficient it will be. You should test for both evenness and efficiency in resistance.

The trick to effectively testing for evenness of response is not to adjust as you play. You want to see how well the clarinet works, not how well you work. In any and all testing, you should use the sensitivities of your playing techniques as gauges to measure, weigh and compare the various qualities of the instrument you may be investigating. The more subtly and sensitively you test, the more information you will obtain. The less you adjust, the more objective the information will be.

Play slowly, listening carefully for changes in tone color. Take note of any resistance changes you feel in your air and embouchure. Listen for tones which tend to jump out and sound louder and brighter than those around them and tones which are hesitant or sluggish in response and sound duller. If a particular tone seems slow to respond, retest it to see whether the response problem was caused by a failure of the fingers to coordinate properly rather than the clarinet itself rather.

Make sure you test how smoothly and predictably the clarinet responds in the middle and high break areas (see page II-V). Be especially careful to test each of these areas at different dynamic levels. Many times flaws in a clarinet's response which are not noticeable at fuller dynamics show up when you try to play the same passage softer.

Finally, make sure your reed is well balanced. A poorly balanced reed can cause a clarinet to play unevenly. So don't end up confusing reed problems for clarinet problems! Make sure the equipment you use in testing has high integrity.

The Clarion Register

The clarion register extends from third line B natural to the C immediately above the staff. It is the solo register of the clarinet.

The clarion register presents the clarinetist with three initial challenges:
1) Making smooth connections in color and response *to* the clarion from the low (chalumeau) register.
2) Making smooth connections in color and response *from* the clarion to the third (altissimo) register.
3) Making smooth connections, securing response and matching color and shape of the tones within the clarion register itself as well as eliminating undertoning in the left hand pitches.

These three tasks can be particularly challenging, especially when playing at extreme dynamic levels. Generally speaking, the clarion register should be superbly beautiful, providing the clarinetist maximum stability in tone color, shape and tuning and great security, with dependability in response and evenness in resistance. Let's look at each of these elements in more detail.

Response and Resistance in the Clarion

For optimum beauty, security and playability the resistance "recipe" of the clarinet should cause the right and left hand pitches to relate to one another in the following way: the right hand tones need to be clear, free blowing and flexible, while the left hand tones must have adequate resistance and "hold" for stability and fullness. Such a resistance relationship will yield the following playing benefits.
1. Elimination of dull, stuffy, inflexible right hand clarion tones which are both sluggish in response and lack clarity.
2. Either an elimination *of* or a significant reduction in the need to make embouchure/air pressure exchanges while slurring from long pipe to short pipe tones within the clarion register. In short, playing legato intervals becomes effortless and secure.
3. Creation of a smoother, more secure connection from the left hand throat tones to the right hand clarion pitches at all dynamic levels.
4. A significant reduction in or elimination of tendency of the clarinet to "grunt" or "undertone" in the left hand pitches of the clarion, especially at soft dynamic levels and in wide legato leaps.

5. Rounder, fuller upper clarion tones which allow the embouchure the relaxation needed to accomodate the increased flow of air demanded by higher dynamic levels and still remain stable in shape, color and pitch. In other words, upper clarion tones that retain a quality timbre and pitch integrity, even in loud passages.

6. Upper clarion tones that can be attacked or slurred to at softer dynamic levels without fear of undertoning or the sound responding too quickly or coming out louder than the long pipe (right hand) tones.

Testing for Tone

Tone color is what first strikes your ear when you play or hear someone else play the clarinet. Any clarinet you select should have a tone that you like. But in the selection process you should analyze the tone of each clarinet in great detail and not just rely on your initial impressions. Remember, the tone must not only *be* something, it must do something as well.

The first tones we usually play on a clarinet are low register tones. Low register tones which are flexible, resonant and free, and which are "easy on the air" have an instant appeal, because they seem to yield a "big sound" with little effort. Because of this, they usually make a great first impression, but all that resonance and flexibility in the chalumeau comes at a price. This price is almost always exacted in the second and third registers, which, due to too little resistance, will tend to be thin and bright in tone, as well as unstable in tone color and pitch.

You will find that other clarinets, not quite so resonant and free in the low register, will produce deeper, rounder, fuller and more stable second and third register pitches, giving you a better sounding and more comfortable playing solo register.

Each person has his or her preference in this regard. The point here is that in considering tone, you need to be aware of the tone in every register, examining it in detail, and not just allowing yourself to be allured and enamored by a particular, isolated area or aspect of the clarinet tone. The acid test for tone, of course, is that of playing music with all of its artistic and technical demands.

Here are some of the questions you might ask yourself as you play slow scales and intervals at different dynamic levels throughout the range of the clarinet, as well as some of the music you are familiar with. (Don't choose music that is difficult for you to play. It will take your attention from how well the clarinet plays and put it on how well you don't. Always choose music you can "play in your sleep" so you can give your full attention to the clarinet).

1. When I blow a steady stream of air pressure, is the tone consistent in color and shape throughout? Or is there a noticeable change in the second register unless I alter my playing techniques?
2. Does the tone get brighter in color and thinner in shape as I play higher and/or louder?
3. When I sustain upper clarion tones and crescendo on them does the color and shape remain stable? Or do I have to back off on the air or use more embouchure pressure to hold the sound together and avoid harshness and brightness?
4. Can I relax my embouchure and know that the envelope or shape of the sound will remain intact? Or does the shape spread unless I maintain a certain amount of pressure on the reed?
5. Can I relax my embouchure as I increase the air in a crescendo without the shape spreading or shattering and/or the tone color becoming harsh, strident and metallic?
6. Can I play at softer dynamics without a loss of substance and body in the tone (and the pitch sailing sharp) and play louder without a loss of quality and refinement in the tone (and without the pitch sagging flat)?

If, after testing, you answer "No" to most or all of these questions, you may be better off looking for another clarinet within that model type, or looking into another model or brand altogether, no matter how good the clarinet may sound in certain registers or areas or when played at moderate dynamics. An instrument that tends to be unstable in tone color and shape can be a real disappointment in performance, no matter how good it may sound in particular areas of its range.

The Bottom Line

The true value and success of any instrument or machine (and don't forget, the clarinet is a machine!) can only be determined by examining the product it was designed to produce. The "product" the clarinet produces is not just a musical sound but musical phrases. This means that how the clarinet phrases music should be the final and deciding "hoop" each clarinet must to jump through.

Therefore, as a final test you need to play music on each clarinet that has not been eliminated in the process of your other tests. As we've already said, make sure you play music that you know very well and feel comfortable playing, so you can put more of your attention on how the clarinet responds and sounds. Select a variety of short passages which run the technical and expressive gamut, so to speak. The clarinet which enables you to do the most with the greatest ease, security and artistic satisfaction has got to be the winner and the one you take home.

FREQUENTLY ASKED QUESTIONS CONCERNING CLARINETS AND CLARINET SELECTION

Should I select a generally resistant or free blowing clarinet?

Many players are enamored by easy, free blowing clarinets, while more experienced players understand the great virtues that more resistant clarinets offer. Some of these virtues are as follows:

1. Resistance helps maintain focus and center in the tone and enable the embouchure greater relaxation.
2. Resistance helps maintain pitch, shape and color stability in dynamic changes.
3. Resistance darkens and adds roundness and depth to the tone, especially in the higher registers.

As a second consideration you should keep in mind that the resistance a player feels in performance is a composite. That is, it is the result of a combination of factors: The player's own playing techniques, the mouthpiece facing and design, the reed, the barrel and the bell and finally the upper and lower joint of the clarinet itself. Changing any one of these factors affects all the others, as well as the basic resistance of the clarinet. This simply means that you, by your choices of equipment, can make most well designed clarinets have a comfortable blowing resistance, whatever the clarinet's own inherent resistance characteristics may be.

Should the clarinet you choose be basically resistant or free blowing? If you need an agile, efficient instrument, which has excellent tonal center, keeps the roundness, darkness and depth of sound (even with lighter reeds) and enables you to relax the embouchure more without the shape of the tone spreading or pitch sagging, you may be a candidate for a more resistant clarinet.

If, on the other hand, you need a resonant instrument which gives great variability in tone shape and color, a rich vibrant low register and you don't mind using some embouchure pressure to prevent the shape, color or pitch from deteriorating as you play in extreme dynamic levels, then a freer instrument may be right for you.

There is no right or wrong answer to this question. But you do need to be aware that free and resistant clarinets each require not only different "recipes" of equipment, but also somewhat different playing techniques for the best results. Put simply, a resistant clarinet is easy on the embouchure but makes the air work. A free blowing clarinet is hard on the embouchure but easy on the air. It's your choice. Few people split the difference perfectly, but most choose nearer the middle than the extremes.

Whatever you may prefer in basic blowing resistance, you can never remind yourself enough that the most important thing is the clarinet's overall uniformity and evenness in blowing resistance. Without that, a clarinet can be frustrating to play and control.

Are there any special testing tips that will help me select a clarinet?

If you are testing several clarinets of the same model it will be a good opportunity for you to find the best clarinet barrel/bell combination, if the dealer permits. You can do this by taking the best barrel from your initial testing, and retesting all the clarinets with that barrel. Then take what you think is the best barrel/clarinet combination and retest it with all the other bells. This process may frustrate and confuse you. If so, dispense with it. On the other hand, it may be very helpful and enable you to walk out with the very best combination of barrel, bell and clarinet. Nothing ventured, nothing gained.

Should I be able to test clarinets with only the information in this chapter?

This question can be answered with a qualified, "Yes." Many of the tests in this chapter assume a certain sensitivity and skill level that is usually only gained by years of experience. Without this sensitivity and skill, you will not be able to distinguish good and bad qualities as well as you should.

If you are an unskilled player, you should rely upon a more advanced and experienced player to help you select a clarinet. It will be worth paying someone to spend the time to select a fine instrument for you. Even if you are a skilled player, it might be good to ask a colleague to help you select an instrument--- There's nothing like an objective ear.

If I am trying to decide on a student model instrument should I only look at wood clarinets?

No. Just because a clarinet is made from wood does not mean it will be automatically superior to a clarinet made of synthetic material. The only way to tell is to test each clarinet as we have described in this chapter. There are some synthetic clarinets which are surprisingly good in most every respect, and which will enable the beginner to advance quickly.

Are there differences in professional and beginner clarinets I should be aware of?

Yes. The needs of advanced players and beginners are very different, and professional and student clarinets reflect these differences in the playing features each provides.

A beginning instrument should be very efficient and very even in blowing resistance with a very well defined, even tone, and good, but set, tuning. A professional instrument, on the other hand, needs more resonance and depth in tone and more flexibility in tuning than is normally found in student models.

A professional will tend to be frustrated with the high degree of "set" in tone and tuning in the student instrument, while the beginner would be lost in the degree of flexibility in many professional instruments.

Should I buy a clarinet with the added left hand Ab/Eb key?
This key is a relatively new, but long needed addition to the clarinet mechanism. For those who have taken the time to retrain themselves in its use, it has proven invaluable. If you can afford a clarinet with this mechanical addition, you should seriously consider it. But you will not likely become comfortable with its use without a period of deliberate practice in its use.

Is there no correction for the spread of twelfths in the lowest right hand tones?
The tones being referred to are the low "E-B," "F-C." Yes this tuning spread can be completely corrected, but not without adding keys to the right hand. A fine craftsman can make such additions, but it can be expensive to do.

There are a few recently designed models which have corrected this tuning problem to the degree that it is hardly a problem, and with nothing more than the standard 17 key 6 ring mechanism! But if you desire absolute perfection you will still need to add mechanisms to the right hand.

Should I consider clarinets made of woods other than Grenadilla?
There are other exotic woods which have very attractive tonal and responsive qualities. Honduran Rosewood, for instance, is very vibrant and responsive and produces a very warm tone.

The problem with many of these woods is that they are often prone to cracking more frequently than Grenadilla. They do not always hold their machined dimensions as well either, and this can cause negative changes in tone and tuning as well. These problems and the expense of such instruments rule them out for most clarinetists.

Should I play a small or large bore clarinet?
Clarinets which have diameters ranging from 14.80 to 15.00 millimeters for the cylindrical section of the bore are commonly regarded as large bore clarinets. The cylindrical section takes up approximately the middle three fifths of the clarinet's

bore. It is often referred to as the "central cylinder." Small bore clarinets are those which have diameters ranging from 14.55 to 14.70 millimeters for the cylindrical section of their bore.

A few generations ago most everyone played large bore clarinets. However, since the mid-twentieth century this trend has been dramatically reversed to the point that the vast majority of serious clarinetists now play small bore clarinets. The primary reason for this sea-change is that small bore clarinets provide much better overall tuning than large bore clarinets. This is a critical feature to have in a clarinet, since recent decades have seen increasing demands upon players to play with greater tuning precision.

Ultimately, whether you should buy a small or large bore clarinet needs to be decided by the type of music you wish to play. Generally speaking, where tuning demands are not strict, such as in some popular forms of music, large bore clarinets can work well. Where tuning demands are precise, such as in chamber music and recital playing, small bore clarinets are the better choice.

Does key plating make a difference?
Keys come in two common types of plating; silver and nickel. Most clarinets sold in America, including professional clarinets, have nickel plating. However, in recent years there has been a trend towards silver plating. This is following the tradition in Europe, where virtually all clarinets have silver plating, even the student instruments.

Some prefer the cosmetic look of silver as well as the touch, which is more positive than nickel. Silver will sometimes blacken and tarnish badly. There are sliver polishing cloths which help remove and prevent tarnishing. You should use such a cloth to clean the keys each time you are through playing.

Silver will also corrode due to acids in the perspiration. Such a process can be slowed by cleaning the keys properly. But if the acidic content in your body is high, no amount of wiping will stop the process.

Nickel plating is more slippery to the touch than silver and perhaps marginally more subject to wear due to corrosive acids in body perspiration. Otherwise, the difference between the two is simply cosmetic. Which one is better is a matter of taste.

Some players think there is a difference in the sound of the clarinet due to key plating, and perhaps there is. But whatever degree of tonal difference there may be between silver and nickel plated clarinets, it is microscopic compared to the other acoustical elements of the clarinet. In any case, the difference is only one perceived by the player but can't be heard.

Conclusion

The clarinet is an acoustical machine; a machine to which the playing techniques must adapt. The more dependable, efficient, stable and predictable the clarinet is, the less adaptation will be needed from the clarinetist's playing techniques to produce the full range of musical and technical effects.

Because clarinets which respond unevenly present unnecessary performance difficulties to the clarinetist, learning to test, evaluate and select clarinets is not ancillary, but <u>central</u> to the whole pedagogical process: <u>Clarinets which play and respond poorly can frustrate and even arrest the student's technical and musical development.</u> It is hardly possible to overstress the importance of having an instrument which plays, responds, sounds and tunes as perfectly, predictably and securely as possible. While the attainment of absolute perfection is an elusive item in a contingent, relative world, there are most definitely instruments which come much closer to the Ideal than others. The only way to find such models with any predictability is to learn how to objectively test and evaluate each of the clarinet's playing qualities, rather than simply buying an instrument because of its label.

Chapter VIII

ALL ABOUT CLARINET MOUTHPIECES

In this chapter you will learn......

About the various parts of the mouthpiece and how each affects tone color, tone shape, tuning, resistance, response and flexibility.

    About facings and how they affect and determine response and resistance.

        About symmetrical and asymmetrically faced mouthpieces and how each affects response and resistance and one's ability to properly adjust reeds.

        How to match reed strength and mouthpiece resistance curves to achieve comfortable blowing resistance.

        How tip and side rail thickness affects the response and color of the tone.

            Abour the interior aspects of the mouthpiece and the influence each has upon tone color, shape, tuning and flexibility.

                How you can choose various "recipes" or combinations of features in a mouthpiece to achieve the kind of playing qualities you prefer.

The Mouthpiece and the Elements of Music
The clarinet mouthpiece is designed to help produce music, and each of its parts affect different elements of the musical sound. Once you have a basic understanding of how the different parts of the mouthpiece relate to and affect the various elements of music, you can begin to make more objective, intelligent choices in mouthpieces. With this knowledge you can select mouthpieces for yourself and/or your students which have just the "recipe" of tone color, resistance and tuning you need or prefer.

Common Mouthpiece Materials and Tone Quality
Mouthpieces are made from various grades and types of plastics, mixtures of hard rubber and plastics, molded glass (crystal), as well as various exotic woods.
Of these, the most common material used in the making of professional mouthpieces today is hard rubber usually combined with a certain mixture or "recipe" of plastics. What is the relationship between materials and tone quality?

Generally speaking, heavier, denser, softer materials produce darker tones that tend toward dullness, while lighter, harder, less dense materials produce brighter tones that tend toward shrillness. In either instance, intelligent design can offset extreme acoustical tendencies in materials to some degree. Therefore, it is possible to make mouthpieces which sound and respond well from lots of different materials, and of course, not everyone prefers the same feel, quality of tone and response either. Viva la difference!

Parts of the Mouthpiece
The clarinet mouthpiece has three basic parts: The facing, the tone chamber and the bore. Let's discuss each of these and see which musical and/or technical elements each influences.

The Mouthpiece Facing
The facing is made up of three parts:
1) The reed table. 2) Two side rails. 3) The tip rail (see example 1).

The facing influences response and resistance more than any other part of the mouthpiece. Let's look at each of its parts in detail.

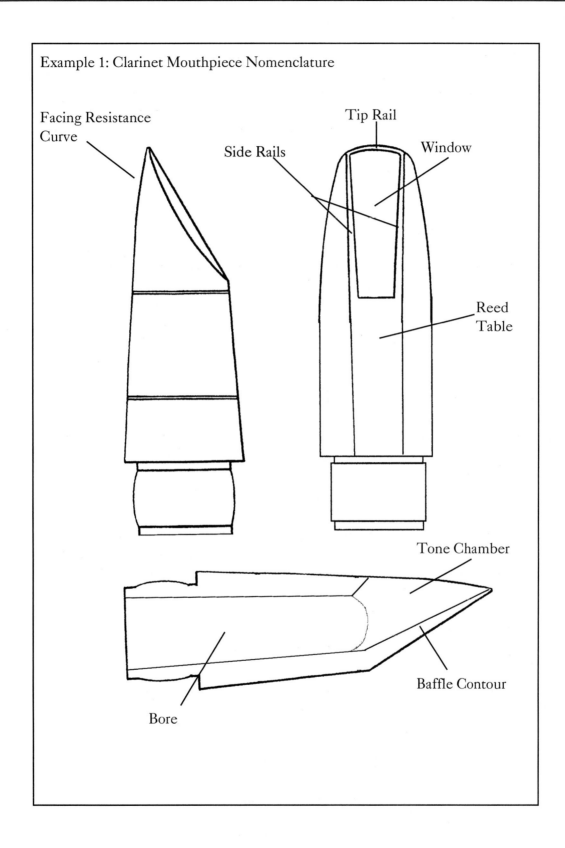

Example 1: Clarinet Mouthpiece Nomenclature

The Reed Table

The reed table is the area of the facing upon which the non-vibrating part of the reed rests. It should be true and level. If the surface is not true the vibrating part of the reed will not be able to correctly relate to the facing curve and tip opening. This causes a whole variety of problems in both tone and response.

Concave and Non-Concave (completely flat) Mouthpiece Reed Tables

Some mouthpiece makers like to build a concave area into the reed table because they believe it makes the reed more vibrant and responsive and helps the mouthpiece accept more reeds by being somewhat forgiving of any reed swelling or warpage that may occur. Others think the reed table should be as flat and true as possible, with no concave area whatsoever.

This debate of "with" or "without" a concave flat table is a largely subjective one. Objectively speaking, the table must allow the reed to do two things:
1. Seal properly on the facing, without any leaks. (Just ask any oboist how leaking reeds play).
2. Relate properly to the curve of the side rails and tip rail. This simply means that the areas of the reed table which do contact the reed must be true in relation to the resistance curve and tip opening.

Fortunately, most manufacturers do a fairly good job of providing these two essentials in their products. If however, you are in doubt about a particular product or products you have two alternatives:
1. Take the mouthpiece(s) in question to a skilled mouthpiece maker for analysis and evaluation.
2. You can check the reed table yourself by placing a straight edge on the surface of the mouthpiece reed table and holding it up to a light source. Any inequities will be shown up by light appearing between the reed table and the straight edge. Only a little practice is required to learn to check reed tables effectively. Just make sure you have a good straight edge.

Convex Reed Tables

Some reed tables have high spots that actually pull the reed away from the surface of the rest of the facing. These are called convex reed tables. Convexity in the table makes it impossible for the reed to properly relate to the facing curve and seal on the facing. Such tables cause a whole array of problems. Insecure response, stuffiness, chirps, squeaks, brightness without resonance, dullness without darkness and leakage of the reed are only a few of the characteristics caused by convex reed tables.

Mouthpieces which have such tables should be given only one of the following fates: either have a skilled mouthpiece maker refinish the entire facing, discard it or drill a hole in the beak and use it to make a key chain. Whatever you do, don't play or continue to play such a mouthpiece without correction. It is nothing but an acoustical liability.

The Mouthpiece Facing Resistance Curve

If you look at the profile of a mouthpiece, you will notice the rails form a curve which gradually departs from the flat table and increases in acuteness almost exponentially as it nears the tip of the mouthpiece. This curve provides the opening between the mouthpiece which allows the reed room to vibrate. It also adds resistance. The shorter and more acute the curve, the greater the resistance. The longer and more gradual (less acute) the curve, the lower the resistance.

Most manufacturers provide information charts that list the various mouthpiece facing curve lengths and tip openings they produce and suggest reed strengths which play best with each facing.

Measuring Mouthpiece Facings

Mouthpiece measuring tools can be purchased from various places. Though helpful, such tools are not really necessary for mouthpiece selection and are probably best left in the hands of the mouthpiece specialist.

However, if you are a stickler for detail and distrustful of a mouthpiece manufacturer's ability to consistently produce true facings, you might, for your own peace of mind, think of purchasing the tools for measuring facings and learn how to use them. Otherwise, you must trust the makers, or take the mouthpieces to someone who knows how to measure and finish mouthpieces.

Asymmetrical Side Rails

While there is one reed table and one tip rail, there are two side rails. Most makers try to put an identical resistance curve on each of these side rails.

However, some mouthpieces are made with rails which do not share the same curve. We refer to such facings as asymmetrical or "crooked" facings. Makers who make such facings are usually seeking to achieve something specific in tone color and/or to mask defects which may be present in other parts of the equipment. However, achieving such tonal or timbral goals by means of facing askewity creates serious problems in the areas of response as well as upper register tone color.

Further, it should be understood that the askewity begun in the side rails extends into the tip rail, causing the most open part of the tip to be off-center. An off-center tip rail opening makes reed adjustment very difficult and has a very negative effect on high register response and tone color.

In order to plot the curve of the side rails, mouthpiece makers place a reading glass on the mouthpiece facing and drop different thicknesses of flat gauges between the facing and the mouthpiece curve. Example 2 shows the plotting of two facings, one asymmetrical, the other symmetrical. A simple visual comparison of them should make it easy to understand why an asymmetrical facing is not "reed friendly."

Playing Characteristics of Askew Facings

Whatever their virtues, askew or crooked facings contribute to many of the following playing problems:

1. They force the habit of biting (upward jaw pressure) in order to control, center, and/or clarify the tone, especially at softer dynamics.
2. They make it difficult to find good reeds, make reed balance precarious and may even frustrate the reed balancing process altogether.
3. They cause insecurity and unevenness in slurring and/or playing attacks in the third register or upper clarion, especially at softer dynamic levels.
4. They make it difficult to play the full dynamic range of the clarinet with a pure, clear tone color. (Breathiness is often a chronic problem, especially at softer dynamic levels.)
5. They make the tone difficult to center, especially at softer dynamic levels.
6. They require an inordinate degree of embouchure/air pressure exchange to produce the full dynamic and pitch range of the clarinet.
7. They cause a tendency toward stridency, brightness and edge in the upper register.

Example 2: Askew and Symmetrical Side Rails

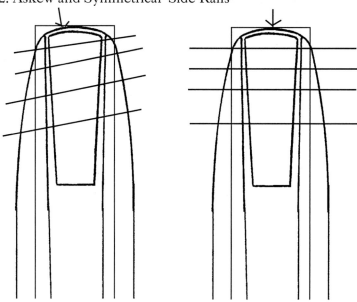

Analysis:
The diagram shows the angles at which the various thickness gauges used to plot the facing curve drop on an asymmetrical and symmetrical mouthpiece facing. The arrows designate the point at which the tip rail is most open. Notice in the asymmetrical example that the rails are not only askew, but the most open part of the tip is off-center. In reality, what you see in the asymmetrical example is essentially two facings, one on the left rail and one on the right rail.

8. They can cause a feeling of perpetual stuffiness, even when softer reeds are used.
9. They reduce endurance because they demand so much embouchure strength to maintain basic tonal focus and secure the semblance of a predictable response.
10. Their playing and response properties are radically unique. This means that finding a second mouthpiece which will use the same reeds as your first mouthpiece is difficult, if not impossible.
11. Few, if any reeds play well on them in a straight up position. In addition, optimum reed placement is both difficult and precarious.

For these and other reasons, such facings should be avoided.

Symmetrical Facings

Symmetrically faced rails completely eliminate the whole litany of problems caused by asymmetrical facings. Reed adjustment becomes much simpler and more straightforward and biting is not required to center the sound, clarify the tone or make the reed speak dependably. All that is needed is to match the resistance of the facing curve with the proper reed strength, balance the corners of the reed and play the reed "straight up" on the facing, and Voila! Everything works!

In addition, all that might be gained timbrally by playing crooked facings can be achieved in other ways, without sacrificing the response, security and "reed friendliness" inherent in symmetrically faced mouthpieces.

As we said, most of the major manufacturers and private makers produce only symmetrically faced mouthpieces. The fact that some commercial mouthpiece facings can be found that measure asymmetrically is largely due to misadjustment of machines rather than any purposed design on the manufacturer's behalf.

The Tip Rail

The two side rails terminate in the tip rail. The tip rail forms the opening that the air passes through. The most open area of the tip rail should be in the very center of the tip. Otherwise, response and color problems may crop up.

The more open the tip, the more flexible the reed must be to produce the sound. The closer the tip, the stronger the reed must be.

Tip Openings, Resistance Curves and Reed Strengths

Unfortunately, the idea that a specific reed strength is the only strength to use, no matter what mouthpiece is played is all too common. This notion does not correspond to reality. Facings are manufactured with a wide range of resistance curves and tip openings, and a reed strength which may play comfortably on one might be altogether too hard or soft for use on another.

The simple fact is there is no "one size fits all" reed strength that can automatically be expected to work in every case. The mouthpiece's resistance curve and the reed strength need to be properly matched to provide a predicatble response and comfortable resistance for the clarinetist. Here is the basic formula:

1. Shorter facing curves and more open tips provide greater resistance and therefore require softer reeds to play comfortably.

2. Longer facing curves and closer tip openings provide lower resistance and require greater reed strength to play comfortably.

Therefore, for the great majority of players, the following "recipes" or combinations of resistance curves and reeds strengths play best and are most comfortable.

Example 3: Basic Facing Resistance Combinations			
Tip	Curve Length	Resistance	Reed Strength
Open	Short	High	Soft
Medium	Medium	Medium	Medium
Close	Long	Low	Hard

Of course, the chart is very basic. There are ways of changing curves and tip openings to further vary resistance. Such combinations are usually arrived at by changing one aspect of the facing while the other remains the same. Here's how:
1. If the resistance curve is lengthened while the tip opening remains unchanged, the total facing resistance will be decreased. If the curve is shortened, the resistance will increase.
2. Opening the tip while the resistance curve remains the same will increase blowing resistance, while closing the tip will decrease blowing resistance.

With this simple two part formula, facings can be designed that provide resistance and response qualities which fall somewhere in between the three basic categories listed in example 3.

So, What's the Difference?!?

You may be thinking to yourself, "If all these different resistance curves combined with the proper strength reed yield the same basic feel of comfort, what is the difference? Why have different facing lengths and tip openings at all ?"

The truth is, on a more subtle level, they do yield different results. These differences may be briefly summarized in the following way:
1. Low resistance (closer/longer) facings combined with harder reeds give the player more control, better articulation (especially in the upper register) and create a darker, more velvety tone.

2. High resistance (more open/shorter) facings combined with softer reeds allow for more brightness in the tone and can perhaps be played a bit louder, but with a sacrifice of delicacy in terms of articulation, control, and refinement in tone.

Beyond these subtle, albeit objective consequences of facing curves and tip openings, the differences in the physical make up of each player must also be considered. Among other things, these physical differences mean that some players get decidedly better basic results with one resistance curve length/tip opening style than they do any other. Also, technical and musical needs can vary significantly.

Rail Thickness
Besides the facing curve and tip opening, the thickness of the rails affects resistance and tone color. The thicker the rails, the darker the tone and greater the resistance. The thinner the rails, the brighter the tone and lower the resistance.

Excessive tip rail thickness can cause the response to be sluggish and unpredictable, especially in the high register. Generally, the tip rail should be no thinner than one half millimeter (.020") or no thicker than 1.25 millimeter (.050"). It is a good rule of thumb to avoid extremes in either thickness or thinness of the rails.

The Mouthpiece Window
The size of the mouthpiece window has a decided effect on resistance, tonal focus and most significantly, how much volume can be produced. Two mouthpieces which are the same in every other respect except window size will play very differently. The mouthpiece with the larger window will blow more freely and play more loudly. (If you need to play loudly without strict consideration of refinement in tone quality and shape, a mouthpiece with a large window may be your tool of choice).

While a louder, freer blowing mouthpiece may be attractive to some, oversized windows often fail to provide adequate resistance, causing a loss of center and an increase of brightness in the tone. One who plays such a mouthpiece and is at all sensitive to tonal focus, usually finds he or she can't seem to find reeds which are hard enough to properly center the tone.

Keep in mind that most possibilities in mouthpiece configurations contribute good things to the playing qualities. It is only when musical myopia drives one to extremes that negative effects begin to creep in and take over. The window is a good example: The freedom and increased volume it gives is good. But when overdone, it can rob the mouthpiece of the "hold" or resistance needed to maintain proper focus and color. Facing length is another example. Lengthening the curve can decrease resistance and make the tone more flexible and mellow. But excessive length can cause loss of efficiency and agility in response. The best advice for the greatest number of players is to choose according to their tastes and needs, but try to make sure your concepts are not so myopic that they drive you to extremes.

The Mouthpiece Tone Chamber
The tone chamber is made up of the baffle and side walls. These two parts of the mouthpiece have the greatest influence on the color and shape of the tone.

The Baffle and Tone Color
Baffle dimensions affect tone color in two ways. First, by its shape or contour. Secondly, by its depth. The straighter, flatter (across) and shallower the baffle is, the brighter the tone will be. The deeper and more concave the baffle is, the darker and deeper the tone will be. It's that simple.

Example 4 : Three Common Baffle Designs

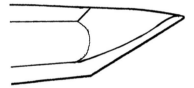

Ski Slope Baffle Contour: This style combines something of the power of the straight baffle with the tonal depth of the concave style.

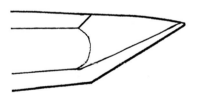

Straight Baffle Contour: This contour gives the most projection of tone, and is often, but not always combined with a medium chamber width.

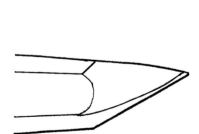

Concave Baffle Contour: The depth of this coutour produces the deepest tone color of the three baffles represented here. This is usually combined with a narrow chamber width to preserve tonal center. The style of this baffle is usually concave side to side as well as tip to bore, and is commonly referred to as a " double concavity."

Vices and Virtues Encountered in Baffle Design

Each baffle design has its virtue and proper purpose. However, going to extremes can create problems, especially in tuning and tone color. For example, shallow baffles not only cause brightness in the tone, but sharpness in the pitch, especially when a shallow baffle is coupled with a small bore. Deeper baffles are just the opposite. They tend to play low in pitch, and when combined with a large bore, cause the throat tones to play flat. Ski slope shaped baffles are characterized by a convexity immediately below the mouthpiece tip rail. This feature can make the response and articulation very lively. But if the convexity below the tip is exaggerated or extreme it can cause stuffiness, resistance and even a tendency towards whistles, squeaks and chirps.

The Side Walls (Chamber Width)

The side walls of the tone chamber control the shape and concentration of the sound by means of their proximity to one another. That is, the further apart the side walls are, the more breadth and flexibility there will be in the shape of the sound. The closer the side walls are to one another, the more concentration and "set" the tone will have.

Most players play something in between the two possible extremes of chamber width. This is generally good advice. Chamber music clarinetists and soloists often prefer more flexibility to the sound and tend to gravitate towards somewhat wider chambers. Orchestral players, on the other hand, usually prefer a narrower chamber to help the sound carry in large halls and maintain focus while playing at the high volume levels sometimes required in orchestral playing.

The side walls can take various shapes. They may be parallel to one another or angled. Angled side walls create what is called an "A" frame style chamber. There are two genres of "A" frames, the German and the French. The French "A" frame is only slightly angled, while the German "A" frame is much more acute and squat in appearance.

The French "A" frame design seeks to strike a balance between focus and flexibility. This style of side wall design has many attractive features, however, most players play mouthpieces which have parallel side walls or side walls which have only very slight angling. The German "A" frame is not recommended for the French clarinet because it doesn't focus the sound adequately. The compatibility problem lies in the bore concept of most French clarinets. Most have a great deal of tonal flexibility built into the bore design. This means the mouthpiece used on the French clarinet needs to supply much of the tonal focus. The German clarinet is exactly the opposite. The bore design allows for less flexibility and variation in tone color. Therefore, the German mouthpieces must add much of the ingredient of flexibility to the sound. When you put a German style "A" frame mouthpiece on the French clarinet you are essentially coupling flexibility to flexibility. The result is a tone that is almost impossible to properly focus into a characteristic shape.

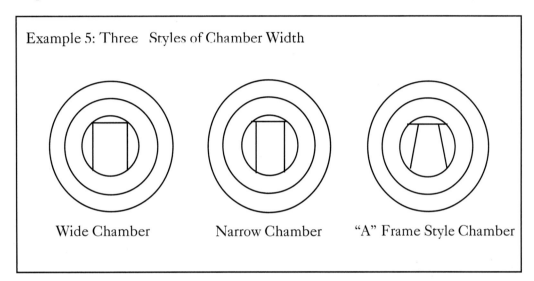

Example 5: Three Styles of Chamber Width

Wide Chamber   Narrow Chamber   "A" Frame Style Chamber

The Bore

The bore is that part of the mouthpiece directly below the tone chamber (see ex. 1). The bore exerts the greatest influence on tuning, but also has a significant effect upon "body resonance," tonal depth, color and flexibility.

The bore of the French mouthpiece is conical and has a length of around 5.5 centimeters (2.200"). Bore diameters of the French mouthpiece range from 14.82 to 15.00mm (.581 to .590 inches). Bores which fall below or rise above these dimensions can cause serious tuning problems on most clarinet models.

Smaller bores tend to play generally sharp, produce sharp throat tones and lower the third register pitches. On the other hand, larger bores produce a generally lower overall pitch, low throat tones and higher third register pitches.

Besides being the most important factor in the clarinet mouthpiece's tuning, the bore contributes to the overall resonance and depth of the clarinet tone. Bigger bores drop the pitch, and they also add depth, flexibility and resonance to the tone, while smaller bores raise the overall pitch and contribute to the concentration and definition of the tone.

Possible Bore and Chamber Width Combinations

Bores also contribute somewhat to the focus of the sound. The clarinet mouthpiece is a recipe that combines all its features to make a balanced, harmonious whole. For instance, combining large bores with wide chambers creates a mouthpiece which does not focus the sound well at all.

Conversely, small bores combined with narrow chambers result in mouthpieces that focus well, but are unbearably bright. Such mouthpieces lack virtually any shape and color flexibility.

Considering these facts, it is probably better to avoid these extreme combinations. The recipe that seems to work best in most every condition is to combine smaller bores with wider, shallower chambers, and larger bores with narrower, deeper chambers.

Mouthpieces and Tuning: An Important Consideration

The mouthpiece interior design not only affects the tuning relationship of various areas within the clarinet itself, but the general pitch level as well. Two mouthpieces of different design can make a difference of as much as twenty to thirty cents in the general pitch level of the same clarinet!

One of the more popular mouthpiece acoustical types preferred by professionals in America is what has come to be known as the *Chedeville-style mouthpiece.* This acoustical type is the basis for a number of mouthpieces presently available on the market, including the Gigliotti, the Vandoren M13 and M14, the Gennusa, and the Ridenour ZMT36, to name only a few. The double concave baffle and large bore of the Chedeville-style mouthpiece has some very attractive playing characteristics, but is quite low in pitch. And purposely so: it is designed to play in a disciplined organization which holds the pitch well down to 440 Hz. Because most concert and symphonic bands do not hold the pitch that low, and because large numbers of young clarinetists are not sufficiently developed with their tone production techniques to play at the top of the clarinet's pitch level as they should, and because clarinets playing flat can be a frustrating problem for both conductor and clarinetist; because of all these things, such low pitched mouthpieces, their tonal virtues notwithstanding, are probably not appropriate for young players to use, certainly not initially. Therefore, it is recommended that low pitched mouthpieces, fine as they are, be introduced only after students have achieved sufficient discipline in their tone production techniques (especially the maintaining of the high/back tongue position). Of course, if the teacher insists upon the use of such mouthpieces and flatness results, it is suggested that the student be allowed to use a shorter barrel. Most often, this means going to a 65 or 64 millimeter barrel rather then the 66 millimeter length, which is the standard length barrel for most models of Bb clarinets. Barrels shorter than 64 millimeters are not recommended, for they can throw the Bb clarinet seriously out of tune with itself, especially driving the throat tones unmanageably high in relationship to the rest of the clarinet.

Mouthpiece Length: More about Tuning

Mouthpiece length is critical to overall pitch. The mouthpiece should be no less than 88 millimeters or no more than 90 millimeters in total length. Mouthpieces which are shorter can cause serious problems with sharpness and can also make the clarinet play quite out of tune with itself. Make sure you check the total length of any mouthpiece you are considering for use. There are a few commercial mouthpieces which are shorter than they should be to play at a 440-442 pitch level. Though they may be useful in some types of playing, they should not be used for most band or orchestral playing.

HOW TO SELECT A MOUTHPIECE

Now that you understand the parts of the mouthpiece and something about how each affects tone, resistance, response and tuning, you are ready to approach the task of selecting a mouthpiece. The knowledge you now have should give you more confidence in your ability to objectively judge and analyze the properties of each mouthpiece you test. There is more than one way to skin a cat, and there is more than one way to go about selecting a mouthpiece. In this section we will present only a single, basic method. This will give you a start. Of course, as you gain more experience and confidence you will no doubt come up with your own variations on the theme presented here.

STAGE I: Clarifying Your Needs

The first thing to do is decide upon the style of mouthpiece you think will be best for you. This will determine what models you will be considering. At this stage, the previously shared information about how design affects tone, tuning and response will be very helpful.

What Sort of Tone, Tuning and Shape Would You Prefer?
If you want a brighter sound and greater tonal volume, with more power and a higher pitch you will be looking for models with medium bores, less concave baffles and perhaps more open facings.

On the other hand, if you want a well focused, dark tone with a lower pitch you should most likely be looking at mouthpieces which have deep, double concave baffles, narrow chambers and larger bores. Players who prefer this type of mouthpiece also usually prefer a somewhat longer facing curve and closer tip, since this combination enables them to play heavier reeds with relative ease, and produces a woodier, darker tone. (This was the style of facing that the redoubtable Harold Wright used for years with such great success).

Finally, you may want a mouthpiece to help you produce a warmer, more flexible and lyrical tone; one with more breadth in the shape. If so, you will probably prefer mouthpieces with wider chamber designs, perhaps even a French style "A" frame chamber configuration may be what you would prefer.

What Strength Reeds do You Wish to Play?
You may already have an idea of the strength of reeds you prefer. If so, this will narrow down the facing types you will care to test. As we have already mentioned, most mouthpiece makers provide information to help you select a facing resistance curve that is compatible with your choice of reed strength. Unless you are prepared to endure the heartache and frustration of finding only a few reeds out of many which work, and don't mind the necessity of biting to make the reed speak and maintain the center and purity of sound, it is suggested that you consider only symmetrically-faced mouthpieces.

Hand-made vs Machine-made Mouthpieces
At some point you may find yourself wondering whether it would be better to try only commercially made, machine-faced mouthpieces or those which are hand-faced and finished. The ultimate question is, "Are hand made mouthpieces better?" The answer is a resounding, "Yes and no". "Yes", when you consider the best mouthpieces finished by a skillful artist/craftsman. "No", when you consider mouthpieces made predicated on bogus or erroneous acoustical principles (such as rail askewity) or which are carelessly finished by someone who does not really know what they are doing. If you finally decide to get a hand-made mouthpiece the best advise is to find out who the best mouthpiece makers are and try their products. Hand-made or machine-finished, the smart advise it never to compromise on the symmetry of the facing. Be up front in demanding the facing be symmetrical and you will not be dissappointed in the long run.

STAGE II: Examining the Mouthpiece

Once you've narrowed down the models which best meet your needs, the selection process can begin in earnest. Try the following procedure and see how it works for you:

Visually Examining the Facing

1. Visually inspect the facing for any obvious flaws. Mouthpieces which have facings with chips or burrs should be eliminated.
a) Remember, thinner rails and larger windows will give you a more lively response and brighter sound, and thicker rails and smaller windows will create more resistance and help darken the tone.
2. Look more closely at the tip of the mouthpiece.
a) If the tip rail is extremely thick it may cause problems in response and articulation. Try to avoid tip rails which are much more than 1.25 millimeters (.050") wide.
b) If the tip rail is extremely thin it may cause brightness, edge in the tone and even squeaks and chirps. Tip rails which are under one half millimeter (.020") should probably be avoided.
c) Notice the left and right corner of the tip rail. Are they on the same plane, or is one corner higher than the other? If the shape of the tip looks uneven or asymmetrical it will cause difficulties in reed adjustment, and may also cause other sound and response problems.
d) Any mouthpiece with an uneven tip rail thickness should be avoided altogether.

Of course, there are exceptions to these guide lines, but generally, following them is a safe bet and will save you time and money in most cases.

Measuring the Mouthpiece (Optional)

1. If you have the tools, measure the facing to see if the rails are symmetrical. You may find that the facing measures somewhat differently from the manufacturer's designation. Not to worry. Some degree of variation is to be expected in commercial mouthpieces, but if the integrity of the rail symmetry and the flat table are good, you still have a viable candidate.
2. If you have a bore gauge, check the bore. If you have no bore gauge, a vernier caliper can be used to measure the end of the mouthpiece bore. Otherwise, you will have to rely on the maker's information, which is usually reliable.
3. Check the overall length of the mouthpiece. Most classical mouthpieces, with few exceptions, are around 89 to 90 millimeters long. A short mouthpiece can make the clarinet play unacceptably sharp and even throw it badly out of tune with itself.

Using a Model
It can be helpful to have a good mouthpiece as a reference point as you test, but keep in mind that no two mouthpieces in the world play exactly the same. The model mouthpiece should be used as a general standard for the response, reed resistance, feel and color you hope to find in a mouthpiece. You can get close, especially if you are testing mouthpieces of the same type and design, but don't expect to walk away with a clone of your favorite mouthpiece. It won't happen. That's the bad news. The good news is that you may actually find a mouthpiece that is superior to your model!

STAGE III: Play Testing
Once the mouthpiece has jumped through and passed the visual and measuring hoops take out some reeds of appropriate strength and begin the playing tests.

What Materials Should be Used for Testing?
Start with long tones, slow scales, arpeggios and overtones. Try some slurs at softer dynamic levels from the upper clarion to the third register. Remember, you are trying to listen to the tone color, check tuning and test response. You can't really do that very well when you are playing fast passages which are technically difficult for you. Therefore, play slowly!!! Carefully *listen* to the sound. Feel how well the mouthpiece responds to changes in register and dynamics. *Note* how dependably the mouthpiece slurs throughout the pitch range.

If the reed is well balanced and the mouthpiece's facing is symmetrical, it should respond evenly when slurring throughout the pitch and dynamic range without any inordinate embouchure/air pressure exchange.

Test the mouthpiece to see how well it does crescendos and decrescendos. See how well it "holds" the sound at louder dynamics, and how well it supports the core of the tone in softer playing. Also test how well it speaks in slurs and soft attacks, especially in the higher register.

If all seems well, play some passages from music you know well. Try to choose three or four selections of different character; lyrical and singing, technical and agile, articulated sections, and passages which encompass the entire dynamic and pitch range of the clarinet. **Whatever you do, don't just play the mouthpiece fast and loud!** Whenever you test a piece of equipment, test how well it does the really difficult things, such as playing softly and responding well in delicate attacks, and slurring dependably in the second and third registers. Loud, fast playing gives you no information of any value concerning the real quality of the mouthpiece.

Don't forget to check the tuning to see if the mouthpiece plays at the pitch level you need. The mouthpiece which passes all the visual and measuring checks and plays and sounds the best is the one for you. See, it's not as hard as you though it would be.

A final piece of advice; <u>seek advice!</u> If possible, take a clarinet playing friend or your teacher with you. An unbiased, objective ear can be of great help.
In any case, if you don't feel confident in your own testing skills, it will pay for you to pay someone else to help you select a fine mouthpiece. The worst thing you can probably do is to disregard all this information, waltz into a music store and begin blindly testing mouthpieces. Your chances for success would be little better than going to Honest Eddie's Used Autos without knowing the slightest thing about cars, yet hoping to get a good deal on a great car.

One Final Consideration

As you become more experienced with mouthpiece selection, you may run into a situation where you find a mouthpiece which has a great interior design, is made of good material and has a great basic sound, but feels and responds poorly. Don't despair! Response/resistance problems are almost always caused by faults in the facing.

This means such mouthpieces can be made to respond sensationally in the hands of a fine mouthpiece maker. So don't give up on a mouthpiece which sounds good, but feels badly. Just take it to someone whom you know does good mouthpiece work, and you may end up with a real jewel!

Your Second Mouthpiece

Most clarinet players do not have a second mouthpiece, even though they know if they broke their first mouthpiece and had to play a rehearsal or concert in the next moment they would be in a <u>w o r l d</u> of hurt! This is nothing more than thumbing your nose at fate: *Not* a good idea. The odds are ultimately stacked against you, no matter how careful you are with old No. 1.

The message here is simple: whether you are in beginning band or soloing with the Philharmonic tonight, you need a good and workable second mouthpiece; one which will get you through that next performance or rehearsal you have to play right after having broken the tip of your first mouthpiece while trying to pry open the lid of a tomato soup can (bet you'll never do that again!). So the question is not whether you should have a second mouthpiece. The question is, what should your second mouthpiece play like?

The answer is that it should be similar enough to your first mouthpiece that the same reeds will work well on both. Many players like to have the second mouthpiece play as much the same in resistance as the first. However, a second idea may be just as valid. That is, choose a second mouthpiece which will take the same reeds are far as response, but has more or less resistance than your first. The reason for this is that reeds as well as playing conditions change from day to day. This means that if, on a given day, your reeds feel too soft to play comfortably on one mouthpiece, they may be ideal for the other.

Whatever you decide in regard to matching resistances, the reeds need to be interchangeable as far as evenness and dependability of response go. **That is the one essential!** Without it, you don't really have a second mouthpiece that is usable. All you have in your case is what the Claricognoscenti commonly call an M.S.O. (Mouthpiece shaped object).

Conclusion

The mouthpiece is not only critical in itself, but also dictates what is acceptable and possible in other pieces of equipment. A poor mouthpiece can make the greatest clarinet play, tune and sound terribly. Defects and faults in mouthpiece design and finish hurt performance. Specifically, poorly faced mouthpieces (mouthpieces with askew, or crooked rails) can frustrate the reed balancing process altogether. They are also a cause of the development of poor, mechanically inefficient playing habits, in that they virtually *force* the destructive habit of biting to both produce and maintain the tone. This, in turn, severely limits the clarinetist's ability to develop both technically and musically. Furthermore, the deeply ingrained habit of biting also clouds the clarinetist's judgment, making him or her incapable of recognizing, appreciating and taking advantage of the great benefits good equipment always provides. In other words, clarinetists who use defective equipment, especially in regard to mouthpiece facings, will always gravitate towards equipment that enables them to continue the practice of biting. Only equipment which both forces and feeds the disease of biting will seem plausible to them until someone with an acoustically sane view of the clarinet shows and demonstrates to them a better, less physically (and emotionally) taxing way to approach clarinet tone production. Time spent on intelligently selecting a mouthpiece is time well spent. Everything which makes great mouthpieces great may be beyond the scrutiny of mere empirical observation, but what makes excellent mouthpieces excellent is not. Learning and referring to the criteria for fine mouthpiece design in the selection process will both reduce post-purchase frustration and help insure one's long-term satisfaction with the mouthpiece(s) finally selected.

Chapter IX

THE FUNDAMENTALS OF REED BALANCING

In this chapter you will learn.....

Why such a low percentage of commercial reeds play well.

Exactly what the difference between a balanced and unbalanced reed is.

The responsive and tonal characteristics between balanced and unbalanced reeds.

How to save time, money and reduce frustration when it comes to reeds.

The distinction between resistance and response and how it can help you balance the reed.

The two tests which help evaluate the balance of the reed.

A simple and quick method of reed balancing which almost anyone can master.

Introduction

Okay, you've got a great clarinet and an excellent mouthpiece which has a fine, "reed friendly" facing. You've got your breathing, blowing, voicing, embouchure and tonguing act together. Now all you need is a few good reeds which both sound and feel right and you're on your way. Easier said than done, right? What isn't?!? But it's not as hard as you might think and it's not nearly as hard as some might make it. With a good testing method to detect the reed's faults and a reliable means of correcting those faults, you should be in good shape to master reeds rather than allow reeds continue mastering you. In addition, you can be confident that you and your students will always have excellent reeds to play. In this chapter we will be studying information which, with a little practice, will assure that both you and your students will have good, well balanced reeds to play all the time!

Our purpose here is to make reed finishing less frustrating, less time consuming, less expensive and less complicated. Therefore, though some clarinetists make their own reeds from scratch, we will avoid these complications, and concentrate solely on learning to how adjust commercial reeds. So before we proceed let's talk about them briefly.

Just What's Wrong with Commercial Reeds!?!

Every clarinetist has experienced the frustration of buying a box of reeds only to find that a few play well, while the rest are unusable (unless, of course, you are one of those grace-filled few who is actually good at reed adjustment). Why are so many reeds so bad? Why do so few play well? The problem is commonly and erroneously thought to be caused by poor cane quality. No doubt, poor cane quality can be a cause of poor reed performance. But it is not the cause for such a high percentage of reeds playing so poorly. Actually, poor cane quality is more related to the durability of the reed than its playability out of the box.

In reality, there are two main causes for poorly playing reeds: badly faced mouthpieces and improperly balanced reeds. These two problems, rather than bad cane, account for the vast majority of unplayable commercial reeds. *In short, many, many more reeds are bad due to bad cut than due to bad cane.* Once you learn to balance reeds properly you'll be amazed at how much the cane quality "improves."

Just What is an Unbalanced Reed?

Both the left and right corners, or "ears" of the reed *should* vibrate as a single unit to produce the sound. An unbalanced reed is simply one whose corners react differently to the energy of the air and embouchure. This means each "ear" has a different response, tone color, resistance, resonance or "ring," and most significantly, a different rate of resonance decay. The reed balancing process is primarily involved in discovering and correcting these inequities. <u>Its goal is simple: to make both corners of the reed respond and sound as identically as humanly possible, so that the tip can vibrate efficiently as a single spring-form unit.</u> The reed can then respond uniformly to the excitation of the air column and the controling energies of the embouchure.

Example 1: Vibrational Patterns of Balanced and Unbalanced Reeds

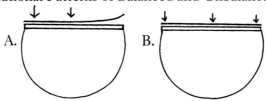

Analysis: The two examples above show how balanced and unbalanced reeds respond differently to composite energy created by embouchure and air..

<u>Example A</u> shows one "ear" of the reed closing while the other ear lags behind. This kind of behavior in an unbalanced reed is common, causing a breathie quality to the tone and making response sluggish and undependable, especially when beginning tones at softer dynamic levels. Soft attacks and articulated passages in the high register can be particular treacherous with an unbalanced reed. Additionally, the clarinetist hardly has any other choice than to continually be adding various amounts of clamp-like, verticle jaw closure to such reeds in order to keep the tone centered, eliminate breathiness and other impurities in the sound and to secure response. This, of course, is commonly known as biting and is the quintessential "no-no" of tone production. The real bottom line here is that a poorly balanced reed precludes the clarinetist's ability to play correctly and efficiently, and the more poorly and inefficiently he plays the more difficult it is for him or her to appreciate or even recognize a well-balanced reed. Playing correctly with well balanced reeds is the only thing which breaks this kind of vicious circularity.

<u>Example B</u> shows how a well-balanced reed responds. Notice the uniformity of the reed's response to the composite energy of the air and embouchure. All a well-balanced reed requires of the embouchure is simply to create an adequate seal around the mouthpiece and lightly cushion the reed as it is snugged against the lips. The use of verticle jaw closure to center the tone or secure tonal response and clarity is neither warranted nor required in the least degree! In addition, a well-balanced reed produces an even, predictable response throughout the clarinet's pitch range, and requires only minimal embouchure/air pressure exchange to produce the full range of dynamic effects. If the clarinetist aspires to consistently play without biting, that is, to play correctly, a balanced reed is essential! Many clarinetists use "bad reeds" for practice and save the good ones for performance. No doubt, the better reeds should be reserved for performance, but playing on unbalanced reeds both requires and perpetuates the habit of biting which can't help but carry over when the "good reed" is put into use. Clearly, whether in practice or performance, a well-balanced reed is the clarinetist's *sine qua non*.

Why Should the Reed be Balanced?

You only have one air column. You can only apply one pressure on the reed at a time with your lip. Yet, as we can seen, there are two vibrating corners to the reed. If they fail to respond the identically to the energy of the air and embouchure, your practice and performance will be made unnecessarily difficult, and the results will more than likely be disappointing. But even beyond the concerns of a single performance, consistently playing on poorly balanced reeds will cause you to develop bad tone production habits (the worst of whcih is biting); habits which, once ingrained, will actually prevent you from getting the best results from a balanced reed and perhaps even being able to appreciate and recognize one.

Playing Characteristics of an Unbalanced Reed

An unbalanced reed is characterized by one or more of the following playing characteristics:

1. A tendency towards a breathie, "airy," spread tone quality, even if the reed is easy to blow.
2. A sluggish and unpredictable response (especially in the high register and/or softer dynamic levels).
3. Uneven, undependable response in attacks and slurs.
4. A tendency to require inordinate embouchure pressure simply to maintain the center of the sound and minimally control the response. (Because of this, most who play unbalanced reeds are biters and play with material between the lower lip and teeth to keep from cutting themselves. The "unbalanced reed/biting syndrome" is a self-perpetuating one, forming a vicious circle of bad habits which are often very difficult to break).
5. Requires lots of added embouchure pressure to either keep the sound going or to eliminate the airy quality which invariably creep into the tone at softer dynamic levels.
6. A loss of roundness and depth in the high register, as if only half of the reed is vibrating, which, in point of fact, is the reality of the matter.

LEARNING TO TEST THE REED

Beginning the Process of Correcting Reed Imbalance: Learning to Test the Reed

How do you effectively correct reed imbalance and eliminate the many problems listed above? First, don't head for the reed rush, files, sandpaper and knives. Before you do any thing as drastic as that you need to begin thinking about the reed correctly. This will help reduce the amount of guess work in reed adjustment.

The "scrape and see" method usually ruins more reeds than it fixes. Put yourself in the reed's place. How would you feel if you were about to be operated on by a surgeon that has no idea of what he or she is doing?!?

Basic Reed Resistance and Response

Before you begin working on the reed there are two important aspects of its playing characteristics you need to learn about; response and resistance. Though these qualities are strongly related, they are not exactly the same. Let's consider the matter of resistance first.

Reed Resistance

Reed resistance concerns itself with how easy or difficult the reed is to blow. What you need is a basically comfortable blowing resistance in your reeds, one which is not too easy or too hard. Therefore, the first step to successful reed adjustment is relatively simple. All you need to do is find the brand and strength of commercial reeds which seem to yield the greatest number of reeds which have a comfortable blowing resistance. Since the reed balancing process unavoidably reduces the reed's overall resistance, it might be best to choose a strength which tends to be a little harder than you find perfectly comfortable. You don't want to end up with a reed that is too soft once it is properly balanced.

Reed Response

Once you have found reeds that are in your resistance "comfort zone" you will need to consider the reed's response. This involves learning how to accurately evaluate and test how the left and right corners of the reed play in relation to one another. The balancing process is almost completely occupied with equalizing their response to the combined action of the embouchure and air pressure.

Reed Response and Mouthpiece Facings

You will notice that the facing of the mouthpiece has two side rails and a tip opening. It is recommended that you have a mouthpiece with identical resistance curves on right and left rails. We call such mouthpieces symmetrically faced mouthpieces. (For a more complete explanation of symmetrical and asymmetrical facings and their playing characteristics, please see chapter eight). This is a complex subject, but it will serve our purposes here to say categorically that symmetrically faced mouthpieces not only simplify reed adjustment tremendously, but they enable you to reach a higher degree of perfection in balance than is possible with asymmetrically face mouthpieces. If you own one of the more commonly used commercial mouthpieces you are probabl in good shape since most commercial mouthpieces are symmetrically faced. However, if your mouthpiece seems suspect to you, ask someone who can measure mouthpiece facings to check the rails of your mouthpiece.

Example 2: Reed Response and Resistance

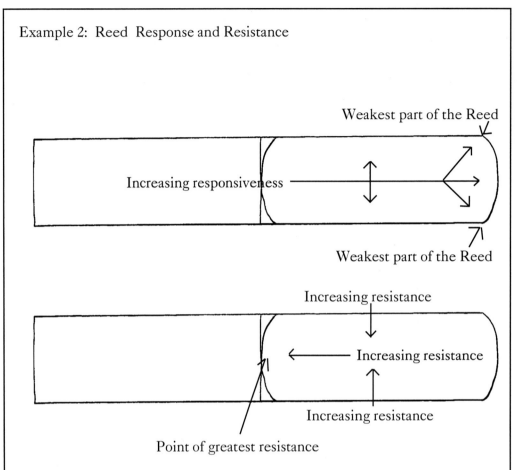

Analysis:
The above examples show the paradoxical nature of the reed. The oppositional qualities of resistance and response meet in the small piece of grass we call a reed. The object in reed finishing is to optimize both qualities in the reed, not to compromise them. Working on the resistant center area, or heart of the reed to increase response can rob the reed of its springiness and life, just as failing to make the reed as responsive or as well balanced as it might be to retain resistance for tone color robs the reed of clarity, resonance and the dependability of response necessary for secure performance.

This means that response needs to be increased by working in the areas which are characteristically responsive, progressing only as needed into the resistant areas. Practically speaking, it means the proper sequence of finishing should progress from the tip to the end of the vamp, and from the rail to the center.

Criteria for a Well Balanced Reed
A reed is well balanced when it meets the following criteria:
1. Each "ear" vibrating on its respective mouthpiece rail, produces identical resistance, response, tone color and "ring" or resonance decay.
2. Responds equally well in all three registers without need to change embouchure and air pressure.
3. Plays with a comfortable, even resistance throughout the pitch range of the clarinet.

When a reed does these three things well it is balanced.
Let's proceed now to see what needs to be done to get the reed to meet these criteria.

The Dynamic and Pitch Range Response Tests
There are two tests you will need to learn to perform if you are to correctly evaluate a reed's balance. These tests are :
1. The dynamic response test.
2. The pitch range response test.

These two tests take some practice to learn, but it is time well spent. Remember, your reed "operation" will be no better than your diagnosis of the reed's problems. The tests enable you to objectively analyze the reed's response characteristics. The better you fine tune your skills at performing them, the better you will know what to do to correctly balance the reed. To better understand what these tests are and how to perform them let's examine each in detail.

Performing the Dynamic Response Test
Many players will recognize the Dynamic Response Test as a variation on "the side to side test." It is similar, but much more refined, and much more effective in detecting the flaws and imperfections in the balance of the reed.

The Dynamic Response Test is performed as follows:
1. Wet the reed adequately and place it on the mouthpiece. Make sure it is on straight.
2. Play the reed for a few moments, just to get your air going and get the reed vibrating on the facing.
3. Next, rotate the reed to one side of your lower lip about 30 degrees. This will do two things. It will put pressure on one corner of the reed, damping it and preventing it from vibrating. It will free the other corner of the reed, enabling it to freely respond to the air column (see ex. 3).

9-8   Chapter IX: The Fundamentals of Reed Balancing

> Example 3: The Side to Side Test
>
>
>
> Explanation:
> The drawings show two views of the way the mouthpiece is tilted to perform the "side to side test." The first example shows the mouthpiece tilted to the player's left. The left corner of the reed is being damped by the lip and cannot vibrate. The second example shows the mouthpiece tilted to the player's right, damping the right corner of the reed so that it cannot vibrate. Damping each corner in turn enables you to isolate the playing qualities of each free corner for the purpose of comparing them. The comparison will show you the objective state of the reed's balance and give you the clues you need to improve it.

4. On an open "G," "aim" a burst of air at the corner of the reed which is free to vibrate, as if you were playing a sFz>P. Feel how quickly and easily the reed responds, listen to the tone color and feel and listen to how the ear or corner "rings" as you taper the air for the sforzando. The whole resonance decay should be no more than three or four seconds. The player's discipline is not to maintain the sound at all costs, but simply to evenly taper the burst of air and let the reed ring and respond as it will. In short, the object of this and all other tests is to see how well the particular piece of equipment works, <u>not</u> how well you work.

> Example 4: The Dynamic Response Test
>
>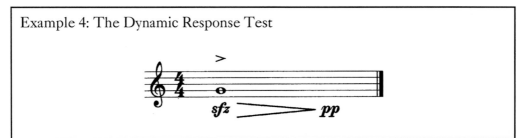

5. Next, reverse the reed rotation, play the burst of air and see how the other ear responds to the air.

You have now performed the dynamic response test. That is, you have seen how each ear of the reed responds and "rings" throughout the full dynamic range from the loudest sound to the softest whisper.

A Word About Biting and The Dynamic Response Test

If you bite or clamp the reed to control it, you will not be able to do the Dynamic Response Test accurately. The reason is that biting virtually kills the reed's ability to "ring" or resonate on the resistance curve, and optimum "ring" or resonance decay in the reed is essential if you are to learn what you need to learn from the Dynamic Response Test. Because of this you might find it helpful to do this test "double lip." That is, test with your upper lip under your upper teeth, even if you are a single-lip player. Doing this helps free the reed so the test can be done better.

Evaluating the Dynamic Response Test

Once you have performed the test on both ears or corners, think about what you have just felt and heard. Compare the resistance, response, tone color and (most critically) resonance decay of each corner. Were they the same in every respect? Or was one more responsive than the other? Which corner produced the clearest tone? Which one blew easiest? Which one rang better and longer than the other as you tapered your air?

If they were not the same, material from the more resistant, less resonant corner of the reed needs to be removed until its playing qualities match that of the lighter corner. (Working on the reed is like cutting hair: you can only take it off). Remove the material from the hard corner, place the reed straight up on the facing and retest. Continue this process of testing, thinning, and retesting until the ears have an identical response, tone color and resonance decay.

The Pitch Range Response Test

Once you have improved the basic balance of the reed, you are ready to perform the Pitch Range Response Test. This test is done to see how well the reed plays throughout the full pitch range of the clarinet. Here's how it's done:

Play low "C." Open the register key and slur to clarion "G." Pick up the first finger of the left hand while depressing the low "Ab" key and slur to "E" above the staff, then lift the low "Ab" key as you open the low "F#" key (left hand pinky "F#" lever) and slur to high "A" (see ex. 5).

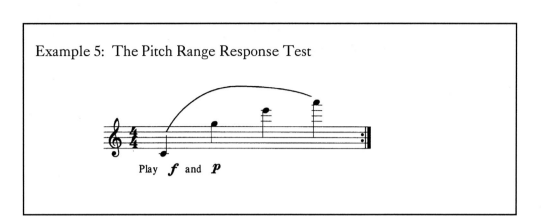

Evaluating the Pitch Range Response Test

Does every tone in each register immediately respond in a similar fashion and with the same tone color while you keep your embouchure and air pressure constant? Or do the higher tones exhibit a sluggish response or "narrowed" tone color unless you make a noticeable change in air and/or embouchure pressure? If so, the reed is still imperfectly balanced somewhere near its very tip.

If the reed seems to be somewhat unbalanced, do two things in this order:
1. Perform the dynamic response test once again, only on a more detailed and subtle level to see if you can't detect which corner is less responsive. This will usually mean testing each ear at even softer dynamic levels (the softness reveals the subtle flaws in balance).
2. Check the corners for identical flex by supporting the reed from underneath with the index finger of one hand, so that you can gently push up on each corner of the reed with the other index finger to compare their strengths and the degree of flex. Try to get the index finger which supports the reed very close to the tip area. This will help isolate the tip and make it easier to compare the corners. As you flex, hold the reed up to a light source so you can see as well as feel how the corner flexes.

If you have found one corner to be somewhat less responsive after testing with step one, your flex test should support this evidence. That is, if you have found a subtle imbalance in the side to side test, the corner that is most resistant should also be the least flexible in the flex test.

Once you are sure of your information, thin the unresponsive tip area and re-perform both the dynamic and pitch range response tests again. Repeat this procedure until the reed plays <u>both</u> tests perfectly.

A SIMPLIFIED, EASY TO LEARN, YET HIGHLY EFFECTIVE METHOD OF REED FINISHING

Reed Balancing Made Simple

No, you haven't misread the heading title incorrectly. Reed balancing can be simple and predictable, and can be done without expensive equipment. You already have your two diagnostic tools. Now, all you need is a good method to correct the balance faults you have discovered by performing each of these tests. Of course, there are lots of effective ways to work on reeds, but we will be presenting only one method here. This method has been chosen because it requires the least amount of skill and is so simple most anyone can learn it relatively quickly.

It has also been chosen because it is the method least likely to ruin reeds in the finishing process (a common occurrence). And finally, it has been chosen because it is a time saver, giving you more time with the clarinet in your hands and less with a reed knife.

What You Will Need for Reed Balancing

For most of us, reed knives and files in our hands become a license to kill when it comes to reed finishing. Neither is absolutely essential for the reed balancing process. Instead, you will only need the following to effectively balance reeds:

1. A piece of 1/4 inch plexiglass or regular glass. The size can vary, but no less than 4 X 5 inches is recommended. Lay out three grades of abrasives on the glass. 320, 400 and 600 grit will do fine. The abrasive strips can be affixed with contact cement, glue stick or even double stick tape. (Norton Tufbak abrasive is recommended over all others. It lasts forever and cleans effortlessly (see ex. 9 for more information on how to make and use this reed surfacing tool).

2. Some reed rush, an emery board, or a small double cut flat file and a small round file are optional. (Okay, a knife may also be used if you insist. If you do use a knife make sure you remove material from the reed by planing the reed, not by scraping it with a rotating wrist motion. Keep the wrist stiff and straight).

That's it! You're on your way at a total cost of under five bucks (even less if you use a piece of broken glass or mirror, and borrow the strips of sandpaper)!

How to Use Your New "Sophisticated" Reed Tools

Earlier in the chapter we mentioned that there were two aspects to the reed; response and resistance. We have largely eliminated the resistance problems by simply purchasing reeds which play closely to the blowing resistance we find most comfortable. This saves us the time of practically having to reprofile the whole reed in the process of finishing it. This means the time we do spend can then be used primarily in refining the reed by simply testing for and correcting imbalance in the corners of the reed.

Correcting the Response: Balancing the Tip Area

Once you have tested the reed you will probably find that one corner is harder, less responsive and doesn't ring or decay as well as the other. This harder corner must be thinned. You will need to use your reed finishing tool to thin the hard corner and do the lion's share of any other work which may need to be done.

If the imbalance is not great you will probably want to use the strip of 600 grade abrasive exclusively. Drastic imbalance sometimes calls for drastic measures. (Usually, the "brick wall maneuver" quickly eliminates horribly unbalanced reeds from further troubling you). You may even use the 320 grade, but it will probably be best to avoid the 320 until you have a bit more experience.

Here's how to remove material from the hard, resistant corner of the tip area.
1. Place your index finger on the <u>flat side</u> of the reed, just below the tip area, and off center. Your finger should be behind the hard corner of the reed (see example 6).
2. Place the reed on the 600 grade abrasive **with the beveled side down,** *and tilt the reed slightly toward the hard corner where your index finger is placed.*
3. While maintaining a light pressure with your index finger, draw the reed **<u>straight back</u>** *about an inch, thinning only the hard, unresponsive corner and tip rail. Do this one or two times, depending upon how badly your testing showed the reed to be out of balance.*
4. Now place the reed straight up on the mouthpiece carefully and perform the Dynamic Response Test again. Continue repeating this process until the corners play identically.

Adjusting the Resistance

Once you are satisfied that the corners are balanced you may find that the reed responds well, but the resistance is still too great. If this is the case, two things need to be done in the following order:
1. Turn your reed flat side up, place your index finger on the rail of the left side of the reed, just below the tip area, place the beveled side of the reed onto the 600 abrasive, tilt the reed toward the rail your index finger is placed on and draw

the reed <u>straight back</u> lightly. Place your finger on the right side of the reed and repeat the process, only thinning the right side (see example 7).

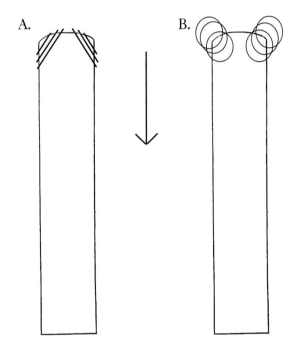

Example 6: Step I: Adjusting the Response of the Tip of the Reed.

Explanation:
The hash marks in reed "A" represent the areas of the tip that are thinned in balancing the tip. The circles in reed "B" represent the placement of the index finger used to thin the corresponding tip areas. Finally the arrow between the two reeds represent the motion the reed is to be pulled when finishing these areas. Notice you only remove material with the fibers of the reeds, never against them or diagonally to them. The thinning of the tip can be done with either 600, 400 or even well worn 320 abrasive.

Chapter IX: The Fundamentals of Reed Balancing

Example 7: Step II: Thinning the Rail Just Below the Tip Area

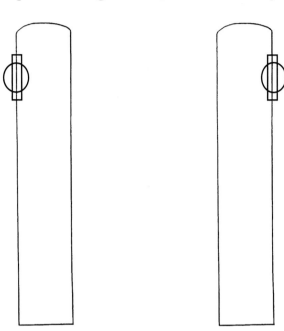

Explanation:
Rectangals represent the areas of the rail which need to be thinned just below the tip. The circle designates the placement of the index finger. Once the rail has been thinned, place the reed straight up on the mouthpiece and perform the side to side test for best placement. Then play the reed to see if the resistance is now more comfortable than before the rail area was thinned.

2. If the reed is still too resistant after the rails below the tip area have been thinned, material lower on the vamp will have to be removed. This material needs to be removed from the top, or vamp side of the reed with a knife (here's your big chance), a round file or some reed rush (see example 8). Once the material is removed in equal amounts from both sides, place the reed once again straight up on the mouthpiece, perform the side to side test to find the best playing position and retest the reed. The reed should now begin to feel comfortable in resistance, as well as responsively well balanced.

Example 8: Step III: Thinning the Lower Half of the Reed to Reduce Resistance, Increase Clarity and Further Improve Response.

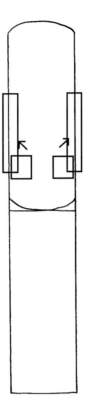

Explanation:
The boxes indicate the area to be thinned. The arrows show the direction material should be move. If you use a knife make sure you plane the reed rather than scraping with a rotary wrist motion. Such motion gouges and produces uneven areas in the reed.
Once these areas are thinned, the reed needs to be retested the same way as before.

Example 9: The Reed Finishing Tool

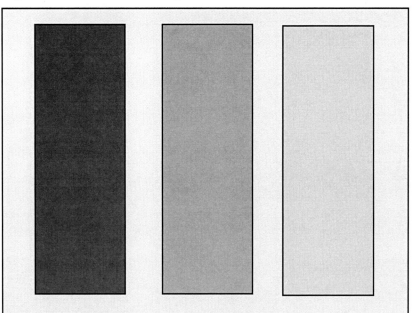

Explanation:
This is the reed finishing tool you can build very inexpensively. The abrasive grades are 320, 400, and 600. The materials are commonly available. Norton abrasive is best, by far, and may be obtained at some hardware stores. The flat surface may be made of glass, plexiglass, ceramic tile, or stone, obtainable at any home store.
The tip area will be finished almost exclusively with the 600 grade, while the rail finishing described in ex. 8 can be done with the 400 grade and the 320 when drastic measures need to be taken.
With this method, very soft reeds may be clipped back so that they are quite hard and then completely resurfaced surprisingly quickly. If the reed is really hard after clipping you may need to do your first few initial strokes on the heavier grade paper and then go to the lighter paper as you near final refinement.
The advantage of thinning the tip and the rails with this method rather than the traditional knife and files is that the flat surface yields a more perfect, uniform finish, with all high spots removed from the finishing area and prevents you from gouging or removing material unevenly. Further, it is much easier to learn to use this tool and fewer reeds are ruined in the finishing process.

Final Finishing

Once the reed is finished to your satisfaction you may further improve the reed by a *very* light sanding with 220 garnet paper to remove rough areas and smooth the surface of the reed. If you decide to do this, sand only the lower two thirds of the vamp and avoid any contact with the tip area. This light sanding will not only smooth the surface of the vamp, but will also smooth and refine the tone as well as adding both purity and darkness to the sound.

Practicing Your Reed Finishing Techniques

Since you are not able to actually see the area you are working on, it is understandable that you may initially feel unsure about what areas you are actually removing material from when you first begin using the tip and rail finishing methods described in examples 6, 7 and 8. If so, you will need a method to help you develop the skill of "seeing" with your fingers. (Don't worry. It's not that hard, and no genetic restructuring is necessary). The way to do this is to select several reeds which are beyond hope and practice with them. Take a sharp pencil, hold it at an angle to the reed and rub the side of the pencil point all over the vamp until the whole reed has a light coating of graphite on it.

Once this is done, you are ready to practice your finishing techniques with these reeds. Take one, turn it flat side up and begin the finishing process by performing the techniques described in the previous examples. After each finishing operation, turn the reed vamp side up and inspect the reed to see where and how much of the pencil lead has been removed. Just a short bit of practice is all that is needed to know where you are removing material on the reed, and gain the confidence you need to work on your "hopefuls" and more "talented" reeds.

Clipping the Reed

All of us have had the experience of clipping the reed only a slight amount, and have it play horribly as a result. The reason this happens is because the closer any imbalance gets to the tip of the reed, the more devastating its effect upon tone color, resistance and response. Clipping the reed often moves an imbalance in the area where it wreaks havoc on the reed's playing qualities. Such a drastic result from the removal of so little material from the tip is exhibit "A" in the case for how important the fine balance and finish of the tip area really is: <u>Poorly balanced reeds always go "bananas" when they are clipped.</u>

You may have had so many negative experiences with clipping the reed that you have become "gun shy" about using the reed clipper at all. You may not even know where your reed clipper is! Find it, because once you have done all the reed balancing on a particular reed, you may find it is now too soft, even when you place it higher on the facing. Your only choice is to clip the reed to achieve adequate resistance and acceptable tone color. Don't despair! If you have done your balancing job well you should have little to fear. A well balanced reed usually only increases in resistance and darkens in tone color when clipped, and requires only minimal additional finishing or rebalancing.

New Reeds and Reed Balancing

Many clarinetists are of the opinion that they should play the reeds "in" for a period of time before they begin doing any work on them. But a reed which is unbalanced at the beginning will not become any better balanced as it is played; it will only become an older, unbalanced reed. What's more, the reed will not break in as well if it is unbalanced.

Therefore, the best thing to do with new reeds is to begin by playing them for a few moments and then perform the Dynamic Response Test. Then use the reed balancing method we have just described to bring the reed into better balance. Afterwards, place the reed in a proper storage case and let it rest overnight. The next day, repeat the procedure, balancing the reed even more finely.

Reeds that are balanced well at the "git go" break in more quickly, are more stable and last longer than reeds which are played for a time in a state of poor balance.

Wetting the Reed and Warpage

Of course, the reed needs to be wetted properly each time you test or play it. There is some disagreement upon how much of the reed should be wetted, and what wetting medium should be used. Some players wet only the vamp or beveled section of the reed, while others soak the whole reed. Some players only use water to soak the reed, while others use only their saliva. Individual experimentation should answer which method is best for you. A few things, however, can be said objectively.

First, the wetting/drying/wetting cycle reeds endure can cause perpetual warping of the flat area which rests on the mouthpiece reed table. When this area warps, it affects the vibrating part of the reed's relationship to the mouthpiece facing, causing leakage and other things which harm both tone and response. Because of this, it is probably best to do as little as possible which might destabilize the flat, non-vibrating area of the reed.

Sanding the Flat Side of the Reed

Many players meticulously sand the reed and insist that the flat side have a high polish. They argue that the reed must be as flat and true as possible and that all warpage needs to be removed. Flatness is important, however, obsessive adherence to this notion is likely to cause most of your reeds to end up functioning better as toothpicks. (Remember, it's a clarinet reed, not the surface of the Hubble telescope!)

Others think that if a reed warps once, it will warp again, ad infinitum, ad nauseam, and that such reeds are not worth all the pampering and time they require. Also, they think that the highly polished flat side causes negative effects in tone, such as a hard, harsh and bright quality. These players would rather do all they can do to avoid destabilizing the flat area of the reed which contacts the mouthpiece reed table, and satisfy themselves with the general flatness and trueness of the reed surface.

This, again, is an area that only personal trial and error can decide. Perhaps the best approach is something between these two extreme positions, using your intelligence and experience to decide which to do on a case by case basis.

Reed Placement for Practice and Performance

Once you have learned to test and balance reeds, care still needs to be taken with placement of the reed on the mouthpiece facing. The ideal situation is to play the reed "straight up" on the facing, tilting it to neither left nor right. Fine reed balancing can help this be a practical reality. This fact notwithstanding, the best playing "spot" must still be found for each reed every time you place it on the mouthpiece.

Of course, if the reed feels too soft or too light, it needs to be moved slightly higher on the mouthpiece and retested. Conversely, if the reed feels too hard, it needs to be moved down. Also, you need to use the Dynamic Response Test to help you incrementally move the reed side to side to find the place where both corners perform the test identically. Here's how:

1. Place the reed "straight up" on the mouthpiece and play it for about half a minute.
2. Now perform the Dynamic Response Test.
3. If you find that one corner is less responsive than the other, tilt the reed incrementally toward the lighter corner. This will have two beneficial effects:
 a) It will <u>decrease</u> the amount of the mouthpiece's rail beneath the less responsive corner of the reed. This "thinning of the rail" will cause the hard corner to blow freer, sound clearer, and respond more quickly.
b) It will <u>increase</u> the amount of mouthpiece rail beneath the lighter corner of the reed. This "thickening of the rail" will increase the resistance of the lighter corner.
4. Now, perform the Dynamic Response Test once more to see if the new placement of the reed has brought the corners into a more equal response, resonance and tone color.
5. Continue this process until the corners have identical resistance and resonance.
6. Finally, play the Pitch Range Response Test.

If the reed:
a) Passes the two response tests and
b) Has a comfortable blowing resistance, you are set for performance or practice.

CONCLUSION

In this chapter we have concentrated upon "objectifying" and "simplifying" the reed as much as possible. We have looked at the reed in terms of its most elemental aspects and showed how they relate to what the clarinetist hears and feels in actual performance. We have established simple, yet effective tests which yield hard information which then may be used to predictably adjust and correct the reed's balance.

The bad news is that the tests, techniques of analysis and adjustment methods described here are by no means automatic solutions to the reed problem. Even after they are understood their successful use depends upon how well the player learns to perform them. This takes thoughtful practice. The good news is that these tests and techniques become increasingly useful and effective as the clarinetist matures musically and develops technically.

Chapter X

CLARINET CARE AND MAINTENANCE

In this chapter you will learn.....

The importance of having the clarinet in good condition and adjustment.

    How to care for the mechanism.

        Why it is important to oil the springs as well as the keys.

        How to clean the key mechanism.

            How to care for pads and make them last longer.

                How to see if the pads are covering well enough.

            How to care for the wood.

                Pros and cons about oiling the bore, and how climate may influence your decision of whether to oil or not.

                    What to do if the clarinet cracks.

                        How to clean tone holes and the register tube.

                            How to clean the mouthpiece and socket joints.

Introduction: The Importance of Clarinet Maintenance

The condition of your clarinet is critical to your development and success as a player. Unlike the oboe, which will not play at all if the slightest thing goes awry, the clarinet unfortunately continues to "play" in a variety of states of disrepair. Playing a clarinet which is in poor condition will cause you to develop both poor finger and tone productions habits. Once the clarinet is fixed, these habits can linger on and be very difficult to break. For this reason alone, you should make sure your clarinet and those of your students are always in excellent playing condition.

Routine inspection of clarinets being played by beginners is essential. Generally speaking, manufacturer's do an amazingly good job on clarinet preparation, but no one is perfect, and not every instrument shipped makes the trip completely unscathed. Perhaps a young player is unfortunate enough to get an instrument which has some padding or mechanical fault for some reason. These young players don't know the difference, and when they are unable to do something the teacher asks, they think it is their fault rather than a problem with the clarinet.

Clarinets need to be checked periodically by a real clarinet specialist, to make sure that they are in fine adjustment. Most professional players, whose livelihood depends upon their success at playing, will have their clarinets checked about every six months. It might be reasonable to follow their lead. If you feel you are inexperienced in judging the playing condition of your clarinet ask a professional or your private teacher to test it to make sure it is really working as it should.

Clarinet Care: General Remarks

The clarinet is easy to care for, and regular maintenance should take only a small amount of your time. Routinely, all you need to be concerned about are three things: the keys, pads and the wood (if your clarinet is made of wood). Let's look at key maintenance first.

Care of the Clarinet Key Mechanism

You'll need to oil the keys periodically. When you do, take care not to over oil them to the point that the oil gets on the body of the clarinet and into the pads. Just put one small drop on the point of a needle, place it where the key hinge and post intersect and work the key up and down several times. The motion of the key will draw the oil into the shaft. It's that simple.

Be sure to place some tissue paper at the base of the key post during oiling to help prevent oil key oil from getting on the wood and pads. The tissue will absorb any excess oil that might happen to run down the post and prevent it from touching the body of the clarinet.

There are a number of oils out there which lubricate the clarinet mechanism very well, and which (and this is important) stay where you put them. Some oils, such as those used for clocks, are oils from animals rather than petroleums. They are very good and have the added advantage of retaining the same viscosity at all sorts of temperatures. (This should take a load off your mind if you happen to be called at the last minute for an outdoor performance on the fourth of July in Antarctica).

Oiling the keys does more, however, than lubricate. It can help quieten the mechanism. Thinner oils not only tend to run, but they also do little for quietening the mechanism. Clock oil is thicker than watch oil and most commercial key oils and does an admirable job of quietening the keys. In general, you should not fear that thicker oils will slow your mechanism. Don't worry, be happy, and oil away!

Finally, oiling the keys can do yet another very important thing for some of us: it can protect the metals from corroding due to the natural acids in the body perspiration. Those who have a high acidic content in their perspiration can ruin the clarinet if they fail to oil the mechanism. If the acid problem is bad, it can cause keys to become completely frozen. Odds are that this is not a great problem with you. But for an unlucky few routinely oiling their mechanism with a fairly heavy oil, as well as coating their flat and needle springs with oil or grease makes the difference between a clarinet mechanism that works or one that completely freezes up. However, for most of us, a routine oiling once every month or two usually suffices.

Those who feel confident in removing steels (screws) may want to consider the following oiling option.

1. Purchase a bottle of "Smoke Begone" or "Engine Honey" from the local auto parts supply place.
2. Unscrew the steel, wipe it clean and dip the threaded part into the lubricant.
3. Replace the steel in the post and key.

Lubricants such as "Smoke Begone" and "Engine Honey" are very thick, but very, very viscous. What's more, they stay exactly where they are put and, like high quality clock oils, won't break down, dry out or gum up. Their heavy weight also does a superior job of quietening the keys. They are ideal for lubricating clarinet mechanisms. But in order to do so the player needs to feel comfortable in pulling the steels which mount the keys.

Which oil to use it ultimately a personal matter. <u>The important thing is that once you decide on a key oil, use it!</u> Oiling the keys is very easy. So easy in fact that many clarinetists don't do it at all. This is a mistake that can have serious and expensive consequences. Specifically, failure to oil the keys over a sustained period of time can result in excessive wear of the mechanism, and in some cases the screws even becoming frozen in the shafts, making them difficult to impossible to remove.

Cleaning the Key Mechanism

The key mechanism needs to be cleaned periodically. At least every six months. Never let cleaning go over a year. In order to clean the mechanism you will need to unscrew the steels, and remove the key. Wipe the steel off with a soft, lint free cloth, take a pipe cleaner and run it through the key shaft, put some oil in the key shaft, remount the key and replace the steel. Before you begin screwing the steel in back it off as if you were unscrewing it until you hear and feel a click. This means the screw and post threads are properly lined up, and you can begin screwing the key in without stripping either post or screw threads.

If you don't feel confident disassembling the clarinet, take it to a repair tech who can do the job for you.

Care of Key Plating

Clarinets usually come in one of two kinds of plating: nickel and silver. Over time both of these materials will tend to wear off the keys and/or corrode and discolor.

Nothing will completely prevent this, but there are things which will slow the process. Here are a few:

1. Make sure you wash your hand before you play.
2. Make sure you wipe your keys off after you play it.
3. Use a polishing cloth to eliminate tarnish. These can usually be found in any music or jewelry store. Just make sure you get the appropriate cloth for the plating type.

If the acid in your fingers is very strong you may find the plating and even the keys are being dissolved over a period of time. There are a few things which can help prevent this.

1. Have the keys your fingers are most in contact with gold plated. The gold plating will resist all body acids, will not corrode (that's what makes gold gold!) and the only thing which will remove it is the wear from your finger motion. If the gold plating is applied heavily enough it should last for years and year and protect the nickel silver keys very adequately.
2. If gold plating is not your cup of tea, have a technician coat the keys with lacquer, epoxy or super glue. This may have to be repeated periodically but it is a better option than having the keys slowly dissolve under your very fingers!
3. Make sure you are very faithful at lubricating springs and key mechanism. People with high acidity can cause steels to corrode and freeze in the key shafts, making them impossible to remove, ruining the mechanism. This can be prevented with routine lubrication.

Flat Spring and Needle Spring Maintenance

Most flat and needle springs are made of blue steel. It's easy for these springs to rust and break, especially in places where there is a lot of salt air, such as coastal cities. They can also rust due to corrosive acids in your own body fluids. For this reason you need to protect them from rust by lubricating them as well. Use a thicker lubricant for this that will stay where it is put and not run. Heavy motor, grease or lawn mower oil is very good. The "Smoke Begone" or "Engine Honey" recommended above for keys is good for springs as well. Even cork grease can be used to protect the spring from rust. The best way to apply most of these heavy lubricants is with a sharp, pointed tooth pick.

Pad care

Pad Care is simple. Usually, the only pads to be concerned about are the left hand low C# key pad, the side trill "Eb" and "F#" pad, and the throat "A". These pads tend to fill with water from playing. You can help prevent this by the way you hold the clarinet when you are not playing it. Try to hold the clarinet at such an angle that the moisture in the bore is directed away from these tone holes.

You can also help prevent water from getting into these tone holes by running a stream of saliva down the bore, forming a channel which is directed around the tone holes.

A third method, is to take a cotton swab, dip it in oil or cork grease and swab it on the inside of the bore around the tone holes which get filled with water most often. The idea is to have the moisture coming down the bore to hit the oil barrier encircling the tone hole and proceed around it.

Sometimes a combination of all these things can eliminate tone holes filling with water. This makes the pads last longer and can save the day at a performance as well.

Many players prefer to put cork pads in the keys which are most prone to get water soaked. If the pads in your clarinet are not already cork pads, it's an idea you might seriously consider. Otherwise, always inspect the pads after playing and place cigarette paper under them while the clarinet is in the case.

Always be on the look out for damaged pads. A torn pad leaves nothing but the felt to cover the tone hole. This causes leaks which seriously affects the performance of your clarinet. Playing a clarinet which leaks will cause you to develop bad playing habits which may be very hard to break, even after the clarinet is properly repaired.

The large, lower pads are often exposed to hitting and rubbing against foreign objects, the case and clothes. This wears the skin over time and causes it to tear. You can help protect these pads by lining the edge of the pad with clear nail polish. If you do this be careful not to get nail polish on the flat side of the pad or on the tone hole.

Pad Inspection and Compression Testing

You should routinely inspect the pads for wear and tear. Any pads with torn skins should be replaced. Also, give each joint a compression test to see how well the pads are holding. Here's how to test each joint.

1. Place your fingers on their respective tone holes.
2. Take the palm of your free hand and place it over the bottom end of the joint, to seal it air tight.
3. Place your lips on the other end of the joint and begin blowing into the clarinet section. Blow gently at first and then gradually increase blowing pressure.

As the pressure builds listen for any soft, hissing sounds coming from the pads. If the bore seems to offer no resistance to the air you put into it you may have leaks which are seriously affecting the clarinet's performance. If so, take it to a clarinet tech ASAP to get the leaks corrected.

Wood Care

Today most professional clarinets are made from a very dense Rosewood or Palisander commonly called Grenadilla wood. It is found in a tree which grows in Mozambique Africa called the Mpingo tree. After many decades of experimentation Grenadilla (or Mpingo) wood became the choice material for clarinet building, not, as many erroneously think, primarily for its superior tone and responsiveness, but in great part because of its machinability and its ability to hold precise dimensions. Most clarinet manufacturers season the wood well, which greatly reduces the number of clarinets which crack. Despite this, there is no guarantee a particular clarinet will never crack. There are, however, a few common sense things which can be done to help prevent it. Some of these are as follows:

1. Never leave a clarinet in extreme temperatures. If the clarinet does happen to get cold, open the case and allow it to gradually acclimate itself to room temperature before you play it.
2. Never play a clarinet when it is cold. Warming the bore with your breath while the outside of the clarinet remains cold can cause the clarinet to crack on the spot.
3. Never leave the clarinet unswabbed on a stand in an air conditioned room after having played it. Do not play the clarinet which is cold from air conditioning.
4. Keep orange peels in the case in the winter. This will hydrate the whole clarinet, balancing the moisture throughout. (Often a clarinet will crack because the outside is very dry and the bore is very moist. "Orange peel therapy" prevents this from happening).
5. Regularly inspect the rings for looseness and check the movement of the keys of the upper joint. If the throat "A" key, the upper side trill keys, or the register key bind, or the action becomes stiff and sluggish it most likely means the wood is moving. If this is the case, the clarinet needs to be taken to a repair technician ASAP to free the key(s) in order to relieve the pressure from the contracting wood. Not immediately correcting this situation puts the clarinet in danger of cracking.
6. Avoid playing a wood clarinet in direct sunlight or at activities where it will be exposed to the slings and arrows of outrageous weather and temperature changes. Instead, use a synthetic clarinet for outdoor playing. Weather will not harm it.
7. Do not assemble a clarinet with loose rings because the joints could crack due to lack of support from the rings. If you find the rings to be loose, have a technician tighten the offending rings ASAP. If you can't get to a repair tech, then you can use clear tape, paper or teflon tape as a shim to help tighten the ring. Simply wrap the tape or paper around the recessed area of the joint and push the ring back on. You may have to experiment to see how much paper or tape is needed to create a snug fit. If the fit is good, it may serve as a more or less permanent solution to the problem and a visit to a repair tech will not be necessary.

Oiling the Bore

There is no consensus on whether the bore of the clarinet should be oiled or not. In most cases it seems not to be necessary. Perhaps the single most important factor which determines whether the clarinet needs to be oiled or not is the climate the clarinet is played in.

High, dry climates deplete the wood's natural moisture, and playing clarinets in such areas causes a disparity of moisture in the wood, with one area (the bore) usually being very damp and another area (the outside of the body) becoming very dry. This disparity of moisture needs to be eliminated and a more uniform distribution of moisture restored and maintained in the clarinet. Oiling can certainly help in such instances.

Most commercial oils should probably be avoided. Some good oils are commercially available, but the oils you can commonly obtain are just as good and probably less expensive. It is better to use natural vegetable oils such as almond oil, linseed oil or olive oil. Mixing these oils with a few capsules of vitamin E will help prevent the oils becoming rancid.

Besides periodic oiling of the bore, another good way to hydrate the clarinet evenly in cold dry seasons is to keep orange peels in the case. Commercial hydration devises are sold, but they are no better for your clarinet than orange peels. What's more, they lack vitamin C, which is better for you.

Also, there are commercial devises some clarinetists leave in the bore of the clarinet while it is in the case. These devises hold the moisture in the bore, rather than letting it dry out naturally. It is probably a good idea not to use such devises since the usual problem is a lack of moisture on the outside rather than the inside of the clarinet. This means devises which prevent the bore from drying and equalizing its moisture with the outside of the clarinet probably do more harm than good.

How to Oil the Bore

The biggest problem in oiling the bore is going overboard with the amount and getting it on your pads. You can help prevent this by being conservative with the amount of the oil, but sometimes even the best preparations go awry. Therefore, as insurance it is a good idea to place cigarette paper between the pads and the tone holes. The paper will protect the pads from any excess oils which get into the tone hole in the oiling process.

Once the papers are in place between the pads take a wire swab (one which has the wire part taped to protect the bore) and dip it into some oil. Or, if you have a small spray bottle, spray the oil evenly on the swab and insert it into the clarinet bore and move it in and out a few times. Then look into the bore and see how evenly the oil is distributed. Repeat the process until the whole bore is evenly covered with a film of oil. Let the clarinet set for several hour to enable the oil to be absorbed. Check the bore to see if all the oil has been absorbed. If so repeat the oiling process again. Continue oiling and checking until you see the bore is no longer absorbing the oil.

How Often to Oil the Bore
There is no guarantee that oiling will prevent a clarinet from cracking. Some clarinets which have been oiled crack anyway, while others which have not been oiled have no cracking problems whatsoever. Oiling frequency is a judgment call, largely determined by how you think the wood is fairing in the climatic and seasonal conditions in which the clarinet is played. As we have already observed, dryer climates require more frequent oiling, while more humid, moderate climates may require no oiling at all.

Loose Bell Rings
Sometimes the bell ring becomes loose in extremely dry periods. The bell ring is strictly ornamental and there is no need to worry about assembly when it is loose. It can, however, become a nuisance and need to be tightened. Take is to a repair tech who has a bell ring shrinker to take care of the problem.

What Happens if Your Clarinet Cracks?
A relatively low percentage of clarinets actually crack. When it happened years ago it was a big deal and required pinning and extensive crack repairs. And even after all that, there was no guarantee that the crack would not reopen at some inopportune time, such as your debut at Carnegie Hall.

Today the problem of cracking is not so serious. So if your clarinet cracks, don't go postal or fall into a blue funk. The advent of high grade super glues have made the danger and expense of pinning a thing of the past. What's more, these super glues make a repaired crack virtually invisible!

Will the repaired crack ever reopen? There is no guarantee. But if it does it is very easy to correct. The fly in the ointment, as far as cracks go, remains the crack which goes through a tone hole. There glues are largely inadequate, and the tone hole will leak from the pad seat. The only choice in such cases is to replace the tone hole. That's the bad news. But the good news it that the repair is usually good for the life of the clarinet, and will never need to be done again.

If a crack goes through a tone hole and you have no immediate access to a repair tech, there are a few things you can do in the interim.

You can fill the cracked area with a hard wax, or hard bees wax. You can probably get a small tin of hard wax from your dentist which will last several lifetimes (just in case your grand children take up the clarinet). Make sure you have a hard wax, otherwise, the wax will be gummy and will cause the pads to stick.

Filling the crack is child's play. Just put a small amount of wax on the crack, heat the end of a pocket knife blade or screw driver, melt the wax into the cracked area and smooth it over, reheating the knife or screw driver as needed.

Tone Hole Maintenance

The tone holes of the clarinet need to be cleaned out about once a month. Debris from the swab, the case and the fingers all tend to collect in the tone holes. These incremental amounts finally build up into amounts significant enough to affect the tone, tuning and response.

Cleaning the tone holes is easy. Just use a cotton swab to go over the inside of the hole thoroughly. Make sure you get down into the tone hole to clear out any debris which has possibly collected in the recessed, undercut section of the tone hole.

Cleaning the Register Tube

The register tube is always getting rubbed by the swab as the bore is cleaned. As a consequence, lint and debris easily collect in its already small diameter. Because of this, register tubes can become quickly clogged up, affecting the way the throat Bb and entire clarion register respond and sound. (Some register tubes actually get so clogged that the entire upper clarion will not speak at all)!

Therefore, the register tube needs regular cleaning. It's simple to do. To clean the tube, remove the register key, take a pipe cleaner and put it in the tube, moving it in an out several times. Look in the bore after this is done to see if any debris was pushed out of the tube and into the bore. If so, put a puff of air down the bore to clear it out. Replace the register key and go on living as normal. It's that easy.

Cleaning the Mouthpiece

The mouthpiece needs to be cleaned routinely, if for no other reasons than health and just plain human decency. Avoid wire swabs. Use a soft cloth instead. Terry cloth is perfect. Clean the facing, baffle and bore area by hand. Don't swab the interior with a tight fitting cloth since repeatedly doing so will change the mouthpiece interior and cause it to play differently.

Some players get lots of calcium build up on the tip of the mouthpiece. Unchecked, this can get on the facing and seriously affect the way the clarinet plays. This needs to be cleaned with hydrogen peroxide and an old toothbrush. It can also be buffed off, if you have a buffer. If so, be very gentle, using only as much buffing as is needed to remove the residue.

Periodically it is a good idea to clean the mouthpiece thoroughly. Here's how:
1. Place a towel or large wash cloth in a sink to protect the mouthpiece from possible damage from the sink's hard surface.
2. Fill the sink with warm, soapy water.
3. Place the mouthpiece in the warm water and let it soak for ten minutes or so. Soaking the mouthpiece will help remove any encrusted particles which the swab could not remove in normal cleaning.
4. Remove the mouthpiece and wipe it dry with a terry cloth towel.

Cleaning Joint Sockets

Joint Sockets, especially the barrel joint sockets, easily get filled with moisture from playing. Keep a cloth in your case for the express purpose of cleaning joint sockets. Don't use the bore swab to clean the sockets, because the residue from cork grease and other materials can get on the swab and then be transferred to the bore and tone hole undercutting recesses.

Conclusion

The formula for successful playing is not just correct techniques and correct equipment, but correct equipment in good condition! While any serious repair needs to be attended to by a professional, there are many things most any one can adequately and safely do that will keep the clarinet playing well and which will extend the life of any repairs a skilled craftsman may do.

Chapter XI

ACCESSORIES FOR THE CLARINET

In this chapter you will learn.....

All about clarinet barrels and how they affect the tuning, shape, resistance and color of the tone.

The use and abuse of adjustable barrels.

All about clarinet ligatures.

How different bells can change the clarinet's tone and response.

About mouthpiece caps, how they can damage the mouthpiece and how to prevent this from happening.

How mouthpiece patches can improve tone and comfort.

How clarinet neck straps can ease the work of the right hand thumb and help the embouchure as well.

How all swabs are not equal and how to choose the best one.

How to select a reed clipper.

Reed storage methods, the advantages and disadvantages.

Synthetic reeds and their value.

Introduction

We have now discussed the clarinet, the mouthpiece and the reed rather thoroughly. Now we turn to accessories. There are many different products on the market which are very helpful and make life easier for the clarinetist. On the other hand there are others that not only don't help, but can actually create problems. In this chapter we hope to share some ideas and considerations with you which should help you better separate the sheep from the goats, so to speak.

As you proceed you will notice no refferences have been made to specific products. The reason for this is that products come and go, and they also change in design and quality. The fluidity of the market makes it hard to discuss a specific product with the assurance that the information will remain current. However, the tasks that products must perform never change. Therefore, what we will concentrate on is establishing a clear set of standards and criteria for each accessory which should help you make intelligent product choices with greater confidence and objectivity.

Barrels

The clarinet barrel is the most changeable part of the clarinet. Most professional clarinetists choose to play different barrels for three primary reasons; tuning, resistance and tone. Let's look at each of these.

Tuning
Various groups play at different pitch levels (ie. 440 Hz, 442 Hz, etc.). When clarinetists encounter the vagaries of pitch in the "real" world they usually find that one barrel isn't adequate to enable them to play well in tune in all circumstances.

The standard length of the barrel for most brands of Bb clarinet is 66 millimeters. Bb barrels range from 64 to 68 millimeters. The various lengths enable the clarinetist to play in tune at a relatively wide variety of pitch levels. However, extremes in barrel length can cause problems with the throat tones (Open G, Ab, A and Bb). These pitches do not rise or fall at the same rate as the rest of the clarinet as barrel lengths change. They fall faster and rise faster. Here is how it works:
 a) *The shorter the barrel is, the sharper the throat tones become in relation to the rest of the clarinet.*
 b) *The longer the barrel is, the lower the throat tones become in relation to the rest of the clarinet.*

Mouthpieces can greatly influence the choice of barrel length. For instance, if some extreme dimension in the mouthpiece causes the throat tones to be either flat or sharp, a shorter or longer barrel may actually be mandatory if the clarinet is to play in tune with itself. The point here is that if you have a piece of equipment that is extreme in some way you will doubtless need to compensate for that extreme by making changes in another piece of equipment. The relationship and influence barrel and mouthpiece exert on one another regarding pitch make up the locus classicus for proof of this principle.

Resistance

Because of design or use, many times clarinets do not provide enough working resistance to maintain the integrity of the shape. Such clarinets are commonly referred to as "blown out." In order for some of the hold to be restored to the sound some compensation must be made in another piece of equipment. Logically, the barrel is the first place to look, along with considering a different mouthpiece.

Tone Color

Barrels also profoundly affect tone color, depth and flexibility. Often a clarinetist's search is aesthetically and artistically, rather than technically motivated. Better tone can be a perfectly valid reason for going on a barrel search. However, if this is ever your case, try to avoid becoming so obsessed with tone that you forget to consider tuning.

Barrel Bores

The standard Bb barrel on most clarinets is a cylinder, usually of around .585" or .586" diameter. However, clarinetists often play with barrels with various types of tapers. These tapers are larger at the top of the barrel and smaller at the bottom. This is called an inverse taper barrel.

The classic inverse taper barrel is the Moennig taper barrel, which tapers 0.009" from top to bottom. Originally, this taper was used on the Buffet clarinet to compensate for tuning problems caused by the use of the larger bore mouthpieces many professional clarinetists in America prefer playing.

The Moennig taper is sometimes thought of as having some magic formula for the clarinet tone. This is just stuff and nonsense. Perhaps this attitude has developed because the Moennig taper has the effect of creating more center and focus in the sound, and since many players use poorly designed clarinets which are generally too free and fail to hold the tonal shape adequately in the upper register, this feature of the Moennig taper is most often a positive one. However, if the clarinetist plays a smaller bore mouthpiece the taper of the Moennig can have the negative effect of increasing tonal brightness and will probably not be a positive contribution to the sound.

Barrel Outer Dimensions

Barrels are also used to change tone color. This is done by a combination of things; bore taper and total mass. The more mass in the barrel, the darker the sound will be. Therefore, "fat" barrels are usually darker than "skinny" barrels, all other things being equal. Conversely, "skinny" barrels are usually more vibrant, responsive and efficient than "fat" barrels.

Barrels Made of Synthetic Material

There are a number of barrels on the market made from various types of synthetic materials. These should in no way be written off in one's search. Synthetic barrels offer a number of advantages, the primary one being stability in dimensions. This can be especially helpful in climates with extreme dryness in the cold winter months. Bore dimensions can change dramatically in that time and cause what used to be a very good barrel to play very poorly. A synthetic barrel, on the other hand, is stable, and using it in combination with the rubber or synthetic mouthpiece material stabilizes the first eighty or so millimeters of the bore. Also, some synthetic barrels have surprisingly fine tones, though it must be admitted that as a genre, there is a tendency towards brightness. This is primarily due to the light weight materials from which most are made. Perhaps they are not for everyone, but they do have their advantages. The carrot at the end of the stick in the search for a fine synthetic barrel is simply that once you find a good one, you can be assured it will remain so for years.

Adjustable Barrels; Their Use and Abuse

Adjustable barrels have been used for decades, but recent years have seen somewhat of an increase in their popularity. This is an accessory which has usefulness, but can be easily abused. Using an adjustable barrel to play generally in tune in various performance situations in "the real world" constitutes proper use. For example, on Monday night you rehearse with the local concert band which plays at 441, but tends to go a little sharp in the heat of battle. On Thursday night you meet with your chamber music ensemble which has an oboist who insists on A=440 Hz and not a vibration higher! On Saturday night you play in Dieter Schmieter's Oktoberfest Funf polka band. Dieter's accordion is pitched at A=443 Hz (and he's threatening to buy one that plays at A=445 Hz!). In such diverse playing circumstances you might find an adjustable barrel quite useful... especially on Saturday night.

On the other hand, using an adjustable barrel to fix an isolated tuning problem which is, in reality, due to poor tone production techniques constitutes an abuse of the product. For instance, let's say your clarinet students play flat in the high register and you're unaware that a combination of proper snugging of the mouthpiece and a high/back tongue position solves this problem in virtually every case.

As a consequence, in search of a solution in the form of a change in equipment instead of playing techniques, you purchase adjustable barrels for the section. Now the high tones are in tune with a simple adjustment. The only problem is that the change of the barrel length has now thrown the clarinet terribly out of tune with itself! One thing has been fixed at the expense of messing up four other things! This, clearly, is abuse of the adjustable barrel in two ways.
a) It seeks to use the barrel as a substitute for rather than a supplement to correct playing techniques.
b) It only "solves" one problem by creating several others, which, is really no solution at all, but the proverbial changing of headache for an up-set stomach.

For the above reasons, adjustable barrels are recommended to educators only with grave reservation and caution. The smart money says that they should be used only when all other aspects of equipment and pedagogy been examined thoroughly and found to be correct.

Tuning Socket Rings

Barrel rings are used to fill up the gap between the bore of the barrel and upper joint when the barrel is pulled for tuning. The rings can be helpful in preventing the throat tones from dropping proportionately faster than the rest of the clarinet when the barrel is pulled. Beyond that, tuning rings have other practical uses. For instance, many clarinets play better in tune when the middle joint is pulled a certain amount. Players who have such instruments often put a socket (tuning) ring between the upper and lower joints to keep them from wobbling and to make sure the space is always consistent.

Finally, sometimes a player may prefer to pull out the mouthpiece for tuning. A socket ring can be very useful there to help keep the mouthpiece from wobbling. One word of warning about tuning at the mouthpiece: the mouthpiece cork needs to be very tight and pulling should be limited to no more than one and a half millimeters. More than that can cause misalignment of the mouthpiece with the barrel bore and cause leaks.

Most clarinetists, however, seem to get along rather well without socket rings. You may or may not find them helpful, but they are worth consideration.

Bells

Of course, bells are tested with much less frequency than barrels, primarily because of their greater expense. But if you would like to optimize your clarinet's playing and tonal qualities, it is worth the time it takes to check out different bells. Clarinet bells can make a significant difference in a clarinet's response, resistance, tone color and tuning. A simple change of bells can cause a clarinet to blow more freely, produce more flexible right hand pitches and make the bell tones clearer, more flexible and responsive. Just the right bell can even change a so-so clarinet into one which has a unique sparkle and "ring." If you go on a bell search in the wooley wilds of Clarinet Accessory Land (it's a jungle out there!) one bit of warning is worth keeping in mind. There are bells available on the market with the English horn style excavation in the bore. Such bells often give a positive impression because they quicken response and make the right-hand clarion pitches play with greater ease, flexibly and clarity. But these improvements come at a price which is usually exacted in two ways. First, the bell is often found to produce too much loss of focus and agility in right-hand clarion tones. In fact, the change in tonal shape can be so great that it noticeably reduces the carrying power and presence of the sound in actual performance situations. Second, and most importantly, these bells usually cause serious detuning (sharpness) of both "E" and "B" bell notes, and can similarly affect right-hand clarion "C" and "D". Such detuning is, practically speaking, really impossible to correct and probably precludes the use of such bells on clarinets for which they were no expressly designed. You may find such a bell to be just what you've been looking for. But before you invest, make sure you check out the two concerns mentioned above.

Nothing Up my Sleeve: Tricks with the Bell:

You may want to try the following little trick to improve the bell you presently have:
1) *Put your bell on the clarinet with the stamp in the front, and test the clarinet.*
2. *Rotate the bell one quarter of the circumference and retest.*
3. *Continue this process until you have tested the bell in all four positions.*

You will no doubt find that the bell plays and responds better in one of these radial positions. When you assemble your clarinet, try to remember to place the bell there. Some clarinetists even go so far as to mark small dots on the right hand and bell joints and align them whenever they assemble the clarinet. The same trick works with the barrel as well.

Finally, you may try testing your clarinet with the bell all the way in and then with it pulled about one millimeter. Most clarinets, with few exceptions, produce clearer bell tones and play with more presence and flexibility when the bell is pulled slightly. (Just for the record, pulling the bell slightly has little or no effect on the tuning).

Clarinet Ligatures

More than any other accessory, with perhaps the one exception of mouthpieces, the ligature market presents the clarinetist with the greatest number of types and styles from which to choose.

There are inexpensive ligatures almost any budget can handle and ligatures priced to blow most any budget. There are thick and thin metals ones, gold ones, silver ones, ligatures made of plastic, ligatures made of neoprene, rigid ones, flexible ones, ones where the screws are on the bottom, others with the screws on the top, ones with two screws, one screw and even ones with no screws! There are ones which only allow two narrow rails to touch the reed, ones with four pressure points on the reed, ones with variable pressure points, ones with rubber liners, ones with interchangeable liners and on and on. Some players have even resorted to using "O" rings, and others use string, just as many of the European players have done for generations.

To add to the confusion, there are all sorts of claims and counterclaims made by manufacturers about the acoustical advantages of one over another. It's enough to discourage, confuse and dismay even the most seasoned of professionals.

Perhaps the best solution to this perplexity is to make a list of what you regard as necessary in a ligature and then another list of what would be nice. No two people's list would be exactly the same, since everyone has somewhat different priorities, tastes and needs.

For instance, the professional's concern is the ultimate artistic result the ligature provides in response and tone. Ease of use is not a great importance, and price is no object. Practically speaking, being able to switch his or her mouthpiece from the A to the Bb clarinet in the midst of a performance without the reed and ligature coming loose can be a serious priority for orchestral players.

A music educator, on the other hand, has a whole different set of priorities. These may include the following:

1. Price: The price of a ligature has to be reasonable enough so that all of the students can afford one.

2. Ease of Use: The ligature must be easy to use, so that the possibility of incorrectly tightening the ligature and damaging the mouthpiece and reed are minimized.

3. Durability: The ligature must be durable. For this reason, perhaps a ligature whose screw(s) and threads are made of high quality steel that will not strip is preferable. The ligature itself must also be able to take a beating and still perform correctly. This may rule out many plastic ligatures, which are relatively easy to break, and many metal ligatures, which are easy to bend out of shape. The last thing a director wants is to find out that his star clarinet player just stepped or sat on his or her ligature only minutes before the band is to go on stage.

4. Number of screw(s): Ligatures usually have one or two tightening screws. Unless the students take care, they can tighten a two screw ligature unevenly or even fail to tighten one at all! The length of the screw should also be a consideration. If the screw and thread part of the mechanism are short, it might be easy to lose the screw.

Mouthpiece Caps:

The metal mouthpiece cap may seem innocent enough, but it can become deadly in the hands of a distracted young clarinetist (or even an old one). All that is needed is a moment of distraction when the cap is being placed on the mouthpiece and its metal edge can ruin the tip of the mouthpiece, making it unplayable. For this reason, a cap which is made of softer material than the mouthpiece should be used: Better safe than sorry.

The design as well as the material of the cap is of importance. The cap must not only protect the reed and mouthpiece, but it should also keep the reed moist when the clarinet is not being played. Some plastic mouthpiece caps have a large slit which allows the reed to dry out quickly. If these caps are used, the slits should be modified in some way to prevent the reed from drying out.

Admittedly, this approach to ligatures and caps does not sound very romantic or "artistic," but its practicality can save the day. So what we recommend here for music educators is to make sure that their choice of ligature meets at least some of the above criteria as a bottom line, whatever the aesthetic considerations might be.

Lip Savers; Their Use and Abuse

Lip savers are made of various materials. They are used to cover the lower teeth in order to prevent them from cutting of the inside of the lower lip. Players who routinely cut their lower lips are most likely biting. In such instances, all the lip saver does is allow biting and encourage its perpetuation with impunity, at least as far as lip pain goes. The lip may cease to suffer...but the tone doesn't. <u>This is a clear abuse of the product!</u>

The lip saver can, however, be a legitimate and proper accessory for a young player who must wear braces for a time, or a professional whose lip becomes a bit raw (not cut) due to heavy performance and practice demands. However, the use of lip savers to reduce the pain of biting is a serious abuse of the product and should not be allowed.

Bore Savers or "Shove Its"

These are rigid bore swabs which are designed to remain in the bore of the clarinet when the clarinet is in its case. The problem with this concept is that after a while they actually hold moisture in the bore. In the dryness of winter months this can mean that the bore gets continual moisture while the outside of the clarinet is progressively drying out. This can create a problem which can lead to cracking. Please see the section on clarinet wood care for a full explanation of the problem of moisture disparity and its affect on wood. No doubt, analogous products are valid for flute and saxophone, for which they were orginally designed. But their usefullness for the clarinet seems dubious at best. Perhaps the safest thing is to tell the makers of such products to shove them in something other than the clarinet bore.

Clarinet Neck Straps

Neck straps can be very beneficial for those who play standing a great deal and run the danger of over stressing the right hand thumb which must support the whole weight of the clarinet all the time it is being played. There are several brands of clarinet neck straps on the market. Some are plain and inexpensive and others pretty fancy (with a fancy price tag too). Fancy or simple, the bottom line is this: The best type of neck strap is one that has some elasticity. <u>A neck strap that does not assist in the lifting action the thumb must do in actual performance is virtually useless.</u> Therefore, whatever choice is made, make sure there is some elasticity in the strap. Only such a strap will really save your thumb and be "pedagogically correct."

Thumb Supports or "Rests"

As with neck straps, you can go fancy or plain, high priced or low, adjustable or not. The only way a clarinetist can know which is best for him or her is trial and error. The bottom line here is comfort. If there is tension in the hand, physical discomfort, or problems with technical facility it might be good to look into different thumb supports as part of the solution. Otherwise, if it ain't broke, don't fix it.

Thumb Cushions

If a clarinetist plays any length of time, his or her thumb will soon send the signal that it is now time to look for a thumb cushion. The thumb needs as much cushioning as possible, for it is in constant contact with the thumb support devise and often must bear the weight of the clarinet for sustained periods of time.

There are many types of thumb cushions on the market, some made of great material. With a little experimentation your can find the one which suits you best.

Mouthpiece Cushions

Mouthpiece cushions are placed on the top of the mouthpiece. A generation ago they were not in such common use. Nowadays, they are widely used by professionals and students alike.

Cushions are made of various materials and in various thicknesses. They have several significant benefits, some obvious and some not so obvious.

Mouthpiece cushions protect the surface of the mouthpiece from damage and cushion the teeth as they contact the mouthpiece. But those made of a rubbery, textured material can greatly facilitate the snugging/wedging action of the mouthpiece necessary for the proper control of the reed.

Another benefit of mouthpiece cushions is that of damping the vibrations of the mouthpiece. This allows the clarinetist to hear the sound more clearly, purely and objectively.

In addition, adding patches to increase beak thickness allows the mouth to open a bit more, and this too, may be beneficial to the sound. Added thicknesses also do one more thing; they decidedly darken the sound. This can be taken too far, however, negatively affecting resonance.

In addition, those who use mouthpiece patches should know that placing the patch at the very edge of the mouthpiece, especially if a thick patch or double thicknesses are being used, can create resistance and stuffiness in the sound and cause sluggishness in the response. Therefore, it is recommended that patches be placed no closer than a millimeter (0.040") to the tip of the mouthpiece.

As a final note on mouthpiece patches, it needs to be said once again that this accessory should not be used as a license to make biting more comfortable. This is abuse of the product and needs to be avoided and corrected.

Swabs

A swab is a swab. Right? Wrong! Some swabs are better than others, and some are definitely to be avoided altogether.

The swab is used to remove excess moisture from the bore after playing. This should be simple and straightforward enough. But the fact that the bore has a number of tone holes as well as a few obstructions (the thumb and register tube) complicate matters.

Swabs are constantly rubbing against these tone holes and the tubes which protrude in the bore. Over a period of time, lint from these swabs can collect in the undercutting of the tone holes and the register tube. Collected lint can significantly change the response, tone color and tuning of certain pitches. For instance, lint can fill the register tube to the degree that the second register will not respond and the throat Bb will hardly speak. Because of this problem, swabs which are as lint free as possible and tend not to carry debris are the only ones recommended.

Finally, some swabs on the market tend to bunch up and can easily get stuck in the bore. Use only swabs which go through the bore with relative ease. It is better to run the swab through a few times rather than get a tight fitting swab which may become irretrievably stuck in the bore and require drastic measures to be removed. It's also better to have a loose fitting swab because it is less likely to rub against the tone holes and leave lint and other debris. Finally, there are also wire handled swabs. Such swabs should never be used because of the danger of damaging the bore of the clarinet with the wire handle.

Reed Clippers

A good reed clipper is invaluable and can save you a lot of money. There are several brands on the market that are adequate for the job. Their prices vary. Some are adjustable as far as the shape they give the tip, others are not. Some have replaceable blades and other replaceable parts.

You will need to decide on just how fancy you want to get, and just how much your budget will allow. In any case, you can pay a lot and still not get a good clipper, and pay relatively little and get the right tool for the job. It all depends upon how diligent you are at testing the clippers you are considering buying.

The best and virtually only way to insure you will get a good reed clipper is to test several of them with some old, worn out reeds. When you do this, you will find that clippers vary considerably in the shapes they cut, as well as the amount of skill and care they require to make a good, symmetrical cut.

You need to look for a clipper which has the tip contour that fits the tip of your mouthpiece best, and that produces a clean, symmetrical cut. You may have to try several to find the one that is best. What ever you do, never buy a reed clipper sight unseen. The odds of you getting a clipper which will be right for your mouthpiece are slim indeed.

Reed Storage Methods

Once you have a good reed you will want to do all you can to make it last as long as possible. There are a variety of methods of reed storage, some very expensive and others inexpensive. Be forewarned, the expense of the reed case is not always commensurate with either practicality or effectiveness.

The criteria for reed storage methods have two classifications: niceties and necessities. Here are the necessities:

1. It needs to keep the reed flat.
2. It needs to protect the tip area of the reed.
3. It needs to prevent the reed from moving around; holding it in a secure, stable place.
4. It needs to remain securely shut, with no danger of opening accidentally and exposing the reeds to possible damage.
5. It needs to receive reeds without danger of being damaged in the process.
6. It needs to hold the reed without damaging or compressing any spots or areas on the vibrating surface.

It would also be nice if :
1. It provided a means of hydrating the reed so that is doesn't dry out completely. (Some players would list this in the necessities column, especially those who live in dry climiates).
2. It were convenient to carry, and could easily fit inside the clarinet case or case cover pouch.
3. It held at least a dozen reeds.

All these criteria can be met by homemade systems which can be fabricated rather easily and inexpensively. However, you can also spend lots of money for reed cases which look fancy, but fail to meet one or more criteria on the list of necessities.

Synthetic Reeds

For years the great majority of clarinetists have regarded synthetic reeds as failing to meet even minimal standards for response and tone. However, there have recently been remarkable advances in synthetic reeds; advances which put them on virtually equal footing with cane reeds in some respects, as well as offering some decided advantages over cane reeds in others. They have improved so much that their use in both practice and performance by advanced and professional clarinetists is noticeably increasing.

It seems that they also have an especially promising future in the context of music education. Here are some of their advantages which are especially useful to the educator and student:
1. They commonly outlast several boxes of cane reeds.
2. They never warp or become waterlogged.
3. They do not require soaking time before they are ready for performance.
4. They are virtually stable throughout seasonal and weather changes.
5. Some brands of synthetic reeds are extremely well balanced, and this makes them an ideal match for symmetrically faced mouthpieces. The reed's fine balance in combination with the uniformity of material significantly increases their playing consistency and virtually eliminates the problem of unusable reeds.
6. They are a dependable backup in case cane reeds are not playing so well on a particular day.

Even if the student and conductor find they prefer cane reeds for actual performance, being able to practice on well balanced reeds and save the best cane reeds for the concert can be very helpful. The synthetic reed has many virtues to consider, but one possible disadvantage. Even though the best synthetics outlast many cane reeds, cost can be a problem if the student is careless and frequently breaks them. For this reason, synthetic reeds should not be given to students until they are skilled and responsible enough to take care of them properly.

Conclusion

Accessories can make big differences in performance comfort, quality of tone, tuning and performance security. The rewards of having the right accessories make it well worth the trouble it takes to wade through the multiplicity of products which continue to flood the market year after year. One point of concern worth reflecting on is the attitude you bring to this search. <u>Suspecting yourself before you suspect your equipment is always a good rule of thumb</u>. In other words, you should not expect any piece of equipment to make up for actual defects and flaws in your own playing techniques; defects and flaws need to be corrected, not indulged! How often have players wasted time trying to find that "magic" mouthpiece or special barrel, when what they really needed was correct voicing or blowing techniques, to stop biting or to correct any number of other problems which were never properly addressed in their study of the clarinet! Such players usually begin their searches for good equipment sadly unaware of two important things; how poor their own playing techniques really are and how poor playing techniques make it virtually impossible to recognize whether a piece of equipment is objectively good or not. Generally, it may be said that players with good fundamental playing techniques look for equipment which will compliment what is already good in their playing, while players with poor fundamentals look for equipment to compensate for what is poor. At the risk of sounding both glib and unkind to the reader, it really needs to be plainly stated that players with poor playing fundamentals may need better equipment, but they need lessons more.

The bottom line is simple: What all clarinetists need is equipment which will suit their aesthetic needs and tastes as well as better facilitate their already-correct-efforts. That notwithstanding, it is never valid to think of equipment as a substitute for the development and application of correct playing techniques. Once, as "The Man" in "Cool Hand Luke" says, you have your "mind right" on this subject along with a set of clear criteria and standards, your approach in examining equipment will be more reasonable and the results more gratifying.

AFTERWORD

Thoughts are neat. Life is messy. The clarinet, with its various systems once understood, is easy to teach. Students, on the other hand, can be difficult to teach, posing a whole array of complications and perplexities.

Sometimes the problems students have can actually tempt teachers into compromising or even abandoning the principles, concepts and methods they have come to know to be true. This is almost always a mistake. The last thing which should ever be done is to abandon or compromise what one <u>knows</u> to be right. One can never be reminded enough that there are no contradictions or exceptions to what it true. However, even though we should never doubt what we know to be true, it is reasonable (and even advisable) to suspect one's understanding of what is true! Truth, in all its multiplied expressions and forms, remains ever and always what it is in its completeness, waiting for our understanding to grow into its fullness and penetrate its depth.

The answer to how we as clarinet teachers may grow into that fullness is simple: We must be willing to be taught by our daily experience of teaching our students. We must enter the class room or studio each day with the expectation of learning something new about what we already know, and not just teaching the same old thing in the same old way, day after day after day. It is the expectation of learning combined with the willingness to think creatively about what is already known which gives someone who has taught twenty years, twenty years of experience, rather than the all-too-common one year's experience twenty times.

Never abandoning the principles in the face of particulars is a key to consistently successful teaching. Rather, application of the principles to the particulars of each student deepens one's understanding of the principles themselves, increases one's appreciation for their consistent workability and bolsters confidence in their rightness. Therefore, moments of initial perplexity are really moments which challenge the teacher's creativity in the use of the pedagogical materials she or he knows. Ultimately, such moments are opportunities to learn and should be gladly and eagerly received rather than dreaded.

It is impossible to put everything in a book. It is hard to explain things well and humbling to try. It is also impossible to avoid controversy. These four facts point to the inevitability of some readers having more questions and being in need of further clarification on one or more of the points we have discussed. Some readers may even need to either vent or assuage their outrage over this or that issue or matter!

I would like to invite those who do run into questions or have comments to contact me on line. I will do my best to respond to your comments, and to either answer your questions or put you in contact with someone who can. (I will even try to respond to your outrage charitably and reasonably....but no guarantees). In this way we can all have the opportunity of growing and perfecting our understanding of the elements of clarinet playing and how they might be best applied and communicated in the process of teaching.

I certainly wish everyone who studies the material in this volume and their students the very best throughout life and the greatest of success in playing the clarinet. I hope you find that you have been both enriched and aided by what you have read.

Good luck and God bless!
Tom Ridenour
Jan. 2000 A.D.